D0090299

BARKING UP THE WRONG TREE

BARKING UP THE WRONG TREE

The Surprising Science Behind Why Everything You Know About Success Is (Mostly) Wrong

ERIC BARKER

HarperOne
An Imprint of HarperCollinsPublishers

BARKING UP THE WRONG TREE. Copyright © 2017 by Eric Barker. All rights reserved. Printed in the United States of America. No part of this book may be used or reproduced in any manner whatsoever without written permission except in the case of brief quotations embodied in critical articles and reviews. For information, address HarperCollins Publishers, 195 Broadway, New York, NY 10007.

HarperCollins books may be purchased for educational, business, or sales promotional use. For information, please email the Special Markets Department at SPsales@harpercollins.com.

FIRST EDITION

Library of Congress Cataloging-in-Publication Data has been applied for.

ISBN 978–0–06–241604–9

17 18 19 20 21 LSC 10 9 8 7 6 5 4 3

For my parents,

who kindly put up with an orchid, hopeful monster, unfiltered leader of a son.

What the heck does that mean, you ask?

Well, we better get started . . .

Nothing important comes with instructions.

—JAMES RICHARDSON

Contents

What Really Produces Success?

By Looking at the Science Behind What Separates the
Extremely Successful from the Rest of Us, We Learn
What We Can Do to Be More Like Them—and Find Out in
Some Cases Why It's Good That We Aren't

Two men have died trying to do this.

Outside Magazine declared the Race Across America the tough-
est endurance event there is, bar none. Cyclists cover three thousand
miles in less than twelve days, riding from San Diego to Atlantic City.

Some might think *Oh, that's like the Tour de France.* They would
be wrong. The Tour has stages. Breaks. The Race Across America
(RAAM) does not stop. Every minute riders take to sleep, to rest, to
do anything other than pedal, is another minute their competitors
can use to defeat them. Riders average three hours of sleep per
night—reluctantly.

Four days into the race and the top riders must debate when to
rest. With the competition tightly clustered (within an hour of each
other), it is a decision that weighs heavily on them, knowing they
will be passed and need to regain their position. And as the race goes
on they will grow weaker. There is no respite. The exhaustion, pain,
and sleep deprivation only compound as they work their way across
the entire United States.

But in 2009 this does not affect the man in the number-one spot.
He is literally *half a day* ahead of number two. Jure Robič seems unbeatable. He has won the RAAM five times, more than any other
competitor ever, often crossing the finish line in under nine days.
In 2004 he bested the number-two rider by eleven hours. Can you

imagine watching an event during which after the winner claims victory you need to wait half a day in order to see the runner-up finish?

It's only natural to wonder what made Robič so dominant and successful in such a grueling event. Was he genetically gifted? No. When tested, he seemed physically typical for a top ultra-endurance athlete.

Did he have the best trainer? Nope. His friend Uroč Velepec described Robič as "Completely uncoachable."

In a piece for the *New York Times,* Dan Coyle revealed the edge Robič had over his competition that rendered him the greatest rider ever in the Race Across America:

His insanity.

That's not an exaggerated way of saying he was extreme. It's a literal way of saying when Robič rode, *he utterly lost his mind.*

He became paranoid; had tearful, emotional breakdowns; and saw cryptic meaning in the cracks on the street beneath him. Robič would throw down his bike and walk toward the follow car of his team members, fists clenched and eyes ablaze. (Wisely, they locked the doors.) He leapt off his bike mid-race to engage in fistfights . . . with mailboxes. He hallucinated, one time seeing mujahedeen chasing him with guns. His then wife was so disturbed by Robič's behavior she locked herself in the team's trailer.

Coyle wrote that Robič saw his insanity as "awkward and embarrassing but impossible to live without." What's fascinating is that Robič's gift was not unknown as an advantage in athletics. As far back as the 1800s, scientists like Philippe Tissié and August Bier noted that an unsound mind can help an athlete ignore pain and push his or her body beyond its naturally conservative limits.

I don't know about you, but my high school guidance counselor never told me that hallucinations, mailbox assaults, and generalized insanity were vital to being a world-renowned success at *anything.* I was told to do my homework, play by the rules, and be nice.

All of which raises a serious question: What really produces success?

This book explores what brings success in the real world. And I mean *life* success, not merely making money. What attitudes and behaviors will help you achieve your goals in whatever arena you choose, career or personal? A lot of books cover one facet of the success diamond or present theory without anything actionable. We're going to look at what works and then learn steps you can use to get where you wanna go.

What defines success for *you* is, well, up to you. It's about what you personally need to be happy at work and at home. But that doesn't mean success is arbitrary. You already know strategies to get you there that are very likely to work (consistent effort) and very unlikely to (waking up at the crack of noon every day). The problem lies in the huge gulf in the middle. You've been told about all the qualities and tactics that will help you get where you want to go, but there's no real proof—and perhaps you've seen plenty of exceptions. That's what we're going to look at in this book.

For eight years on my blog, *Barking Up the Wrong Tree,* I have been breaking down the research and interviewing experts about what makes a successful life. And I've been finding answers. Many of them are surprising. Some seem contradictory on the surface, but all of them provide insight into what we need to do to in our careers and our personal lives to get an edge.

Much of what we've been told about the qualities that lead to achievement is logical, earnest—and downright wrong. We'll explode the myths, look at the science behind what separates the extremely successful from the rest of us, learn what we can do to be more like them, and find out in some cases why it's good that we aren't.

Sometimes what produces success is raw talent, sometimes it's the nice things our moms told us to do, and other times it's the exact opposite. Which old sayings are true and which are myths?

Do "nice guys finish last"? Or first?

Do quitters never win? Or is stubbornness the real enemy?

Does confidence rule the day? When is it just delusion?

In each chapter we'll review *both* sides of the story. We'll see the strengths of each perspective. So if anything seems like a slam-dunk or a contradiction, hang with me. Both angles will present their case, much like a trial. Then we'll settle on the answer that gives the best upside with the least downside.

In chapter 1, we'll look at whether playing it safe and doing what we're told really produces success. We'll learn about what Harvard professor Gautam Mukunda calls "intensifiers." Like Jure Robič's insanity, intensifiers are qualities that, on average, are negative but in certain contexts produce sweeping benefits that devastate the competition. We'll learn why valedictorians rarely become millionaires, why the best (and worst) U.S. presidents are the ones who subvert the system, and how our biggest weaknesses might actually be our greatest strengths.

In chapter 2, we'll find out when nice guys finish first as well as when Machiavelli was right on the money. We'll talk to a Wharton School professor who believes in compassionate business and altruism, and a teacher at Stanford whose research shows hard work is overrated and kissing up is what gets promotions. We'll look at pirates and prison gangs to see which rules even rule breakers follow, and find out how to strike the right balance between ambitiously getting ahead and being able to sleep at night.

In chapter 3, we'll dive into Navy SEAL training and explore the emerging science of grit and resilience. We'll talk to economics Ph.D.s to calculate the best time to double our efforts and when to throw in the towel. Kung fu masters will teach us when being a flaky quitter is a great idea. And we'll learn the silly word that can help us decide when to stick with something and when giving up is the best move.

Chapter 4 looks at whether it really is "what you know" or "who you know." We'll see how the most networked employees are often the most productive but that the greatest experts almost invariably classify themselves as introverts (including an astounding 90 percent of top athletes). We'll get insights from the most connected guy in Silicon Valley and learn how to network without feeling sleazy.

In chapter 5, we'll look at attitude. We'll see how confidence can push us past what we think we're capable of but how that needs to be balanced with a grounded view of the challenges ahead. We'll learn how the emerging science of "mental contrasting" can help us determine when to go all in and when to think twice. Most important, we'll look at new research that shows why the entire confidence paradigm might be problematic at its core.

In chapter 6, we step back to view the big picture and try to see how success in career aligns with success in life—and when it doesn't. Is there any place for work–life balance in our 24/7 go, go, go world? Harvard Business School's Clayton Christensen and Genghis Khan provide examples of how to find peace in a fast-moving office. We'll get lessons from tragic case studies of legends who achieved success but paid too steep a price, sacrificing family and happiness.

Success doesn't have to be something you see only on TV. It's less about being perfect than knowing what you're best at and being properly aligned with your context. You don't need to be literally insane, like Jure Robič, but sometimes an ugly duckling can be a swan if it finds the right pond. The thing that sets you apart, the habits you may have tried to banish, the things you were taunted for in school, may ultimately grant you an unbeatable advantage.

In fact, let's start there . . .

CHAPTER 1

Should We Play It Safe and Do What We're Told If We Want to Succeed?

Does Playing by the Rules Pay Off? Insight from Valedictorians, People Who Feel No Pain, and Piano Prodigies

---

Ashlyn Blocker does not feel pain.

In fact, she has never felt pain. To the naked eye she is a normal teenage girl, but due to a defect in the *SCN9A* gene, her nerves did not form the same way yours or mine did. Pain signals do not reach her brain.

Sound like a godsend? Hold on. The Wikipedia entry on "Congenital insensitivity to pain" puts it quite simply: "It is an extremely dangerous condition." Dane Inouye writes, "Most children dream about being a superhero when they are young. CIPA patients can be considered Superman because they don't feel physical pain but it is ironic that what gives them their 'super powers' also becomes their kryptonite."

As recounted in a *New York Times Magazine* article by Justin Heckert, Ashlyn's parents noticed she had broken her ankle before she did—and that was two days after it occurred. Karen Cann, another woman with the disorder, broke her pelvis giving birth to her first child but didn't realize it for weeks until the stiffness in her hip made it almost impossible to walk.

People with the disorder tend to have shorter lives, often dying during childhood. Of babies with CIPA (Congenital insensitivity to pain with anhidrosis), 50 percent do not live past age three.

Swaddled by well-meaning parents, they do not cry out when they overheat. Those who do survive frequently bite off the tips of their tongue or cause serious damage to their corneas rubbing their eyes raw. Adults with the disorder are usually covered in scars and have repeatedly broken bones. Every day they must check their bodies for signs of damage. Seeing a bruise, cut, or burn may be the only way they know it has occurred. Appendicitis and other internal maladies are of particular concern—people with CIPA often feel no symptoms until the problem kills them.

But how many of us, at one time or another, have not wished we were like Ashlyn?

It's easy to naively see only the benefits of such a condition. No more nagging injuries. No fear at the dentist's office. A life free from the minor discomforts of illness and injury. Never another headache or the limitations of capricious lower back pain.

In terms of health care and lost productivity, pain costs the United States between $560 and $635 billion annually. Fifteen percent of Americans face chronic pain daily, and there's little doubt many of them would happily trade places with Ashlyn.

One of the villains in the bestselling novel *The Girl Who Played with Fire* has CIPA, and the disorder is presented as a superpower. With the skills of a professional boxer and unable to feel pain, he is a seemingly unstoppable force and a terrifying foe.

This raises larger questions: When are our weaknesses actually strengths? Is it better to be an outlier with both handicaps and superpowers? Or do we live better lives at the middle of the bell curve? We're generally encouraged to play it safe, but is doing the normally prescribed "right thing," and not risking the ups and downs of extremes, the path to success—or to mediocrity?

To solve this puzzle, let's first look at those who follow the rules and do everything right. What becomes of high school valedictorians? It's what every parent wishes their teenager to be. Mom says study hard and you'll do well. And very often Mom is right.

But not always.

*

Karen Arnold, a researcher at Boston College, followed eighty-one high school valedictorians and salutatorians from graduation onward to see what becomes of those who lead the academic pack. Of the 95 percent who went on to graduate college, their average GPA was 3.6, and by 1994, 60 percent had received a graduate degree. There was little debate that high school success predicted college success. Nearly 90 percent are now in professional careers with 40 percent in the highest tier jobs. They are reliable, consistent, and well-adjusted, and by all measures the majority have good lives.

But how many of these number-one high school performers go on to change the world, run the world, or impress the world? The answer seems to be clear: zero.

Commenting on the success trajectories of her subjects, Karen Arnold said, "Even though most are strong occupational achievers, the great majority of former high school valedictorians do not appear headed for the very top of adult achievement arenas." In another interview Arnold said, "Valedictorians aren't likely to be the future's visionaries . . . they typically settle into the system instead of shaking it up."

Was it just that these eighty-one didn't happen to reach the stratosphere? No. Research shows that what makes students likely to be impressive in the classroom is the same thing that makes them less likely to be home-run hitters outside the classroom.

So why are the number ones in high school so rarely the number ones in real life? There are two reasons. First, schools reward students who consistently do what they are told. Academic grades correlate only loosely with intelligence (standardized tests are better at measuring IQ). Grades are, however, an excellent predictor of self-discipline, conscientiousness, and the ability to comply with rules.

In an interview, Arnold said, "Essentially, we are rewarding conformity and the willingness to go along with the system." Many of the valedictorians admitted to not being the smartest kid in class, just the hardest worker. Others said that it was more an

SHOULD WE PLAY IT SAFE AND DO WHAT WE'RE TOLD IF WE WANT TO SUCCEED?

9

issue of giving teachers what they wanted than actually knowing the material better. Most of the subjects in the study were classified as "careerists": they saw their job as getting good grades, not really as learning.

The second reason is that schools reward being a generalist. There is little recognition of student passion or expertise. The real world, however, does the reverse. Arnold, talking about the valedictorians, said, "They're extremely well rounded and successful, personally and professionally, but they've never been devoted to a single area in which they put all their passion. That is not usually a recipe for eminence."

If you want to do well in school and you're passionate about math, you need to stop working on it to make sure you get an A in history too. This generalist approach doesn't lead to expertise. Yet eventually we almost all go on to careers in which one skill is highly rewarded and other skills aren't that important.

Ironically, Arnold found that intellectual students who enjoy learning struggle in high school. They have passions they want to focus on, are more interested in achieving mastery, and find the structure of school stifling. Meanwhile, the valedictorians are intensely pragmatic. They follow the rules and prize A's over skills and deep understanding.

School has clear rules. Life often doesn't. When there's no clear path to follow, academic high achievers break down.

Shawn Achor's research at Harvard shows that college grades aren't any more predictive of subsequent life success than rolling dice. A study of over seven hundred American millionaires showed their average college GPA was 2.9.

Following the rules doesn't create success; it just eliminates extremes—both good and bad. While this is usually good and all but eliminates downside risk, it also frequently eliminates earthshaking accomplishments. It's like putting a governor on your engine that stops the car from going over fifty-five; you're far less likely to get into a lethal crash, but you won't be setting any land speed records either.

So if those who play by the rules don't end up at the very top, who does?

*

Winston Churchill should have never been prime minister of Great Britain. He wasn't someone who "did everything right," and it was shocking that he was elected. His contemporaries knew he was brilliant—but he was also a paranoid loose cannon who was impossible to deal with.

Initially rising up through the ranks of British politics at a steady clip (he was elected to Parliament at age twenty-six), Churchill was eventually found lacking and deemed unsuitable for the highest offices. By the 1930s his career was effectively over. In many ways he was a perfect foil to Neville Chamberlain, a leader who had done everything right and was the prototypical British prime minister.

Britain does not choose its leaders carelessly. A review of prime ministers shows they are generally older and more strongly vetted than their American counterparts. John Major rose to power more quickly than almost any British leader but was still objectively more prepared for the role than the majority of U.S. presidents.

Churchill was a maverick. He did not merely love his country; he displayed a clear paranoia toward any possible threat to the empire. He saw even Gandhi as a danger and was beyond outspoken in his opposition to what was a pacifist rebellion in India. He was the Chicken Little of Great Britain, passionately railing against all opposition to his country, great, small—or imagined. But this "bad" quality is the key to why he is one of the most revered leaders in world history.

This Chicken Little was the only one who saw Hitler for the threat he was. Chamberlain, on the other hand, regarded Hitler as "a man who could be relied upon when he had given his word." The entrenched British leadership was convinced appeasement was the way to quell the Nazis.

When it mattered the most, Churchill's paranoia was prescient. He didn't believe the schoolyard bully would leave them alone if they gave him their lunch money. He knew they needed to sock him in the nose.

Churchill's zealotry—the thing that had nearly ruined his career early on—was exactly what Britain needed heading into World War II. And thankfully the British people realized this before it was too late.

To answer the big question of who makes it to the top, let's come at it from another angle: What makes a great leader? For years, academic research didn't seem able to make up its mind whether leaders even mattered. Some studies showed that great teams succeeded with or without a figurehead taking the credit. Others showed that sometimes a charismatic individual was the most important factor in whether a group succeeded or failed. It wasn't clear at all—until one academic had a hunch.

Gautam Mukunda speculated that the reason for the inconsistency in the research was there are actually *two* fundamentally different types of leaders. The first kind rises up through formal channels, getting promoted, playing by the rules, and meeting expectations. These leaders, like Neville Chamberlain, are "filtered." The second kind doesn't rise up through the ranks; they come in through the window: entrepreneurs who don't wait for someone to promote them; U.S. vice presidents who are unexpectedly handed the presidency; leaders who benefit from a perfect storm of unlikely events, like the kind that got Abraham Lincoln elected. This group is "unfiltered."

By the time filtered candidates are in the running for the top spot, they have been so thoroughly vetted that they can be relied upon to make the standard, traditionally approved decisions. They are effectively indistinguishable from one another—and this is why much of the research showed little effect for leaders.

But the unfiltered candidates have not been vetted by the system and cannot be relied upon to make the "approved" decisions—many would not even know what the approved decisions are. They do unexpected things, have different backgrounds, and are often unpredictable. Yet they bring change and make a difference. Often that difference is a negative. Since they don't play by the rules, they often break the institutions they are guiding. A minority of unfiltered leaders are transformative, though, shedding organizations of their misguided beliefs and foolish consistencies, and turning them toward better horizons. These are the leaders that the research said have enormous positive impact.

In his Ph.D. thesis, Mukunda applied his theory to all the U.S. presidents, evaluating which ones were filtered and which unfiltered, and whether or not they were great leaders. The results were overwhelming. His theory predicted presidential impact with an almost unheard of statistical confidence of 99 percent.

The filtered leaders didn't rock the boat. The unfiltered leaders couldn't help but rock it. Often they broke things, but sometimes they broke things like slavery, as Abraham Lincoln did.

Mukunda understood firsthand. His unconventional Ph.D. thesis made him an outlier in the academic job market. Despite a Harvard and MIT pedigree, he received only two job interviews after more than fifty applications. Schools wanted a conventional professor who could teach Political Science 101—they wanted a *filtered* academic. Mukunda's outside-the-box approach made him an unlikely candidate for traditional professorships. Only schools looking for superstar outliers, with the resources to support a diverse and well-rounded faculty, were interested in someone like him. Harvard Business School made him an offer, and he accepted.

When I spoke to Mukunda, he said, "The difference between good leaders and great leaders is not an issue of 'more.' They're fundamentally different people." Had the British seen the failure of appeasement and said "Get us a better Neville Chamberlain," they would have been screwed. They didn't need a more filtered leader; they needed someone the system would have never let in the door. The old ways didn't work, and doubling down on them would have been disastrous. To fight a menace like Hitler, they needed a maverick like Churchill.

When I asked Mukunda what made the unfiltered leaders so

much more impactful, he said often they had unique qualities that differentiated them. Not the flattering descriptors you might expect, like "incredibly smart" or "politically astute." These qualities were often negative at the mean—qualities you and I would consider "bad"—but due to the specific context, they became positives. Like Churchill's paranoid defense of the British state, these qualities were a poison that under just the right circumstances could be a performance-enhancing drug.

Mukunda calls these "intensifiers." And they hold the secret to how your biggest weakness might just be your greatest strength.

*

Glenn Gould was such a hypochondriac that if you sneezed while on a phone call with him, he'd immediately hang up.

The classical pianist routinely wore gloves, and it wasn't uncommon for him to have on multiple pairs at the same time. Speaking about the portable pharmacy of medications he always had on him, Gould said, "One reporter wrote that I traveled with a suitcase full of pills. Actually, they barely fill a briefcase." He'd cancel as many as 30 percent of his concerts, sometimes rebooking them and then recanceling them. Gould quipped, "I don't go to concerts, sometimes not even my own."

Yeah, he was a strange guy. He's also one of the undisputed greatest musicians of the twentieth century. He won four Grammys and sold millions of albums. He even achieved the truest hallmark of fame in our era: he was referenced on an episode of *The Simpsons*.

Gould wasn't merely a hypochondriac. He was called "a musical Howard Hughes" by *Newsweek*. He would go to sleep at six A.M. and wake in the afternoon. If he deemed a flight "unlucky," he'd refuse to get on the plane. He hated cold weather so much he wore winter clothes in the summer and often used a trash bag to carry his everyday items. This eventually led to Gould being arrested in Florida because police mistook him for a hobo.

Of course, his eccentricities affected his relationships. Afraid that getting too close to people might hurt his work, he often kept friends at arm's length. His lifeline was the telephone. In the last nine months of his life, he ran up a phone bill approaching thirteen thousand dollars. His crazy driving earned the passenger seat of his car the nickname the "suicide seat" among his friends. He once commented, "I suppose it can be said that I'm an absent-minded driver. It's true that I've driven through a number of red lights on occasion, but on the other hand, I've stopped at a lot of green ones but never gotten credit for it."

What was even stranger was how he played his famous music. Kevin Bazzana described it in his wonderful biography of Gould: "the rumpled appearance, the simian crouch over the keyboard, the flailing arms and gyrating torso and bobbing head." Remember, this isn't a jazz pianist or Elton John. This guy was playing *Bach*. And he hated performing. His control-freak nature did not lend itself to the touring requirements of changing planes and hotels, and dealing with new people daily. "I detest audiences. I think they're a force of evil," he once hissed.

And then there was "the chair." Because of his playing style, Gould needed a special chair. It was a little more than a foot off the ground and sloped forward so he could comfortably sit on the edge of the seat. He had so many specific requirements that his father ended up having to custom make it for him. Gould would use that one chair for his entire career, shipping it everywhere for his performances. It underwent significant wear and tear over the years, eventually being held together by wire and tape. It can even be heard squeaking on his albums.

Despite his extreme eccentricity, he was electrifying. As George Szell of the Cleveland Orchestra once said, "That nut's a genius."

But his skills, his fame, his success, all could have easily never come to be. Yes, he was a prodigy, having achieved the skill level of a professional at age twelve, but he was so awkward and sensitive as a child that for a few years he had to be homeschooled because he couldn't deal with the pressures of being around other kids.

Gould could have been someone completely unable to function in the real world. So how did he manage to thrive and become one

SHOULD WE PLAY IT SAFE AND DO WHAT WE'RE TOLD IF WE WANT TO SUCCEED?

15

of the greats? Luckily he was born into an environment perfectly suited to his fragile temperament. His parents were supportive—to an almost impossible degree. His mother devoted herself to nurturing his talent and his father spent three thousand dollars a year on Glenn's musical training. (Does three thousand dollars not sound like a lot? This was in the 1940s. That was twice the average annual salary in Toronto at the time, Gould's hometown.)

With such an incredible level of support and an inexhaustible work ethic, Gould's talent bloomed. He would be known for sixteen-hour days and hundred-hour weeks in the recording studio. It wasn't odd for him to be oblivious to the calendar when scheduling sessions and to require a reminder that most people did not want to work on Thanksgiving or Christmas. When asked what advice he would give aspiring artists, he said, "You must give up everything else."

His neuroses-fueled obsessiveness paid off. By the young age of twenty-five, he was performing on a musical tour of Russia. No North American had done that since before World War II. At twenty-eight, he was on television with Leonard Bernstein and the New York Philharmonic. By thirty-one, he was a legend of music.

Then he decided to vanish. "I really would like the last half of my life to myself," Gould said. At thirty-two, he stopped performing publicly altogether. All told, he had given fewer than three hundred concerts. Most touring musicians do that in just three years. He still worked like a madman, but he no longer performed for audiences. He wanted the control that only studio recording could give him. Oddly enough, his retirement from performance did not limit his influence in the world of music—in fact, it enhanced it. Kevin Bazzana notes, Gould went on "maintaining his presence through a conspicuous absence." He kept working until his death in 1982. The next year he was inducted into the Grammy Hall of Fame.

What did Gould have to say about his extreme habits and crazy lifestyle? "I don't think I'm all that eccentric." Biographer Kevin Bazzana says, "That is a hallmark of a true eccentric—not thinking you're all that eccentric, even when your every thought, word, and deed seems to set you apart from the rest of the world."

Gould certainly would not have become a musical legend without that early encouragement and incredible financial support from his parents. He was too fragile and peculiar a creature to withstand the harshness of the world. Without that nurturing he might really have been just an overdressed hobo in Florida.

Let's talk about orchids, dandelions, and hopeful monsters. (I know, I know, you talk about these things all the time and this is nothing new to you. Please indulge me.)

There's an old Swedish expression that says most kids are dandelions but a few are orchids. Dandelions are resilient. They're not the most beautiful flowers, but even without good care they thrive. Nobody goes around deliberately planting dandelions. You don't need to. They do just fine under almost any conditions. Orchids are different. If you don't care for them properly they wilt and die. But if given proper care, they bloom into the most gorgeous flowers imaginable.

Now we're not just talking about flowers, and we're not just talking about kids. We're actually learning a lesson about cutting-edge genetics.

The news is always reporting on a gene that causes this or that. Our first instinct is to label the gene as "bad" or "good." This gene causes alcoholism or violence. *Whew, good thing I don't have that gene.* It's just bad. Psychologists call this the "diathesis-stress model." If you have this bad gene and encounter problems in life, you're predisposed to end up with a disorder like depression or anxiety, so pray you don't have the awful gene that can turn you into a monster. There's only one problem: more and more it's looking like this perspective might be wrong.

Recent discoveries in genetics are turning this bad gene vs. good gene model on its head and pointing toward what looks a lot more like the concept of intensifiers. Psychologists call it the "differential susceptibility hypothesis." The same genes that lead to bad stuff can actually lead to great stuff in a different situation. The same knife that can be used to viciously stab someone can also prepare food for your family. Whether the knife is good or bad depends on context.

Let's get specific. Most people have a normal *DRD4* gene, but some have a variant called *DRD4-7R*. Uh-oh. *7R* has been associated with ADHD, alcoholism, and violence. It's a "bad" gene. Yet researcher Ariel Knafo did a study to see which kids would share candy without being asked. Most three-year-olds are not about to give up tasty treats if they don't have to, but the kids who had the *7R* gene were more likely to. Why were the kids with this "bad" gene so inclined to help, even when they weren't asked? Because *7R* isn't "bad." Like that knife, it's reliant on context. *7R* kids who were raised in rough environments, who were abused or neglected, were more likely to become alcoholics and bullies. But *7R* children who received good parenting were even *kinder* than kids who had the standard *DRD4* gene. Context made the difference.

A number of other genes associated with behavior have shown similar effects. Teenagers with one type of the *CHRM2* gene who are raised poorly end up as the worst delinquents, but teens with the same gene, raised in good homes, come out on top. Children who have a *5-HTTLPR* variant and domineering parents are more likely to cheat, while kids with the same gene who receive kind nurturing are the tykes most likely to obey the rules.

Okay, let's step away from the microscope and the acronyms for a sec.

Most people are dandelions; they'll come out okay under almost any circumstances. Others are orchids; they're not just more sensitive to negative outcomes but more sensitive to *everything*. They won't flourish in the dirt by the side of a road like a dandelion would. But when they're well tended in a nice greenhouse, their beauty will put the dandelions to shame. As writer David Dobbs said in a piece for *The Atlantic*, "the very genes that give us the most trouble as a species, causing behaviors that are self-destructive and antisocial, also underlie humankind's phenomenal adaptability and evolutionary success. With a bad environment and poor parenting, orchid children can end up depressed, drug-addicted, or in jail—but with the right environment and good parenting, they can grow up to be society's most creative, successful, and happy people."

This leads us to hopeful monsters. What are they? Professors Wendy Johnson and Thomas J. Bouchard, Jr. said, "A hopeful monster is an individual that deviates radically from the norm in a population because of a genetic mutation that confers a potentially adaptive advantage." While Darwin said that all evolution was gradual, Richard Goldschmidt put forth the idea that maybe nature occasionally made bigger changes. And he was mocked as a kook. But late in the twentieth-century, scientists like Stephen Jay Gould started realizing Goldschmidt may have been on to something. Researchers started seeing examples of mutations that weren't so gradual and fit the hopeful-monsters theory. Nature occasionally tries something very different, and if that "monster" finds the right environment and succeeds, it might just end up changing the species for the better. Again, it's the intensifiers theory. As writer Po Bronson said, "All of Silicon Valley is based on character defects that are rewarded uniquely in this system."

What if I told you your son's upper body would be too long, his legs too short, his hands and feet too big, and he'd have gangly arms? I doubt you'd jump for joy. None of those things sounds objectively "good." But when a knowledgeable swim coach hears those things, he sees nothing but Olympic Gold.

Michael Phelps should be considered one of the X-Men: a mutant with superpowers. Is Phelps physically perfect? Far from it. He doesn't dance well. Or even run well. In fact, he doesn't seem designed to move on land at all. But Mark Levine and Michael Sokolove both wrote pieces for the *New York Times* describing Phelps's collection of odd traits as making him uniquely suited to being an awesome swimmer. Yes, he's strong and lean, but for a six-foot-four-inch man he's not normally proportioned. His legs are short and his trunk long – making him more like a canoe. He has disproportionately big hands and feet—better "flippers." If you extend your arms out in either direction, the distance between your fingertips should match your height. Not for Phelps. His wingspan is six feet seven inches. Longer arms mean more powerful strokes in the pool. Phelps joined the U.S. Olympic Team at age fifteen. Nobody so young had done that since 1932. His biggest challenge as a swimmer? Diving into the pool. He's slower off the blocks than most swimmers. Phelps simply wasn't built for moving out of water. And this monster is more than just hopeful; he's earned more Olympic medals than anyone, ever.

How does this relate to success outside of athletics? Researchers Wendy Johnson and Thomas J. Bouchard Jr. suggest that geniuses might be considered hopeful monsters too. While Michael Phelps can be awkward on terra firma, Glenn Gould seemed positively hopeless in polite society. But both of them thrived, thanks to the right environment.

We saw that some orchids wilt from bad parenting and blossom when raised well. Why else might some monsters end up hopeless and others hopeful? Why do some people end up crazy-brilliant and others end up crazy-*crazy*? Dean Keith Simonton says that when creative geniuses take personality tests, "their scores on the pathology scales fall in a middle range. Creators exhibit more psychopathology than average persons, but less than true psychotics. They seem to possess just the right amount of weirdness."

Too often we label things "good" or "bad" when the right designation might merely be "different." The Israeli military needed people who could analyze satellite images for threats. They needed soldiers who had amazing visual skills, wouldn't get bored looking at the same place all day long, and could notice subtle changes. Not an easy task. But the IDF's Visual Intelligence Division found the perfect recruits in the most unlikely of places. They began recruiting people with autism. While autistics may struggle with personal interaction, many excel at visual tasks, like puzzles. And they've proven themselves a great asset in their nation's defense.

Dr. David Weeks, a clinical neuropsychologist, wrote, "Eccentrics are the mutations of social evolution, providing the intellectual materials for natural selection." They can be orchids like Glenn Gould or hopeful monsters like Michael Phelps. We spend too much time trying to be "good" when good is often merely average. To be great we must be different. And that doesn't come from trying to follow society's vision of what is best, because society doesn't always know what it needs. More often being the best means just being the best version of you. As John Stuart Mill remarked, "That so few now dare to be eccentric, marks the chief danger of our time."

In the right environment, bad can be good and odd can be beautiful.

*

Steve Jobs was worried.

In 2000, he and the other senior leaders of Pixar were all asking the same question: Was Pixar losing its edge? They'd had huge hits in *Toy Story, Toy Story 2,* and *A Bug's Life,* but they feared that with success the studio synonymous with creativity would grow, slow down, and become complacent.

To try to invigorate the team, they hired Brad Bird, director of the acclaimed animated film *Iron Giant,* to helm Pixar's next big project. Jobs, John Lasseter, and Ed Catmull felt he had the mind to keep the company vibrant.

Did he address the creativity crisis by leaning on Pixar's established top performers? No. Did he recruit top outside talent and bring in new blood? Nope. This wasn't the time to play it safe and look for "filtered" talent. It had made them successful, but it had also gotten them to this sticking point.

As he assembled his first project at Pixar, Bird revealed his plan to address the creativity crisis: "Give us the black sheep. I want artists who are frustrated. I want the ones who have another way of doing things that nobody's listening to. Give us all the guys who are probably headed out the door." Translation: *Give me your "unfiltered" artists. I know they're crazy. That's exactly what I need.*

Bird's new "Dirty Dozen" of animation didn't just make a film differently. They changed the way the entire studio worked:

> We gave the black sheep a chance to prove their theories, and we changed the way a number of things are done here. For less money per minute than was spent on the previous film, *Finding Nemo,* we did a movie that had three times the number of sets and had everything that was hard to do. All this because the heads of Pixar gave us leave to try crazy ideas.

That project was *The Incredibles.* It grossed over $600 million and won the Oscar for Best Animated Feature.

The same traits that make people a nightmare to deal with can also make them the people who change the world.

Research shows that very creative people are more arrogant, dishonest, and disorganized. They also get lower grades in school. Despite what teachers may say, they dislike creative students because those children often don't do what they're told. Does this sound like a great employee to you? Hardly. So it's no surprise that creativity is inversely correlated with employee performance reviews. Creative people are less likely to be promoted to CEO.

H. R. Giger, the man responsible for the eerily brilliant designs of the creature in the *Alien* film franchise, explained: "In Chur, Switzerland, the word 'artist' is a term of abuse, combining drunkard, whore monger, layabout, and simpleton in one."

But as any mathematician knows, averages can be deceptive. Andrew Robinson, CEO of famed advertising agency BBDO, once said, "When your head is in a refrigerator and your feet on a burner, the average temperature is okay. I am always cautious about averages."

As a general rule, anything better aligned to fit a unique scenario is going to be problematic on average. And qualities that are "generally good" can be bad at the extremes. The jacket that works just fine eight months out of the year will be a terrible choice in the dead of winter. By the same token, with intensifiers, qualities that seem universally awful have their uses in specific contexts. They're the Formula 1 cars that are undriveable on city streets but break records on a track.

It's a matter of basic statistics. When it comes to the extremes of performance, averages don't matter; what matters is variance, those deviations from the norm. Almost universally, we humans try to filter out the worst to increase the average, but by doing this we also decrease variance. Chopping off the left side of the bell curve improves the average but there are always qualities that we think are in that left side that also are in the right.

A great example of this is the often-debated connection between creativity and mental illness. In his study "The Mad-Genius Paradox," Dean Keith Simonton found that mildly creative people are mentally healthier than average—but *extremely* creative people have a far higher incidence of mental disorders. Much like with Leadership Filtration Theory, reaching the heights of success requires a dip into qualities that are otherwise problematic.

This is regularly seen across a wide variety of disorders—and talents. Studies show people with attention deficit disorder (ADD) are more creative. Psychologist Paul Pearson found a connection between humor, neuroticism, and psychopathy. Impulsivity is a generally negative trait frequently mentioned in the same sentence as "violent" and "criminal," but it also has a clear link to creativity.

Would you hire a psychopath? No. And the research shows that psychopaths don't do well on average. Most people would just stop there, but a study titled "Personality Characteristics of Successful Artists" showed that top performers in creative fields demonstrate markedly higher scores on measures of psychoticism than lesser artists. Another study from the *Journal of Personality and Social Psychology* showed that successful U.S. presidents also demonstrate higher scores on psychopathic characteristics.

Often intensifiers masquerade as positives because we give successful people the benefit of the doubt. It's the old joke that poor people are crazy and rich people are "eccentric." Traits like obsessiveness are framed as positives for those already in the successful camp and negatives for others. We all know some who benefit from perfectionism and others who are just "crazy."

Malcolm Gladwell popularized K. Anders Ericsson's research showing that it takes approximately ten thousand hours of effort to become an expert at something. There is a natural reaction to so big a number: *Why in the world would anyone do that?*

With the idea framed by the term "expertise," we are quick to associate positive notions, like "dedication" and "passion," but there's little doubt that spending so much time and hard work on anything nonessential has an element of obsession to it. While the valedictorian treats school as a job, working hard to get A's and follow the rules, the obsessed creative succeeds by bearing down on his or her passion projects with a religious zeal.

In his memorably titled study "The Mundanity of Excellence," Daniel Chambliss examined the extreme dedication and unvarying, monotonous routines of top-level swimmers. Considering they put themselves through this day after day for years on end, the idea of dedication rings hollow. But the word "obsession" makes you nod your head.

You may think intensifiers are only relevant to areas of individual artistry and expertise, like sports, or that they just aren't relevant in the regular world. You'd be wrong. Consider some of the richest people in the world. Do you see conscientious rule followers, free from negative outlier traits? No.

Fifty-eight members of the Forbes 400 either avoided college or ditched it partway through. These fifty-eight—almost 15 percent of the total—have an average net worth of $4.8 billion. This is 167 percent greater than the average net worth of the four hundred, which is $1.8 billion. It's more than twice the average net worth of those four hundred members who attended Ivy League colleges.

The hard-charging Silicon Valley entrepreneur has become a respected, admired icon in the modern age. Do these descriptors match the stereotype? A ball of energy. Little need for sleep. A risk taker. Doesn't suffer fools gladly. Confident and charismatic, bordering on hubristic. Boundlessly ambitious. Driven and restless.

Absolutely. They're also the traits associated with a clinical condition called hypomania. Johns Hopkins psychologist John Gartner has done work showing that's not a coincidence. Full-blown mania renders people unable to function in normal society. But hypomania produces a relentless, euphoric, impulsive machine that explodes toward its goals while staying connected (even if only loosely) with reality.

With intensifiers, you have to take the good with the bad. In their paper "The Economic Value of Breaking Bad: Misbehavior, Schooling, and the Labor Market," the authors showed that efforts to reduce aggressiveness and misbehavior in young boys did improve their grades but also reduced their lifetime earnings. Boys who acted out ended up working more hours, being more productive, and earning 3 percent more than boys who didn't.

It parallels the venture capital industry. Noted venture capitalist Marc Andreesen spoke at Stanford, saying:

> . . . the venture capital business is 100 percent a game of outliers, it is extreme outliers . . . We have this concept, invest in strength versus lack of weakness. And at first that is obvious, but it's actually fairly subtle. Which is sort of the default way to do venture capital, is to check boxes. So "really good founder, really good idea, really good products, really good initial customers. Check, check, check, check. Okay this is reasonable, I'll put money in it." What you find with those sort of checkbox deals, and they get done all the time, but what you find is that they often don't have something that really makes them really remarkable and special. They don't have an extreme strength that makes them an outlier. On the other side of that, the companies that have the really extreme strengths often have serious flaws. So one of the cautionary lessons of venture capital is, if you don't invest on the basis of serious flaws, you

don't invest in most of the big winners. And we can go through example after example after example of that. But that would have ruled out almost all the big winners over time. So what we aspire to do is to invest in the start-ups that have a really extreme strength. Along an important dimension, that we would be willing to tolerate certain weaknesses.

In some cases the greatest tragedies produce the greatest intensifiers. What do the following people all have in common?

- Abraham Lincoln
- Gandhi
- Michelangelo
- Mark Twain

They all lost a parent before age sixteen. The list of orphans who became spectacular successes—or at least notoriously influential—is much longer and includes no fewer than fifteen British prime ministers.

There's no doubt that for many losing a parent at a young age is devastating, with profound negative effects. But for some, as Dan Coyle points out in *The Talent Code,* researchers theorize that such a tragedy instills in a child the feeling that the world is not safe and that an immense amount of energy and effort will be needed to survive. Due to their unique personality and circumstances, these orphans overcompensate and turn tragedy into fuel for greatness.

So under the right circumstances there can be big upsides to "negative" qualities. Your "bad" traits might be intensifiers. But how can you turn them into superpowers?

*

In 1984, Neil Young was sued for not being himself.

Music mogul David Geffen had signed the rock-and-roll legend to a major contract but didn't like Young's first album for the label. The lawsuit would say it was "unrepresentative." Plain and simple,

Geffen had wanted Neil Young to be who he'd always been, do what he'd always done, and, quite frankly, sell lots of albums doing it. In Geffen's mind, the album *Trans* was too country. Neil Young hadn't made a Neil Young album.

On the surface, that might be true. But underneath it was dead wrong.

Neil Young had always been an innovator. That's who he really was. As an artist, he'd always tried different things. He wasn't making a quality controlled, consistent product like Coca-Cola. His sound had evolved and would continue to. Neil Young was being himself.

After talking with Gautam Mukunda about Leadership Filtration Theory, I asked the obvious question we'd all want to know the answer to: "How do I use it to be more successful in life?" He said there are two steps.

First, *know thyself.* This phrase has been uttered many times throughout history. It's carved into stone at the Oracle at Delphi. The Gospel of Thomas says, "If you bring forth what is within you, what you bring forth will save you. If you do not bring forth what is within you, what you do not bring forth will destroy you."

If you're good at playing by the rules, if you related to those valedictorians, if you're a filtered leader, then double down on that. Make sure you have a path that works for you. People high in conscientiousness do great in school and in many areas of life where there are clear answers and a clear path. But when there aren't, life is really hard for them. Research shows that when they're unemployed, their happiness drops 120 percent more than those who aren't as conscientious. Without a path to follow they're lost.

If you're more of an outsider, an artist, an unfiltered leader, you'll be climbing uphill if you try to succeed by complying with a rigid, formal structure. By dampening your intensifiers, you'll be not only at odds with who you are but also denying your key advantages.

While improving yourself is noble and necessary, research shows that many of the more fundamental aspects of personality don't change. Traits like verbal fluency, adaptability, impulsivity, and humility are stable from childhood through adulthood.

In *Management Challenges for the 21st Century*, Peter Drucker, probably the most influential thinker on the subject of management, says that to be successful throughout your entire work life—which will likely span numerous jobs, multiple industries, and wholly different careers—it all comes down to exactly what Mukunda said: knowing yourself. And knowing yourself, in terms of achieving what you want in life, means being aware of your strengths.

Consider the people we're all envious of who can confidently pick something, say they're going to be awesome at it, and then calmly go and *actually* be awesome at it. This is their secret: they're not good at everything, but they know their strengths and choose things that are a good fit. Regarding knowing your strengths, Drucker says:

> [This] enables people to say to an opportunity, to an offer, to an assignment, "Yes, I'll do that. But this is the way I should be doing it. This is the way it should be structured. This is the way my relationships should be. These are the kind of results you should expect from me, and in this time frame, because this is who I am."

Many people struggle with this. They aren't sure what their strengths are. Drucker offers a helpful definition: "What are you good at that consistently produces desired results?"

To find out what those things are, he recommends a system he calls "feedback analysis." Quite simply, when you undertake a project, write down what you expect to happen, then later note the result. Over time you'll see what you do well and what you don't.

By figuring out whether you fall into the filtered or unfiltered camp and by knowing where your strengths are, you're miles ahead of the average person in terms of achieving both success *and* happiness. Modern positive psychology research has shown again and again that one of the keys to happiness is emphasizing what are called "signature strengths." Research by Gallup shows that the more hours per day you spend doing what you're good at, the less stressed you feel and the more you laugh, smile, and feel you're being treated with respect.

Once you know what type of person you are and your signature strengths, how do you thrive? This leads to Mukunda's second piece of advice: *pick the right pond.*

You've got to pick the environments that work for you . . . context is so important. The unfiltered leader who is an amazing success in one situation will be a catastrophic failure in the other, in almost all cases. It's way too easy to think, "I've always succeeded, I am a success, I am successful because I am a success, because it's about me, and therefore I will succeed in this new environment." Wrong. You were successful because you happened to be in an environment where your biases and predispositions and talents and abilities all happened to align neatly with those things that would produce success in that environment.

Ask yourself, *Which companies, institutions, and situations value what I do?*

Context affects everyone. In fact, the conscientious valedictorians so good at following rules often stumble the most here. Without an existing passion and being so eager to please, they often head in the wrong direction when they're finally free to choose. Speaking about the valedictorians she studied, Karen Arnold said, "People feel like valedictorians can take care of themselves, but just because they could get A's doesn't mean they can translate academic achievement into career achievement."

Whether you're a filtered doctor or a wild, unfiltered artist, research shows the pond you pick matters enormously. When Harvard Business School professor Boris Groysberg looked at top Wall Street analysts who jumped ship to work for a competitor, he noticed something interesting: they stopped being top analysts. Why? We tend to think experts are experts just because of their unique skills and we forget the power of context, of knowing one's way around, of the teams who support them, and the shorthand they develop together over time. That's one of the things Groysberg discovered: when the analysts switched firms but brought their team with them, they stayed awesome.

When you choose your pond wisely, you can best leverage your type, your signature strengths, and your context to create tremendous value. This is what makes for a great career, but such self-knowledge can create value wherever you choose to apply it.

This was well illustrated by how Toyota helped a charity. The Food Bank for New York City relies on corporate donations to function. Toyota had donated money—until 2011 when they came up with a far better idea. Toyota's engineers had dedicated countless hours to fine-tuning processes and realized that while any company could donate cash, they had something unique to offer: their expertise. So they decided to donate *efficiency*.

Journalist Mona El-Naggar described the results:

> At a soup kitchen in Harlem, Toyota's engineers cut down the wait time for dinner to 18 minutes from as long as 90. At a food pantry on Staten Island, they reduced the time people spent filling their bags to 6 minutes from 11. And at a warehouse in Bushwick, Brooklyn, where volunteers were packing boxes of supplies for victims of Hurricane Sandy, a dose of kaizen cut the time it took to pack one box to 11 seconds from 3 minutes.

You can do this too: know thyself and pick the right pond. Identify your strengths and pick the right place to apply them.

If you follow rules well, find an organization aligned with your signature strengths and go full steam ahead. Society clearly rewards those who can comply, and these people keep the world an orderly place.

If you're more of an unfiltered type, be ready to blaze your own path. It's risky, but that's what you were built for. Leverage the intensifiers that make you unique. You're more likely to reach the heights of success—and happiness—if you embrace your "flaws."

It's like the Turing test. For years, computer scientists have put people in front of computers and had them converse via typing with "someone." After a period of time the people are asked, "Were you communicating with a human or a piece of software?" The program that fools the most judges wins the Loebner Prize. But there's also another prize given out at the competition—it goes to the *human* that is most convincingly human. When the judges look at what the people typed, which person is least likely to be mistaken for a clever computer? In 1994 the winner was Charles Platt. Did he come across as so human because his responses were more emotionally realistic or his use of English more rich and nuanced? Hell, no. He did it by being "moody, irritable, and obnoxious." Maybe that's because our flaws are what make us most human. Charles Platt found success through human flaws. And sometimes we can too.

You've now got a better idea of who you are and where you belong. But life isn't all about you, you, you. You have to deal with others. And what's the best way to do that? Do "nice guys finish last"? Or do you need to cut corners—and maybe a few throats—to get ahead?

Let's look at that next.

CHAPTER 2

Do Nice Guys Finish Last?

What You Can Learn About Trust, Cooperation, and Kindness . . . from Gang Members, Pirates, and Serial Killers

It's not uncommon for people to die while under a doctor's care. What is quite uncommon is for a doctor to deliberately kill his patients.

Michael Swango was not a very successful doctor. But as James B. Stewart explains in his book *Blind Eye,* Swango was one of the most successful serial killers ever.

By his third year in medical school, hospital patients he interacted with were dying at such a rate that his fellow students took notice. They joked that the best way to get rid of a patient was to assign them to Swango. In fact, they gave him a tongue-in-cheek nickname: "Double-O Swango." Like James Bond, he seemed to have a license to kill.

But it was a hospital. People die there. It happens. So it was easy to brush off the deaths as accidental. However, the disproportionate number of fatalities continued when Swango began his neurosurgery internship at Ohio State. After Swango began his rotation on the ninth floor, there had been more patients requiring resuscitation than in the past year.

How did he get away with this? Was he a genius mastermind like Hannibal Lecter? Hardly. While Swango was definitely very intelligent (he was a national merit finalist and graduated summa cum laude from college), it's a huge understatement to say he didn't make much effort to reduce suspicion.

When a mass murder at a McDonald's was all over the news, he told a colleague, "Every time I think of a good idea, somebody beats me to it." He religiously kept a scrapbook of newspaper articles about violent incidents. When asked why, he said, "If I'm ever accused of murder [these will] prove I'm not mentally competent. This will be my defense."

Finally an incident occurred that no one could ignore. A nurse witnessed him inject something into the IV line of a patient, Rena Cooper. And Swango was not Cooper's doctor. She nearly died, but doctors managed to save her life. Once stable, she confirmed Swango's involvement, and an investigation into the incident quickly followed.

This is the part where I'm supposed to tell you that they caught him. That everyone did the right thing. That the system worked. That good triumphed over evil.

But that's not what happened.

Senior management at the hospital closed ranks, more concerned about the hospital's reputation than stopping a murderer. *What if the public found out they had a killer working there? What about their jobs? What if Swango filed a lawsuit? What if patients or their families sued them?* They obstructed the police investigation. Meanwhile, Swango was allowed to keep working. In one form or another, his reign of terror continued . . . for fifteen years.

It's estimated Swango killed sixty people, putting him pretty high up on the list of "successful" American serial killers, though no one is sure exactly how many people he killed. In all likelihood it was far more.

Many educated, intelligent people knew what he was doing and had the chance to stop him. But they didn't.

Now, this isn't a book about successful serial killers, but the Swango case does raise serious questions we all wonder about: Do people who cheat and break the rules succeed more often? Is the world fair? Can good people get ahead or are they doomed to be suckers? *Do nice guys really finish last?*

The answers aren't all peaches and cream, but that doesn't mean there isn't plenty of good news to give us hope.

Although perhaps we should start to unravel this puzzle by starting with the *bad* news.

*

In the short term, sometimes being bad can be very good.

"Work hard, play fair, and you'll get ahead," they say. Um, sorry but there's actually a lot of evidence that shows this just *isn't* the case. People surveyed say effort is the number-one predictor of success, but research shows it's actually one of the worst.

Appearances seem to trump truth at the office. According to Stanford Graduate School of Business professor Jeffrey Pfeffer, managing what your boss thinks of you is far more important than actual hard work. A study shows that those who made a good impression got better performance reviews than those who worked harder but didn't manage impressions as well.

Often this comes down to something we're all very familiar with: good ol' ass kissing. Is flattering the boss effective? Research has shown flattery is so powerful that it works *even when the boss knows it's insincere.* Jennifer Chatman, a professor at the University of California at Berkeley, did a study to see at what point flattery backfired . . . but she couldn't find one.

Pfeffer says we need to stop thinking the world is fair. He puts it bluntly:

> The lesson from cases of people both keeping and losing their jobs is that as long as you keep your boss or bosses happy, performance really does not matter that much and, by contrast, if you upset them, performance won't save you.

For those of us expecting to be rewarded for long hours and fair play, this can be tough to stomach. But hold on—it gets worse. Ass kissers aren't the only ones who thrive. Jerks do too.

Do you approach salary negotiations with a win-win, mutual benefit attitude? Unfortunately people who push for more money out of self-interest do better. The *Harvard Business Review* reports that men low in the personality trait "agreeableness" make as much as ten thousand dollars a year more than men high in agreeableness. Rude people also have better credit scores.

As sad as it sounds, it seems we're all inclined to mistake kindness for weakness.

Eighty percent of our evaluations of other people come down to two characteristics: warmth and competence. And a study from Teresa Amabile at Harvard called "Brilliant but Cruel" shows we assume the two are inversely related: if someone is too nice, we figure they must be less competent. In fact, being a jerk makes others see you as more powerful. Those who break rules are seen as having more power than those who obey.

It's not just an issue of perception; sometimes jerks *are* actually better at their jobs than the nice guys. Research shows some negative traits can actually make you more likely to become a leader. The managers who moved up the ladder quickest—and were best at their jobs—weren't the people who tried to be team players or who focused on accomplishing tasks. They were the ones most focused on gaining power.

To add insult to injury, it's not just that jerks do well; being the downtrodden nice guy can kill you. Being powerless at the office— having little control or discretion over your work—is a bigger risk factor for coronary artery disease than obesity or high blood pressure. Feel underpaid? That increases risk for a heart attack too. Meanwhile, ass kissing results in a reduction of workplace stress, improving happiness as well as physical health.

Are you a nice guy or gal who is having trouble processing all this bad news? Maybe that's because not having a high status position at the office contributes to a reduction in executive function. Want that in English? Feeling powerless actually makes you *dumber*.

We're taught that good conquers all, just like at the end of a Disney film. But sadly, in many scenarios researchers have studied, that's not the case. A study bluntly titled "Bad Is Stronger than Good" shows that in a shocking number of areas bad things are more impactful and longer lasting than good things: "Bad emotions, bad parents, and bad feedback have more impact than good ones, and bad information is processed more thoroughly than good . . . Hardly any exceptions (indicating greater power of good) can be found. Taken together, these findings suggest that bad is stronger than good, as a general principle across a broad range of psychological phenomena." And I can't help but mention that an informal study showed that ethics books are 25 percent more likely to be stolen than the average library book.

I'm going to stop now because my publisher won't let this book be packaged with antidepressants.

Why do jerks succeed? Sure, some of it's duplicity and evil, but there's something we can learn from them in good conscience: they're assertive about what they want, and they're not afraid to let others know about what they've achieved.

Does it sound like I'm encouraging you to be a jerk? Hold your horses. We're just getting started. They do win in the short term. Now we need to hear the other side.

And it all starts with the same thing your mom might say if you told her you were going to lie, cheat, bully, and ass kiss your way to the top: "What if everyone acted like that?"

So what happens when all of us become selfish and just stop trusting one another? The answer to that question is "Moldova."

*

I'm sure many times you've thought you were in the most miserable place on Earth. Whether it was elementary school as a child, a bad job, or just a bad day, you've probably felt at some point like you were in the unhappiest spot imaginable—but unless you were in Moldova, you weren't scientifically correct.

Ruut Veenhoven, the Dutch sociologist known as the "godfather of happiness research," maintains the World Database of Happiness. And when he looked at all the countries of the world in terms of happiness, Moldova came up dead last.

What garnered this little-known former Soviet republic such a dubious distinction? The Moldovans simply don't trust one another. It has reached epic proportions, so much so that it stifles co-operation in almost every area of Moldovan life. Writer Eric Weiner notes that so many students bribe teachers for passing grades that Moldovans won't go to doctors who are younger than age thirty-five, assuming they purchased their medical degrees.

Weiner sums up the Moldovan attitude with a single sentence: "*Not my problem.*" Getting people to act collectively for the benefit of the group seems impossible. Nobody wants to do anything that benefits others. Lack of trust has turned Moldova into a black hole of selfishness.

The usual response to Mom saying "What if everyone did that?" is to say, quite simply, "Well, everyone *doesn't.*" But that's not really true, is it? We all know a company or a department that slid downhill due to selfishness. Research agrees: bad behavior is infectious. It spreads. Soon you won't be the only one scheming.

Research by Dan Ariely of Duke University shows that seeing others cheat and get away with it increases cheating across the board. We start to see cheating as an acceptable social norm. It's a concept we can all relate to. After all, do you really drive under the speed limit all the time? Why not? Well, it's like the old joke about ethics. There are three categories: "right," "wrong," and "everybody does it." Once we see others getting away with something, we assume it's okay. Nobody wants to be the sucker who plays by the rules when no one else does.

Studies show expecting others to be untrustworthy creates a self-fulfilling prophecy. You assume they'll behave badly, so you stop trusting, which means you withhold effort and create a downward spiral. It's not surprising that work teams with just one bad apple experience performance deficits of 30 to 40 percent.

So, yes, individual shenanigans can pay off—but it's only a matter of time before other people start cutting corners too. Then everyone suffers, because you end up with a self-centered Moldova-like culture where there is no value being created by people contributing to the common good. Ruut Veenhoven said, "The quality of a society is more important than your place in that society." Why is that?

Robert Axelrod, a professor of political science at the University of Michigan, explains, "Not being nice may look promising at first, but in the long run it can destroy the very environment it needs for its own success."

Simply put, when you start being selfish and Machiavellian, others will eventually notice. If they retaliate before you rise to power, you're in bad shape. Even if you succeed, you've still got a problem. You've shown others that the way to succeed is by breaking the rules, so they'll break them too, because bad behavior is infectious and people do what works. You'll be creating other predators like yourself. Then the good people leave. That creates a ripple effect: you can quickly create a place where you don't want to work anymore, like Moldova. Once trust goes, everything goes. What quality do people, when surveyed across a number of arenas—work, athletic teams, family members—say they desire most in others? Trustworthiness.

To truly scale effort and succeed means going beyond selfishness to create trust and achieve cooperation. Ironically, even if you want to be successful at *evil* you need to do this. So to learn why selfishness doesn't work in organizations over the long haul and see how essential trust and cooperation are, you need to look at criminals.

*

It's your first day in prison and you're going through all the goodies in your gift basket. Seriously. I'm not kidding.

As David Skarbek of King's College London explains, prison gangs often act as welcoming committees to new inmates who are members of their gang, and it's not unheard of for inmates from the same neighborhood to provide gifts to help new entrants get settled. What could be nicer than that? (I'm not sure whether the gifts are up to Martha Stewart standards, but I can't think of a place where a gift basket would be more welcome.)

We think of gang members as lawless, impulsive psychopaths, and surely there are many who fall into this category, but they know a lot more about trust and cooperation than we give them credit for.

Gangs aren't coalitions dedicated to chaos, led by a nefarious Bond villain. In fact, the data show that street gangs don't create crime. It's the exact opposite: *crime creates street gangs.* Similarly, the majority of successful prison gangs on record were created not as a way to further evil but as a way to provide protection to their members while incarcerated. A study of members of the Aryan Brotherhood prison gang shows that far from being "the worst of the worst," gang members' criminal records or number of violent encounters in prison are nearly indistinguishable from those of non-gang members.

In many ways criminals are more aware of the value of trust and cooperation than you and I. Because within the world they live, trust cannot be taken for granted. You don't go to the office every day and wonder if someone is going to stab you in the neck. So the stakes of trustworthiness are much higher for criminals, and they can't call the cops when someone steals their heroin.

Some people may shake their head at this, thinking that while there is definitely a shortage of trust in the criminal community, it is more than made up for by the increased options criminals have: if someone screws them over they can kill him, and that will keep people in line. But research into organized crime shows resorting to violence is actually highly overrated. What happens when you go total Tony Soprano and start whacking everyone who causes problems? Everyone will respect you and no one will want to work with you. Being a mob boss who is too violent has an inherent irony to it. Would you want to work for someone whose response to late expense reports is two bullets to the head? I didn't think so.

Therefore smart criminals must find alternatives to violent enforcement. They need *more* order, not less, to reduce the increased options on their plate. As an inmate at Corcoran State Prison was quoted as saying, "Without order, we have anarchy, and when we have anarchy, people die here."

How valuable are stability and rules? So valuable that in prison, where much of daily interaction is divided along racial lines, whites actually *encourage* blacks to join black gangs. With more anonymity and separation, violence increases behind bars. When everyone is a part of the system—even if that means joining a rival gang—life is more stable.

Want to cheat a little? Fine. But if you want to do it every day for years, you need a system. Always worrying about being cheated or killed makes transactions too costly, preventing efficient dealings, whether you're selling Pepsi or illegal drugs. You need rules and cooperation, and that means trust.

Economists call it the "discipline of continuous dealings." When you know and trust someone, it makes a transaction smoother and faster. That means more transactions happen, producing a better market and more value for everyone involved. It's no different for prison gangs, really. Think of it like a good eBay review for your heroin dealer. "GREAT SELLER A++++++ would buy again."

Eventually this scaling of order, trust, and rules makes a prison gang look a lot more like a corporation. Gang leaders ("shot callers") often send recently incarcerated members of their gang new-arrival questionnaires. It's good to know what fresh employees have to offer. As crazy as it may sound, all this works. Corrupt countries with Mafia-style groups are more economically successful than countries with decentralized crime, showing higher rates of growth. They put the "organized" in organized crime. And while nefarious groups certainly have negative effects on society, the order they enforce has positive externalities as well. The presence of yakuza in Japanese cities is negatively correlated with civil lawsuits. Research shows prisons in the United States run smoother with gangs than without them.

Don't get me wrong. These are criminals. They're doing bad things. But for any criminal organization to be successful, it needs a level of trust and cooperation inside, even if its members are doing naughtiness outside. Successful criminals know that selfishness, internally, doesn't scale. Eventually this can even lead to criminals treating people—at least those inside the gang—quite well. (When was the last time your boss sent *you* a gift basket?)

This isn't some new thing—even hundreds of years ago criminal groups thrived by looking out for one another. And what might be the best historical example of criminal cooperation? The parrot-shouldered rebels of the high seas. Pirates were so successful because they treated their people well. They were democratic. They trusted one another. And they set up an economically sound system to make sure this would be the case.

These savvy businessmen of the oceans were not all crazed psychopaths with eye patches. In fact, according to Blackbeard expert Angus Konstam, that famed pirate, over the course of his career, killed exactly zero people. And there are no cases on record of anyone walking the plank. Nope. Not one.

So why do we have this impression of them as bloodthirsty savages? It's called marketing. It's much easier, cheaper, and safer to have people surrender quickly because they're terrified of you than it is to fight every battle, so pirates were sharp enough to cultivate a brand image of barbarity.

Of course, pirates weren't all kind sweethearts and Blackbeard was no Robin Hood. They cooperated so well not out of altruism but because it made good business sense. They knew they needed rules and trust to succeed, and they ended up forming a system more fair and appealing than life on tyrannical Royal Navy ships or mercantile boats, where workers were exploited to maximize profit. As Peter Leeson writes in his book *The Invisible Hook: The Hidden Economics of Pirates,* "Contrary to conventional wisdom, pirate life was orderly and honest."

You may be a pirate at heart yourself. Ever get tired of a bully of a boss and think about striking out on your own? Think everyone should have a say in how the company is run? Think a corporation is obligated to take care of its people? And that racism has no place in business? Congrats! You're a pirate.

Much like prison gangs, pirates weren't originally unified to do evil. In fact, one could easily argue they were a *response* to evil. Mercantile ship owners of the period were despotic. Captains routinely abused their authority. They could take any crewman's share of confiscated loot or have him executed. As a response to this predation, and a desire to sail the seas and not worry about being abused by the "management," the life of the pirate was born.

Pirate ships were very democratic places. All rules needed to be agreed to unanimously. Captains could be deposed for any reason, and this turned them from tyrants into something closer to servants. The only time a captain had total authority was in the midst of battle, when quick decision-making was a matter of life and death.

Pirates ended up forming a "company" you might be very happy to work for. Since the boss could be fired at any time, he was quite focused on taking good care of his employees. Captains' wages weren't significantly larger than anyone else's. As Leeson explains, "The difference between the highest and lowest paid person in this pirate crew was thus only a single share." And he didn't get ridiculous perks. Pirate captains didn't get a bigger bunk on the ship or more food.

Pirates Inc. also had great benefits. Fighting bravely or being the first to notice targets was handsomely rewarded with bonuses. Got injured? Just file a claim. Pirates effectively had a disability plan, covering battle-related injuries. And these fantastic HR initiatives worked. The historical record shows pirates had no trouble getting people to join their ranks, while the Royal Navy resorted to compelling men to sign up.

Pirates Inc. even had a diversity program hundreds of years before it was popular or mandated by law. Why? They weren't morally enlightened; racism simply wasn't good business whereas treating people right was. It gave them an advantage in recruiting and retaining talent. It's estimated that the average pirate ship was approximately 25 percent black. Each crewmember, regardless of race, had the right to vote on ship issues and was paid an equal share. This was in the early 1700s. The United States did not abolish slavery until more than a hundred fifty years later.

Did it work? Economists praise pirates for their business savvy. In Leeson's paper "An-arrgh-chy: The Law and Economics of Pirate Organization," he says, "Pirate governance created sufficient order and cooperation to make pirates one of the most sophisticated and successful criminal organizations in history."

So treating those around you well can lead to far greater success than selfishness—even if your goal is to make mischief.

Some may say I'm stretching the point. Talking about prison gangs or long dead pirates may be clever, but how relevant is it to modern life?

We've looked at the selfish bad guys, and we've looked at the bad guys who are smart enough to not be selfish. What about the truly good? What about those of us who really want to do the right thing? Do we succeed? Can nice guys finish first? When you do the right thing—if you put your life on the line to save someone else—will it be rewarded?

*

The young man next to you stumbles off the subway platform and falls onto the tracks below. He is incapacitated, helpless. You can feel the rumble of the approaching train. Do you climb down to help him?

Some would say it's less an act of altruism than an act of suicide. Your two young daughters are standing next to you. How will they fare if you die and they lose a parent? Letting a young man die is tragic, but aren't two deaths and two orphans more tragic? That's a tough question to answer.

Luckily, on January 2, 2007, Wesley Autrey didn't ask it.

As the lights on the front of the number-one train flashed in the tunnel, he jumped down to the tracks where Cameron Hollopeter lay helpless.

But Autrey had misjudged the speed of the train. It was coming *much* faster than he anticipated. There simply was not time to move Hollopeter to safety. Yet he wasn't about to let the man die either. The shriek of the train's brakes tore the air, but the driver couldn't stop its momentum in time.

As the sound of the oncoming train rose to a deafening roar, Autrey shoved Hollopeter into a narrow drainage ditch and leapt on top of him, sheltering him as the train passed over them.

Both were unharmed, though the train had come so close to killing them that it left grease on Autrey's hat. He later said, "I don't feel like I did something spectacular; I just saw someone who needed help. I did what I felt was right."

Wesley Autrey acted altruistically that day. He had everything to lose and nothing to gain. He was the type of hero we think exists only in movies.

So did this nice guy finish last?

No. Autrey received the Bronze Medallion, the highest award that New York City gives to civilians. (Previous winners include General Douglas MacArthur, Muhammad Ali, and Martin Luther King Jr.) His daughters received scholarships and computers. He got backstage passes to Beyoncé and a new Jeep; he was on *The Ellen DeGeneres Show* and received season tickets to the New Jersey Nets. On January 23, Autrey and his daughters were at the State of the Union address as guests of President George W. Bush, who praised Autrey's selfless actions on national television.

It's an amazing story. And that's exactly what cynics might say: we remember stories like this because they are so rare.

When we step aside from both the spectacular stories and the cynical eye rolling, what do the statistics actually tell us? Do nice guys finish last?

Yes. But they also finish *first*.

Confused? It actually makes perfect sense. Stay with me.

When Wharton School professor Adam Grant looked at who ended up at the bottom of success metrics, he found an awful lot of nice guys—"Givers." In studies of engineers, medical students, and salespeople, those who were the most giving to others consistently came up short. They missed more deadlines, got lower grades, and closed fewer sales.

For a guy like Adam, who has devoted much of his research to exploring ethical business and how altruistic behavior can lead to success, this was far more distressing than it might be to you or me. If he had stopped there, it would have been a sad day indeed. But he didn't. When I spoke with Adam, he said:

Then I looked at the other end of the spectrum and said if Givers are at the bottom, who's at the top? Actually, I was really surprised to discover, it's the Givers again. The people who consistently are looking for ways to help others are over-represented not only at the bottom but also at the top of most success metrics.

"Matchers" (people who try to keep an even balance of give and take) and "Takers" (people who selfishly always try to get more and give less) end up in the middle. Givers are found at the very top and very bottom. Those same studies showed that the major-ity of productive engineers, students with the highest grades, and salespeople who brought in the most revenue were all Givers.

When you think about it, it makes intuitive sense. We all know a martyr who goes out of their way to help others and yet fails to meet their own needs or ends up exploited by Takers. We also all know someone everyone loves because they are so helpful, and they succeed because everyone appreciates and feels indebted to them.

Being the most productive or getting top grades isn't the only thing Givers seem to excel at. It also appears to make them rich. When Arthur Brooks looked at the connection between charitable giving and income, he found that for every dollar donated, income for that person went up by $3.75. There was a clear relationship between how much was given and how much was earned that year.

Some of you may be scratching your heads. This seems to con-tradict much of what we saw in the beginning of the chapter, where jerks did better. Yes, on average jerks do better, but at the *very* top we see the Givers.

Income peaks among those who trust people more, not less. In a study titled "The Right Amount of Trust," people were asked how much they trusted others on a scale of one to ten. Income was highest among those who responded with the number eight. This aligns with what Adam Grant found, with Givers at the top of success metrics.

What also matched was that those who responded with a number above an eight had incomes 7 percent lower than the eights. Much like the Givers at the bottom of success studies, these people were more likely to be taken advantage of.

Who suffered the most? Those with the lowest levels of trust had an income 14.5 percent lower than eights. That loss is the equivalent of not attending college.

Surely these Givers can't hack it when they get to be leaders, right? Leaders are supposed to be tough. We saw earlier that some negative traits actually help people who are in charge. However, when we look at the top ranked leaders in the military, where we would expect toughness to be prized, the exact opposite is true: those scoring the best are supportive, not stern.

While some of those studies say the social stress of being a powerless nice guy can give you a heart attack, the big-picture research shows that the old maxim "The good die young" isn't true. The Terman Study, which followed many subjects across their entire lives, found that people who were kind actually lived longer, not shorter. You might be inclined to think that getting help from others would prolong your life, but the study showed the reverse: those who *gave* more to others lived longer.

Finally, there is the issue of happiness. While a number of data points show how jerks get promoted or are financially rewarded, they aren't necessarily any more thrilled with their lives. But research has found that ethical people are happier. People less tolerant of unethical behavior had a higher well-being than those who were okay with a big dose of cheating. The boost was equivalent to the happiness increase one would get from a small increase in income, getting hitched, and going to church regularly.

This is where the Moldovans have it all wrong. By not trusting, by not helping others, they miss out on a lot of what makes us happy. Studies show spending money on others makes us happier than spending it on ourselves. Volunteering even just two hours a week predicts increases in life satisfaction. Even more surprising, those who donate their time to help others feel less busy and like they have more free time.

In a lot of short-term scenarios a little cheating and bullying can pay off. But over time it pollutes the social environment and soon everyone is second-guessing everybody and no one wants to work toward the common good. Being a Taker has short-term benefits, but it's inherently limited. In the end, nobody wants to help you because they know what you're really like. Who are a Taker's worst enemies? *Other Takers,* says Adam Grant's research. While Givers get tons of help from other Givers and receive protection from Matchers—who believe that to maintain fairness kind acts should be rewarded—they have only Takers to worry about. Meanwhile, Takers end up being disliked by everyone, including other Takers.

Unless Takers learn to trust and cooperate, they can never really scale their efforts the way a group of Givers can. Even Matchers, who do benefit from trust and reciprocity, are inherently limited because they often wait for someone else to initiate a good act, which prevents exchanges that could be beneficial for both parties.

You might think I'm glossing over the fact that a lot of the Givers end up dead last. The difference between the Givers who succeed and the Givers who don't isn't random. Adam Grant notes that totally selfless Givers exhaust themselves helping others and get exploited by Takers, leading them to perform poorly on success metrics. There are a number of things Givers can do to build limits for themselves and make sure they don't go overboard. That two-hours-a-week volunteering? Don't do more. Research by Sonja Lyubomirsky shows that people are happier and less stressed when they "chunk" their efforts to help others versus a relentless "sprinkling." So by doing all their good deeds one day a week, Givers make sure assisting others doesn't hamper their own achievements. One hundred hours a year seems to be the magic number.

Grant also points out the other ace in the hole Givers have: Matchers. They want to see good rewarded and evil punished, so Matchers go out of their way to punish Takers and protect Givers from harm. When Givers are surrounded by a coterie of Matchers, they don't have to fear exploitation as much.

This may seem a bit confusing. In the short term, being a jerk has benefits but eventually poisons the well since others become jerks around you. In the long term, being a Giver pays off big, though you risk exhausting yourself helping others. In the war between good and evil, is there a clear winner? Is there a clear way to behave that will let you get ahead and let you sleep at night feeling like a decent person?

Actually, there is.

*

Don Johnson made $6 million in one night. No, I'm not talking about the *Miami Vice* actor. This Don is a gambler. And he took it all from the Tropicana. But that isn't where his winning streak stopped. He ended up taking the casinos of Atlantic City for a lot more.

It's an old saying in the gambling industry: the house always wins. And for a few months in 2011, Don Johnson became the house.

It's one of the most sensational success stories in gambling. Johnson didn't cheat or count cards, and nobody makes that much money due to pure luck. Johnson knew cards. More important, he knew math. His day job was running a company that calculated the odds for horse racing.

You see, top blackjack gamblers don't gamble. They know the odds and won't play straight up. They actually negotiate rules with the house: "If I lose X amount, you rebate me a percentage of it." Or "The dealer has to hit on X instead of Y." After the recession of 2008, casinos were in bad shape, and since a disproportionate amount of casino revenues come from high rollers, they were offering these players rebates of up to 20 percent. By the time Johnson was done negotiating, not only did the casino no longer have an odds advantage at the table but Johnson had reduced his losses to only eighty cents on the dollar. As long as he didn't make any strategic mistakes during play, he was *ahead*. He became the house. In cards, you can never be sure you'll win a particular hand, but once the odds favor you, the gods of math decree that the longer you stay, the better you do.

With that, Don went to work. Playing almost a hand of blackjack per minute and betting $100,000 a hand, he began devastating the Tropicana. At one point he won $800,000 on a single hand. Cutting similar deals with other casinos, he won $5 million from the Borgata and $4 million from Caesars. In six months, he took Atlantic City casinos for a cool $15 million.

It wasn't magic or luck or cheating. And he didn't win every hand he played. But by shifting the odds in his favor and playing right, he came out way ahead in the long run.

Let's handle the issue of ethics the way Don Johnson so marvelously approached the game of blackjack. Let's get the house edge in our favor. Don't worry; you won't have to do any heavy math. The system itself is something you've been familiar with since you were a child. And it works.

*

At this point you know cooperation is vital, but will you get cheated? Should you trust? If you don't, you risk becoming a Moldovan. If you do, you could end up a chump. How do you handle the dilemma of whether to trust?

When scientists look at the issue of trust, they turn to a game called the Prisoner's Dilemma. Here's how it works: Let's say you and your friend rob a bank, and you're not very good at robbing banks so you get caught. The police arrest you both and put you in separate rooms to interrogate you. You have no way to communicate with your friend. The cops offer you a deal: if you testify that your friend was the mastermind and he doesn't testify against you, you go free and he gets five years in prison. If you don't testify against your friend but he testifies against you, you get five years and he goes free. If you both testify against each other, you both get three years. If you both refuse to testify, you both get one year. If you two knew you could trust each other, the answer would be simple: you both keep your mouths shut and get one year. But can you trust your friend? Are the police scaring the heck out of him? Will he testify while you stay silent? That means he walks free and you get five years in prison. In a one-off game, testifying seems like the smart move, but what about when you play the game twenty times? That's more like life, right? Our fate rarely hangs on any one decision.

This is where Robert Axelrod got started. With the Cold War raging between the United States and the USSR, he wanted to explore what it takes to get people to trust and cooperate, what strategy is most effective. So he decided to have a tournament where different computer programs with different strategies play Prisoner's Dilemma together to see which one racked up the most points.

Researchers from psychology, economics, math, sociology, and other disciplines sent in a total of fourteen algorithms plus one program that would behave randomly. One of the programs was insanely nice: it always trusted its opponent even after being screwed over. Another of the programs—named ALL D—was the opposite: it always betrayed its opponent without fail. Other programs rested somewhere in between. Some of the more complex programs played nice for the most part while occasionally trying to sneak in a be-trayal to get a leg up. One program called Tester monitored the other player's moves to see how much it could get away with and then would backpedal if caught betraying its opponent.

Which ethical system reigned supreme in the end? Shockingly, the simplest program submitted won the tournament. It was only two lines of code. And it's something we're all familiar with: tit for tat.

All TFT did was cooperate on the first Prisoner's Dilemma round, then in every subsequent round, it did whatever the oppo-nent did previously—that is, if on the previous round the opponent cooperated, it cooperated on the next round; if the opponent be-trayed, it betrayed on the next round.

This simple program decimated the competition. So Axelrod ran the tournament again. He reached out to even more experts and this time had sixty-two entries. Some algorithms were more complex and some were variants on TFT.

Who won? Simple ol' tit for tat. Again.

What magic power did this humble little strategy have? Axelrod determined it came down to a few key things that made those two lines of code so special. He saw the same thing we noticed when looking at altruistic methods like being a Giver—early on, the good guys got trounced. Much like in the study "Bad Is Stronger than Good," the bad guys quickly seized the high ground in the initial interaction. Even TFT, the eventual winner, always got the short end of the stick early on because it cooperated initially. But as time passed, the bad guys couldn't match the big gains of the cooperators. When TFT met a program that cooperated on every move, the gains were enormous. Even programs like Tester (the backpedaler) learned that playing along was more beneficial than the marginal gains earned from defecting.

TFT had a number of things going for it. By initially cooperating, it showed goodwill. With other "nice" programs, it quickly started cooperating and increasing value. With punishing programs, they effectively became nice programs. With programs like Tester, TFT showed a willingness to punch them in the nose if they betrayed. It was no wimp. So those programs got in line.

TFT also displayed something vital: forgiveness. By not being complex, by only remembering what the other player did most recently, TFT was able to bring out the best in almost any program that was not totally evil or utterly random. TFT was not just a cooperator and a punisher but also a teacher. It showed the other players how to play better. Axelrod says that one of the reasons the not-nice programs performed so poorly is because they could not forgive and got caught in death spirals.

But Axelrod didn't stop there. He and other researchers explored how to build an even better program. TFT had won two big tournaments, but in order to defeat an apex predator, did they need to add more evil to create a superprogram? Hardly. What they needed was more good—specifically, more forgiveness.

Axelrod and others saw that going from straight tit for tat to "generous tit for tat" made the program even more successful. Rather than always repeating the opponent's last move, it would occasionally forgive and cooperate after being betrayed. While this led to it losing a couple more points to evil programs like ALL D, those points were more than made up for by the generous TFT's tremendous gains pulling potentially nice programs out of death spirals.

The main reasons for the success of TFT were that it was nice, it was forgiving, it was easy for the other players to deal with, and it would retaliate when necessary.

I'm sure a number of parallels to things we've talked about are becoming obvious, but let's see how the principles from a simple game can lead to big payoffs in life.

Moldova is like ALL D. If the nice guys of Moldova could meet each other and work together, before too long they would get a foothold, but that never happens. If they signaled niceness to try to find other nice guys, that would be like baby chicks cheeping in a nest: it encourages momma bird to come feed them but it also gives away their location to hungry cats. And the cats vastly outnumber the momma birds in poor, sad Moldova.

Pirates, on the other hand, wouldn't tolerate ALL D. A democratic system with rules in place to assure winnings are shared nearly equally would kick that jerk off the boat. Even if ALL D was the boss, he wouldn't last long, because captains would be subject to the same rules as everyone else, and rules would be agreed upon unanimously. It would be really hard for a total jerk to remain on board.

What if we injected more Adam Grant–style Giver tendencies in there? Instead of robbing everyone who wasn't a pirate, what if they started cooperating, minimally at first, convincing non-pirates to work with them? What if instead of a single pirate ship or a small group of ships they created a far larger network? The Royal Navy might not have stood a chance.

Inherent in the strategies of the bad guys in the tournament were two mistaken assumptions. The first was that later rounds would be like earlier rounds. Yet many programs, including TFT, paid attention to prior moves and responded accordingly, eventually punishing bad behavior. This happens in real life. We get a reputation. The majority of our dealings are not anonymous. Most of us deal with the same people over and over again. Betray them and they remember it. An early edge achieved with betrayal isn't worth much since it poisons what could have been a fruitful long-term relationship.

The second mistaken assumption was that the games are zero-sum. In real life, cooperation can be far more beneficial and far less costly. How? Well, the answer involves orange peels.

Business schools frequently do a negotiation experiment in which two groups are told to decide how a pile of oranges, which both groups need, should be split. Both groups are given specific details the other group can't see. Much like in the Prisoner's Dilemma, the bad guys do terribly. They assume the game is zero-sum: every orange they get is one the other group doesn't get. But the cooperators, the people who share and communicate quickly, discover that the special instructions each person was given include a detail: one group only needs the fruit of the orange; the other group only needs the peels. If the groups talk to each other, they can easily get *everything* they both need. But if they immediately resort to fighting, both groups do worse.

The long-term vs. short-term issue is critical. Used-car salespeople thinks they'll see a customer only one time and that's why they have the reputation they do. Meanwhile, your mom is (hopefully) going to be with you till the end. That's why moms have the reputation they do. The longer the time we anticipate we'll be dealing with someone, the better the behavior we can expect.

Adam Grant's research proves this distinction as well. Givers often take it on the chin in the short term, but over the long term—

when they can meet other Givers and gain the protection of Matchers—their reputation becomes known, and boom. They go from the bottom of success metrics to the top.

But isn't TFT a lot like Adam Grant's Matchers? There are two critical distinctions. TFT starts off with cooperation. Matchers don't necessarily cooperate. Matchers tend to wait until others do something nice before they respond in kind. This passive attitude drastically reduces the number of interactions they have. Meanwhile, Givers run around handing out favors, losing a little to Takers, getting a fair share back from Matchers, and winning the lottery whenever they meet another Giver. Givers can be great networkers by merely being themselves, while the hesitant Matchers wait for an engraved invitation to the party.

Axelrod offers four lessons we can learn from TFT's success:

DON'T BE ENVIOUS

Again, most of life isn't zero-sum. Just because someone else wins, that doesn't mean you lose. Sometimes that person needs the fruit and you need the peel. And sometimes the strategy that makes you lose small on this round makes you win big on the next. Here's the crazy thing: TFT never got a higher score than its counterpart did in any single game. It never won. But the gains it made in the aggregate were better than those achieved by "winners" who edged out meager profits across many sessions. Axelrod explains this by saying, "Tit for tat won the tournament not by beating the other player but by eliciting behavior from the other player [that] allowed both to do well." Don't worry how well the other side is doing; worry about how well you're doing.

DON'T BE THE FIRST TO DEFECT

Influence guru Professor Robert Cialdini says that not only is reciprocity one of the key elements of being influential and winning favor with others but it's also essential that you go first. Matchers wait and miss too many opportunities. And Takers trade short-term gains for long-term losses. Remember, all the big winners were nice and all the big losers started off betraying.

RECIPROCATE BOTH COOPERATION AND DEFECTION

Never betray anyone initially. Why make someone question your motives? But if a person cheats you, don't be a martyr. In the tournament, picking fights resulted in low scores, but retaliating increased scores.

DON'T BE TOO CLEVER

Tester sounds like a rational strategy: see what you can get away with and go no further. But this strategy lacks the clarity of TFT's, and while Tester edged out a gain here and there, it came at the cost of a good reputation. None of the other complex systems fared very well. TFT was the simplest of them all, and adding some occasional forgiveness was the only way to improve it. You need to be able to teach the people you're dealing with because you want the relationship to continue. *You cooperate with me, I cooperate with you. You betray me, I betray you.* It's that simple. Getting too clever muddies the waters, and the other person can quickly become very skeptical of you. Once that person sees clear cause and effect, he or she is more likely to jump on board and realize that everyone will benefit. Now, in zero-sum games like chess you want your intentions to be unclear, but in the iterated Prisoner's Dilemma, it's the exact opposite. You want the other player to see what you're doing so they can join you. Life is more often like the latter.

We've looked at jerks, nice guys, prison gangs, pirates, and computer simulations. You've learned a lot, and that's all fine and dandy, but what rules can you take away from this and use? Let's round up what we've got so we know how to be ethical and successful—but not a chump.

Don't move to Moldova—literally or figuratively. When I asked Bob Sutton, a professor at Stanford's Graduate School of Business, for the best piece of advice he gives to his students, he said this:

> When you take a job take a long look at the people you're going to be working with—because the odds are you're going to become like them; they are not going to become like you. You can't change them. If it doesn't fit who you are, it's not going to work.

As we've established, bad work environments can make you a bad person and can make you unhappy. Cheating is infectious, as shown by Dan Ariely's study "Contagion and Differentiation in Unethical Behavior: The Effect of One Bad Apple on the Barrel." When you see your peers cheat, you're more likely to cheat. And when your peers see each other cheat, everyone is more likely to bend the rules. That's one step closer to Moldova.

Luckily, the influence of context works both ways. The Terman Study, which followed over a thousand people from youth to death, came to the conclusion that the people who surround us often determine who we become. When we see others around us perform altruistic acts, we're more likely to act altruistically ourselves.

This also allows us to more safely be Givers—and get the success benefits that top-ranked Givers get without the fear of ending up a martyr. Connecting with other Givers was what allowed for the incredible success of the "nice" programs in Axelrod's tournament. If you're already in a bad environment, circle the wagons with other good people. It only took 5 percent of interactions between "nice" programs for good to get the edge over bad. That may not translate perfectly to the everyday world, but there's certainly a tipping point.

Picking the right pond can even help you get the benefits jerks get. Kissing your boss's ass isn't immoral or unsavory if the boss is someone you actually respect. At that next job interview find out who you will be reporting to. Ask to speak to that person and do some research on them. Studies show that your boss has a much larger affect on your happiness and success than the company at large.

RULE 2: COOPERATE FIRST

All the successful programs in Axelrod's competition cooperated first. Givers outdo Matchers because they volunteer help without waiting to see what the other person will do. Plenty of other research backs this up. Robert Cialdini says that being the first to offer help is key to engendering a feeling of reciprocity, which is one of the cornerstones of persuasion and ingratiation.

When Harvard Business School's Deepak Malhotra teaches negotiation, the first thing he says isn't "Be tough" or "Show the other side you mean business." His number-one recommendation to students is *"They need to like you."*

This doesn't mean you need to give twenty-dollar bills to everyone you meet. Favors can be quite small. We also often forget that something quite easy for us (a thirty-second email introduction) can have enormous payoffs for others (a new job). Doing quick favors for new acquaintances tells other Givers you're a Giver and can earn you the protection of Matchers. Go ahead and send that new inmate a gift basket. When the knives come out in the prison yard you'll have a lot more people watching your back.

RULE 3: BEING SELFLESS ISN'T SAINTLY, IT'S SILLY

Trusting others works better in general, but like Don Johnson at the blackjack table, having the edge doesn't mean you'll win every hand. You can't predict how successful cooperating will be for any specific interaction, but you'll win more than you lose. Remember, the most successful people in that study on the power of trust ranked themselves an eight—not a ten—as to how much they trusted others.

In fact, there's a newer variant of tit for tat that one researcher says outperforms both regular TFT and GTFT. What tweak does it include? If its opponent always cooperates, no matter what, it exploits that opponent. Kinda sad that it works, but we get it. It's just human nature that when people do too much and don't ever push back, they get taken for granted. So if you're not a total saint, it's okay; being a saint is actually a very poor strategy for getting ahead. (Don't you feel better now?)

Axelrod saw that retaliation was necessary for programs to be successful in the tournament. But what does that mean in the real world? It turns out that the best way to punish Takers in the workplace is good old-fashioned *gossip*. Warning others about Takers will make you feel better and can help police bad behavior.

Also, as Adam Grant acknowledged, giving too much can lead to burnout. A mere two hours a week of helping others is enough to get maximum benefits, so there's no need for guilt or for martyring yourself—and no excuse for saying you don't have time to help others.

RULE 4: WORK HARD—BUT MAKE SURE IT GETS NOTICED

What lessons can you take from the jerks without becoming a jerk? A common trend through the research was that jerks aren't afraid to push a little. They self-promote. They negotiate. They make themselves visible. This can be done without being a jerk. Maybe you won't gain everything the jerks get, but you can benefit from putting yourself out there—and without losing your soul.

You do need to be visible. Your boss does need to like you. This is not proof of a heartless world; it's just human nature. Hard work doesn't pay off if your boss doesn't know whom to reward for it.

Would you expect a great product to sell with zero marketing? Probably not.

So what's a good balance? Every Friday send your boss an email summarizing your accomplishments for the week—nothing fancy, but quickly relating the good work you're doing. You might think they know what you're up to, but they're busy. They have their own problems. They'll appreciate it and begin to associate you with the good things they're hearing (from you, of course). And when it's time to negotiate for that raise (or to refresh your résumé), you can just review the emails for a reminder of why exactly you're such a good employee.

RULE 5: THINK LONG TERM AND MAKE OTHERS THINK LONG TERM

Remember, bad behavior is strong in the short term but good behavior wins over in the long term. So to the best of your ability, make things longer term. Build more steps into the contract. Entice others with ways you can help them down the line. The more things seem like a one-off, the more incentive people have to pull one over on you. The more interactions or friends you have in common with other people, and the more likely you are to encounter them again, the more it makes sense for these people to treat you well. It's why medieval kings married their sons and daughters off to the children of other royals. *Now we're family. We're going to have grandchildren in common. We're going to have to play nice.*

Axelrod calls it "enlarging the shadow of the future." David DeSteno, head of the Social Emotions Group at Northeastern University says, "[People are] always trying to discern two things: whether a potential partner can be trusted and whether he or she is likely to be encountered again. Answers to those two questions, far beyond anything else, will determine what any of us will be motivated to do in the moment."

Remember the thing that made tit for tat even better? Occasionally forgiving. It prevented death spirals.

While Axelrod's tournaments are an abstraction and may seem oversimplified compared to real life, the forgiveness lesson is more important in day-to-day behavior than in the game. Life is noisy and complex, and we don't have perfect information about others and their motives. Writing people off can be due just to a lack of clarity. Face it: you can't even always trust yourself. You say you're on a diet, then someone brings donuts to work and you blow it. Does that mean you're a bad person and you should never trust yourself again? Of course not. TFT never came out ahead in a single game, but it won out in the grand scheme of things. One reason was because it could teach its opponent to behave. That means giving second chances. You're not perfect, others aren't perfect, and sometime people get confused.

One last thing before we move on. Remember Michael Swango? The killer M.D.? Well, they did catch him.

Eventually someone did the right thing. Jordan Cohen sent a fax about him to every medical school in the United States, and this got the attention of the FBI. Swango fled the country, but when he eventually returned in 1997 he was detained at Chicago's O'Hare Airport.

On September 6, 2000, he pled guilty to murder and fraud to avoid the death penalty. Sentenced to three consecutive life terms, he now resides in a maximum-security facility in Florence, Colorado.

Swango was careless, and the people around him were selfish. In the short term, that worked out for them, but in the longer term, he was caught and many reputations were sullied. Even when others are selfish, being a serial killer isn't really a good long-term strategy for success.

So being a nice person can be an effective strategy. But that raises other questions: How do you know how long to hang in there? The old saying is "Quitters never win and winners never quit." But is it true?

We all know someone who wasted years on something that was never going to happen. *(Did she really think that quitting her job and becoming a yoga instructor was going to work out?)* And we've all quit something too early and regretted not sticking it out through the tough spots. *(Why did I drop out of college? I'd be so much better off now.)*

So what makes more sense: grit or quit? How do you know when to give up and when to hang in there? Let's look at that next.

CHAPTER 3

Do Quitters Never Win and Winners Never Quit?

What Navy SEALs, Video Games, Arranged Marriages,
and Batman Can Teach Us About Sticking It Out When
Achieving Success Is Hard

It all started with a comic book.

As a boy growing up poor in the small Mexican village of Palaco, the story of Kalimán was inspirational to young Alfredo Quiñones-Hinojosa. Kalimán fought for justice, and even though he had superpowers, he had achieved them all through hard work and discipline. Alfredo spent many an afternoon trying to emulate the incredible—and impossible—exotic martial-arts kicks of Kalimán so he could be like his hero.

Kalimán is the kind of thing a young boy needs when a recession hits his country. When his family loses the gas station that is their livelihood. When his mother is reduced to making outfits for prostitutes at the local brothel to help feed the family. When his younger sister dies of an illness that would have been easily treatable if they lived in the United States instead of an hour from a rural clinic in Mexico. Alfredo wanted a better life. Then one day, an opportunity presented itself.

When he was fifteen, his uncle was working in California and making good money as a foreman on a ranch. Alfredo saw his chance. He joined his uncle for the summer and worked so hard he dropped down to ninety-two pounds. But after two months he returned home to Mexico with enough money to help support his family for the rest of the year.

The long-term answer was obvious. If he wanted a better life, if he wanted to help his family, he'd have to go over the border again. He planned. He waited. He sprinted . . . and was quickly nabbed by the border patrol. They sent him back home. But he had to help his loved ones. Would Kalimán let the border patrol stop him? No. And so it wouldn't stop Alfredo either.

After a lot more preparation, he executed a *Mission: Impossible*–style plan, crossed into the United States, and ended up in Stockton, California, where he was able to work and send money back to his family.

He couldn't speak English. He knew that would always stop him from really getting anywhere, so despite working twelve hours a day, seven days a week, and initially living in his car, he started taking community college classes at night. He came to class smelling like rotten eggs from shoveling sulfur onto trains, but he regularly made the dean's list in school, and it wasn't too long before he had an associate's degree.

With solid grades and the encouragement of teachers, he transferred to the University of California at Berkeley—one of the top schools in the country. He dealt with discrimination. Now, instead of rotten eggs, he came to class at night smelling like the fish lard he scraped at the port all day, but he completed his bachelor's in psychology and graduated with honors.

After spending his whole life in Mexico and California, winters in Cambridge seemed horrific, but Alfredo eventually learned to deal with them when he started at Harvard Medical School. As if this wasn't daunting enough, consider he'd only learned English a few years ago. But he found time to marry the woman of his dreams and become a U.S. citizen. When he accepted his medical school diploma, he was carrying his six-month-old daughter, Gabbie.

Today, Dr. Q, as he is known, is one of the top brain surgeons in the United States and very likely the world. He performs hundreds of surgeries a year at Johns Hopkins, which is frequently ranked as the top hospital in the country. He has his own lab and teaches oncology and neurosurgery at the medical school. Perhaps he doesn't save lives with kicks and punches, but Kalimán would be quite proud.

All of this raises really important questions: How the heck does an illegal migrant farm worker from a dirt-poor upbringing in the middle of nowhere become one of the greatest brain surgeons in the world? How does he stick with it through all the hard work, suffering, discrimination, and setbacks—when he doesn't even speak the native language? How does he do this when most of us can't seem to stick to a diet for more than four days or hit the gym more than annually?

*

Our culture beats us over the head with the idea that grit—sticking to something, working hard, and not quitting—is the secret to success. Often they're right. Grit is one of the key reasons why we see such differing levels of achievement between people of the same intelligence and talent levels. Remember the 2.9 GPA of millionaires in the first chapter? What's interesting is that despite their lack of impressiveness in academics, when interviewed, millionaires disproportionately say their teachers in school complimented them on being the "most dependable." They had grit.

But what about that notoriously flaky bunch of people we call artists? Howard Gardner studied the most successful artists for his book *Creating Minds* and found:

> Creative individuals frame their experiences. Such people are highly ambitious, and they do not always succeed, by any means. But when they fail, they do not waste much time lamenting; blaming; or, at the extreme, quitting. Instead, regarding the failure as a learning experience, they try to build upon its lessons in their future endeavors.

Again, sounds a lot like grit.

And it's not all dollars and cents either. Angela Duckworth's research at the University of Pennsylvania shows that kids with grit are happier, physically healthier, and more popular with their peers. "The capacity to continue trying despite repeated setbacks was associated with a more optimistic outlook on life in 31 percent of people studied, and with greater life satisfaction in 42 percent of them."

Sounds pretty conclusive: be gritty and we'll be successful. Which leads to a pretty simple question: Why the heck don't we do it?

One reason is that we all think we know where grit comes from— and, as you'll find out in this chapter, we're wrong. The second reason is that while grit *can* produce success, there's a whole other side to the story that no parent tells their children and no teacher tells their students: sometimes quitting is the smartest choice. And giving up, when done right, can make you a huge success too.

Let's start with reason number one: where does grit really come from? The answer is often *stories*. You don't need to grow up in a poor town in Mexico . . . but you may need a Kalimán comic book. Sound crazy? To find out, let's take a look at the people who know more about being tough and not giving up than anyone: Navy SEALs.

*

James Waters had always fantasized about being an All-American, but he had never considered himself more than a mediocre swimmer. He stuck with it, always working hard and being optimistic about his ability to improve. And one day his ability seemed to catch up with his dreams.

As a senior on the college swim team, he was tearing it up in a meet against Brown University. For the first time, his dreams of All-American glory felt within reach. But upon finishing a lap, he hit the side of the pool and felt a sharp pain in his hand. Hours later, x-rays confirmed it was broken. He couldn't swim for two weeks. Once he was back in the pool, he had to train wearing a cast that messed up his stroke. He fell behind in training. And any chance he'd had at his NCAA dreams slipped away.

That wasn't the worst of it. Though his chances had vanished, the dream wouldn't. James told me, "I had nightmares for two years afterward. I dreamt that every time I touched anything, that part of me broke. I couldn't get it out of my head."

James had unfinished business. The optimistic stories he'd been telling himself didn't match the reality, and he needed them to. Maybe he wouldn't be an All-American, but the loop had to be closed.

That's how six years later and three thousand miles away he found himself swimming again, but in a very different scenario: the grueling "Hell Week" of BUD/S (Basic Underwater Demolition/SEAL) training.

One-hundred-ten hours without sleep. Carrying a log over his head for hours. Endless runs and swims. At six feet two, two hundred twenty pounds, with broad shoulders, James looks like Hollywood's vision of a SEAL. Ironically that's not what most SEALs look like, and this only made his life harder. When the team had to run with a boat on their heads, James's height meant he bore more of the weight. And then there was the dreaded "pool comp" . . .

You're underwater with scuba gear. An instructor yanks the regulator from your mouth. He ties your air hose in knots. He antagonizes you relentlessly as you struggle for air. Your brain is screaming, *You are going to die.* You must follow correct procedure to right your equipment as the instructor continues to harass you, simulating the whirlwind a SEAL might deal with when facing the powerful undertow of an ocean current. The whole time your brain is racing with panic. BUD/S candidates are given four tries to pass pool comp—because they *need* four tries. Less than 20 percent can pass this test the first time.

Tomorrow brings more long runs in the sand. More sleep deprivation. Oh, and maybe jumping out of an airplane too. Many guys—statistically *most* guys—ring the bell and quit.

James was being pushed to his limits. But each time he thought of the nightmares, and his dreams, of the optimistic belief that he could get better. And back into the water he went.

SEAL class 264 had a 94 percent attrition rate. Of the 256 men who started, only 16 graduated with the class and had a Navy SEAL trident pinned to their uniform.

James Waters was one of them. And the nightmares stopped.

*

What makes some people pass BUD/S and others ring the bell to quit? Surprisingly, at one time the Navy didn't know. And that was a big problem. After the tragedy of 9/11, the military needed more SEALs, but lowering the standards would defeat the purpose. They needed answers. Who should they be recruiting? And what could they teach guys that would help them pass the punishing gauntlet?

What they eventually found was shockingly counterintuitive. The Navy didn't need more strong or macho guys. But it might have been smarter to recruit a lot more insurance salesmen. Yes, insurance salesmen. Hold on to that thought for a second.

A Navy study revealed a number of things that people with grit do—often unknowingly—that keep them going when things get hard. One of them comes up in the psychological research again and again: "positive self-talk." Yes, Navy SEALs need to be badass, but one of the keys to that is thinking like The Little Engine That Could.

In your head, you say between three hundred and a thousand words every minute to yourself. Those words can be positive (*I can do it*) or negative (*Oh god, I can't take this anymore*). It turns out that when these words are positive, they have a huge effect on your mental toughness, your ability to keep going. Subsequent studies of military personnel back this up.

When the Navy started teaching BUD/S applicants to speak to themselves positively, combined with other mental tools, BUD/S passing rates increased nearly ten percent.

Getting through BUD/S is a lot of physical hardship, but quitting is mental. What does this have to do with insurance salesmen, you ask? Think about how people usually respond when asked to think about insurance salesmen: "Ugh." It's not just SEALs who take a battering; insurance salesmen face constant rejection.

While you may think that the key to being a good salesperson is people skills or being extroverted, research shows that salespeople can be hired based on optimism *alone*. Researchers found that "agents who scored in the top 10 percent [of optimism] sold 88 percent more than the most pessimistic tenth."

It makes sense that optimism keeps us going, but it's hard to believe that it has such powerful effects. For why that is we need to look at man's best friend.

*

The dogs wouldn't move. And the researchers couldn't complete the study if the dogs just sat there.

Martin Seligman and other academics at the University of Pennsylvania were doing a study of Pavlovian conditioning. The dogs were on one side of a large box that had a low wall separating it from the other half of the box. A tone would sound and then the floor would deliver a mild shock. If the dogs jumped the low wall to the other side of the box they could avoid the zapping. The researchers were trying to get the canines to recognize that the tone always preceded the shock, and if they leapt over the wall after hearing it, they could avoid the pain altogether. It should have been easy. Dogs usually pick this up quickly.

But they didn't move. They just sat there and whimpered. The tone sounded, the shock was delivered, and they didn't do anything. (These are the moments when researchers put palms to their foreheads and reconsider career choices.)

Then a lightbulb went off in Seligman's head. He realized that during the early rounds of training the researchers must have screwed up and not made the connection between the tone and shock clear enough. The shocks had felt *random* to the dogs. So instead of making the connection that this was a warning signal, they had learned they had no control. They were helpless. Maybe the pooches weren't thinking between three hundred and one thousand words a minute like you and I, but they weren't dumb either: *These shocks are going to happen no matter what. Why keep trying?*

The dogs had learned the concept of futility. They had become pessimistic. They gave up. So there weren't any big advances made on Pavlovian conditioning that day, but the implications for understanding grit were huge. Similar studies have been tried with humans, and they often react the way the dogs did.

It's perfectly rational. If you went out on your lawn and tried to fly like Superman and every time you ended up facedown in the flower bed, it wouldn't be very long before you wisely concluded you and the Man of Steel have one less thing in common and instead took your car to the grocery store. *I can't do it.*

This is often more insidious and less obvious in daily life. We give up, rationalize, accept our fate . . . but then occasionally wonder why we didn't do better or do more. But we're not always right that we "can't do it." Sometimes there's a way out that we didn't see because we gave up.

What's interesting is that in similar studies of people, one in three did *not* become helpless. They kept trying to figure out why the shocks were happening and what they could do. They thought every failure was an anomaly and they kept going. And it's only reasonable that these people end up either (1) utterly delusional or (2) far more successful than you or I.

It all comes down to the stories you tell yourself. Some of us say "I'm not cut out for this" or "I've never been any good at these things." Others say "I just need to keep working at it" or "I just need better tips on form." In almost any scenario (other than flying like Superman) each of these four could be applied. It's individual which one you are likely to choose, which is your default, and how often and when you vary from your preferred explanation.

Seligman decided that what was at the center of this was optimism and pessimism: feeling you can change things and feeling you can't. Helplessness was the result of a pessimistic attitude. When you believe things will not get better, it's irrational to keep trying. You just shrug and go home. In situations where you truly cannot win, this is the right choice. But in difficult but not impossible situations, when persistence is called for, pessimism kills grit. It says "Give up and go home" instead of "Gimme one more try. I can do it."

Seligman realized he wasn't really studying helplessness. He was studying pessimism. He realized something else too: "depression is pessimism writ large." When you keep down the path of feeling helpless again and again, you end up clinically depressed. You feel helpless at life. You give up in a much more holistic way and stop doing anything.

What's shocking is that when asked to make predictions, depressed people are more accurate than optimists. It's called "depressive realism." The world can be a harsh place. Optimists lie to themselves. But if we all stop believing anything can change, nothing ever will. We need a bit of fantasy to keep us going.

When we're optimistic, research shows we experience a host of benefits:

- Optimism is associated with better health and a longer life. Levels of optimism can even predict which survivors of cardiovascular disease are likely to have a second heart attack.
- Expecting a positive outcome from negotiations makes groups more likely to close a deal and to be happy with it.
- Optimists are luckier. Studies show by thinking positive they persevere and end up creating more opportunities for themselves.

For optimists, this is very reassuring. But what if you're a pessimist? What if you've always been a pessimist and you feel you're just wired that way? Then listen up, Eeyore, because Seligman's research showed this attitude isn't genetic; it all comes from the stories you tell yourself about the world. And that's something you can change.

Optimists and pessimists shape their stories of the world very differently. Seligman called this "explanatory style," and it comes down to three Ps: permanence, pervasiveness, and personalization.

Pessimists tell themselves that bad events

○ will last a long time, or forever (*I'll never get this done*);
○ are universal (*I can't trust any of these people*); and
○ are their own fault (*I'm terrible at this*).

Optimists tell themselves that bad events

○ are temporary (*That happens occasionally, but it's not a big deal*);
○ have a specific cause and aren't universal (*When the weather is better that won't be a problem*); and
○ are not their fault (*I'm good at this, but today wasn't my lucky day*).

Seligman found that when you shift your explanatory style from pessimistic to optimistic it makes you feel better and you become grittier.

This isn't just true for individuals. It also works for groups. Seligman analyzed newspaper quotes from the players on Major League Baseball teams. Could attitude one year predict performance the next year?

> Using their quotes, we computed the 1985 explanatory style for the twelve National League teams. Statistically, in 1986, optimistic teams bettered their 1985 win-loss records, and pessimistic teams did worse than they had in 1985. Teams optimistic in 1985 hit well under pressure in 1986, whereas the hitting of teams pessimistic in 1985 fell apart under pressure in 1986, compared to how well both kinds of teams normally hit.

Sound too good to be true? Seligman repeated the study with 1986's baseball player quotes and again predicted achievement for

1987. Then he did it with basketball. This was no fluke. Optimistic explanatory style predicted success. (Bookies in Las Vegas, you're welcome.)

*

James Waters's optimism wouldn't quit. His stories were stronger than his body and kept him going through BUD/S. And that grit pushed him on to become a Navy SEAL platoon commander. And to complete an MBA at Harvard. And to become deputy director of scheduling in the White House.

So is grit merely the optimistic stories you tell yourself about the future? No, sometimes the stories go much deeper than that. They go way past just helping you succeed—they can keep you alive when you're in the most hellish place on Earth . . .

*

Again, we start with a nightmare.

The man was tossing and turning in his sleep. Viktor reached out to wake him . . . but thought better of it. Whatever the man was facing in that dream couldn't be worse than the reality he would awaken to. It was 1944. And they were in Auschwitz.

Fifteen hundred people in a building meant for two hundred. Visible through the windows, barbed wire. Guard towers. Each prisoner was expected to subsist on just two pieces of bread a week. It was hardly a surprise that a piece of human flesh had been found in a cooking pot. The desperate were resorting to cannibalism.

The horrors had no end.

Many would "run into the wire"—the electrified fence. Suicide. It became easy to tell who would go next: the ones smoking their cigarettes. Cigarettes were money. They could be traded for food, for help, for almost anything. The last thing anyone ever did was smoke them. Those people just wanted some enjoyment now to forget the pain of the hell they were in. And they did not last long.

Unlike BUD/S training, this was not a simulation. Some people lived and some people died. Who survived? The physically strong did not live longer. The young did not. The brave did not. The compliant did not. What Viktor Frankl realized was that in the most awful place on Earth, the people who kept going despite the horrors were the ones who had meaning in their lives:

> A man who becomes conscious of the responsibility he bears toward a human being who affectionately waits for him, or to an unfinished work, will never be able to throw away his life. He knows the "why" for his existence, and will be able to bear almost any "how."

Those who saw their life existing for a reason greater than themselves persisted, while others smoked their cigarettes before making that final run toward the fence.

Viktor always thought of his wife. He didn't even know if she was alive, but that didn't matter. He held one-sided conversations with her as he worked laying train tracks. His stories were greater than his suffering. And that kept him going.

We've all worked harder on something for someone else than we would have for ourselves. Mothers do things for their children you couldn't pay them for. Soldiers die for their country.

If life is all about pleasure, then when it ceases to be fun or immediately beneficial, we quit. When we step outside the wish for comfort, when we live for something greater than ourselves, we no longer have to fight the pain; we accept the pain as a sacrifice. Frankl said, "What is to give light must endure burning."

And we don't give up.

It's the stories we tell ourselves that keep us going. They can be a higher truth. Or, in many cases, they don't need to be true at all.

*

People with Cotard's syndrome believe they are dead. They will sit in front of you, look you in the eye, and say they are deceased. It's a very rare mental illness. And good luck talking them out of it. They'll always have a reason why you're wrong and they're right, why even though the flesh on their arm isn't rotting and they don't roam the streets like *The Walking Dead,* they'll say they kicked the bucket.

Their responses are something psychologists call "confabulation." They're not trying to trick you, and they're not even aware they're incorrect. And sometimes their responses are utterly ridiculous. People with Alzheimer's often confabulate when they can't remember things. They completely reconstruct reality to fill in the gaps. Their minds just make stuff up in order to create logic retroactively.

What they rarely say is "That's a good point. I don't know why I believe this." And I'll bet you know plenty of otherwise normal people who aren't big on saying "I don't know."

Daniel Kahneman won the Nobel Prize for his work on cognitive biases. Those are little hardwired shortcuts in our brains that help speed up decision-making. They're usually helpful but not always rational. One example is loss aversion. Rationally, gaining a dollar should be as pleasurable as losing a dollar is painful. But that's not how our minds work. Losing a dollar bothers us a lot more than earning a dollar makes us feel good. It makes sense; losing too much can mean death but gaining a lot . . . well, it's nice but quickly results in diminishing returns. So evolution has wired us to fear losses a lot more than we love gains.

What's funny is that when Duke professor Dan Ariely, who was inspired by Kahneman, would lecture on biases he frequently got the same response: "Yeah, I know lots of other people who do that—but I don't." Oh, the irony: Cognitive biases prevent us from understanding cognitive biases. So Ariely tweaked his lectures a bit. Before saying anything about our inherent biases, he would show everyone optical illusions. You know the type: two lines appear to be different lengths but when you measure them, they're the same. He needed people to not just hear but *experience* the fact that they can't always trust their brains. After Ariely showed people they were capable of errors, they were open to accepting that biases applied to them too.

Our brains are wired to try to make sense of things. Meaning is part of our operating system. We need to think the world makes sense and that we have control. The brain doesn't like randomness.

So what is meaning? Meaning, for the human mind, comes in the form of the stories we tell ourselves about the world. This is why so many people believe in fate or say things were "meant to be." Having a story about the meaning of life helps us to cope with hard times. Not only do we naturally see the world this way, but frankly we can't *not* tell stories. If I asked you how your day was or how you met your spouse, what would you tell me? A story. What's your résumé? A story. You even tell stories when you sleep: dreams. And research shows you have about two thousand daydreams every day, telling yourself little stories about this or that.

For nearly every area of your life, like career or relationships, you have a story you tell yourself about it. But rarely are these consciously or deliberately constructed.

This may sound like hippie talk, very abstract and out there, but it's the exact opposite. Stories are the invisible undercurrent that promotes success in a shocking number of the most important areas of life.

What best predicts the success of romantic relationships? It's not sex or money or having the same goals. Researcher John Gottman realized that just hearing how the couple told the tale of their relationship together predicted with 94 percent accuracy whether or not they'd get divorced.

What's the best predictor of your child's emotional well-being? It's not great schools, hugs, or Pixar movies. Researchers at Emory University found that whether a kid knew their family history was the number-one indicator.

Who finds their careers meaningful and fulfilling? Hospital cleaners who saw their jobs as "just a job" didn't derive any deep satisfaction from their careers. But cleaners who told themselves the story that this was their "calling"—and that their work helped sick people get better—saw their jobs as meaningful.

Jews and Christians have parables. Hindus and Buddhists have sutras. Nearly all religious leaders give sermons. Stories, stories, stories. They remind us how to behave and help us persist. Even if we're not religious, popular culture fills the gap. UCLA film school professor Howard Suber describes movies as "sacred dramas for a secular society." Just like with religious parables, we act like the heroes of the stories we tell. Studies show that when we relate to characters in fictional stories we are more likely to overcome obstacles to achieve our goals.

And then there's happiness. Studies have shown that many people don't feel good about their lives because they don't see the good times as aligned with their vision of themselves. They want their lives to fit their stories, so when bad things happen they see that as consistent with who they are; the joyful moments are exceptions to be ignored.

This is true even in the most profound and distressing examples of sadness: suicides. Roy Baumeister, a professor at Florida State University, found that people who committed suicide often weren't in the worst circumstances, but they had fallen short of the expectations they had of themselves. Their lives were not matching the stories in their heads. Just as Frankl saw in Auschwitz, the stories determined who would keep going and who would make a run for the wire.

So there's no shortage of evidence that stories rule our thinking and predict success in so many arenas. But how do stories work?

*

Research shows that fiction makes us more "prosocial"—that is, kind and giving. It does this by making our vision of the world *less* accurate. Just as religion and stories of personal meaning help us cope, so do movies, TV, and other stories. Stories not only engage our minds but also quietly slip a pair of rose-colored glasses on our heads.

George Mason University professor and bestselling author Tyler Cowen agrees. He cites research in which people, when asked to describe their lives, often said "journey" or "battle" but few ever replied "mess." And life can be a mess. He says stories are a filter, imposing order on an often chaotic world. Stories remove information. They make recollections *less* accurate. They are deliberately constructed, but life often isn't.

He's right. There are a zillion things going on every second. We cherry-pick certain elements ("That time I gave a homeless man a dollar") and ignore others ("The time I pushed my cousin down a flight of stairs") to arrive at a story about our lives ("I am a good person").

In economics, the term "bounded rationality" basically means that human beings aren't perfectly rational because they always have limitations, such as how much information is available or the amount of time there is to think things through. There is too much going on in the world for our little brains to process; we must distill it.

One study showed that we feel meaning in life when we think that we know ourselves. The key word there is "think." Truly knowing oneself didn't produce meaning but *feeling* one did created the results. The story doesn't need to be accurate to be effective. That's a little unnerving and maybe even depressing, right?

But when it comes to grit, this can be a good thing. If we made all our decisions based on the odds, we'd never achieve anything risky. We'd never even try. But to survive like Viktor Frankl did, in the face of such horrors, stories can keep us going *because* of their inaccuracy.

It aligns with what we saw in the optimism research. Optimists told themselves a story that may not have been true, but it kept them going, often allowing them to beat the odds. Psychologist Shelley Taylor says that "a healthy mind tells itself flattering lies." The pessimists were more accurate and realistic, and they ended up depressed. The truth can hurt.

This is why lawyers are 3.6 times more likely to be depressed than people in other professions. To protect their clients, attorneys must consider every possible thing that can go wrong. They can't tell themselves happy, less accurate stories about how a deal will unfold.

Pessimists outperform optimists in law school. And this same quality makes them very unhappy. Law is the highest paid profession in the United States and yet, when surveyed, 52 percent of lawyers described themselves as dissatisfied with their jobs. You can guess what effects this has on grit: the legal profession has high attrition rates. To quote Liz Brown, "Law is the only career I know that has a sub-profession dedicated to helping people get out of it."

Stories aren't perfect pictures of the world, but they allow us to succeed for this very reason. They can keep us going and become prophecy. You weren't "born" to do anything in particular, but when your story says you were "born" to do something you perform better and persist. After all, it's your *destiny*.

And this is how it connects to career. As Harvard professor Teresa Amabile discusses in her book *The Progress Principle,* meaningful work is the number-one thing people want from their jobs. Yup, it beats salary and getting promoted. How did Steve Jobs lure John Sculley away from his great job as CEO of Pepsi? He asked him, "Do you want to spend the rest of your life selling sugared water or do you want a chance to change the world?" Meaningful doesn't have to be saving orphans or curing the sick. As long as your story is meaningful to *you,* it has power.

So how do you find your story?

There's a really simple way to do it: just think about your death.

In modern America it seems nobody wants to spend time thinking about death. It's not fun. We like to think we're going to live forever. But in many cultures death is a part of life and has a place of respect or even its own holiday. Mexico has *Dia de los Muertos*. Christianity has All Saints' Day. Japan has *Sorei*. Indians engage in *Shraaddha*. And on and on.

Thinking about death reminds us of what is truly important in life. David Brooks makes the distinction between "résumé values" and "eulogy values." Résumé values are the things that bring external success, like money and promotions. Eulogy values are about character: *Am I kind, trustworthy, or courageous?* We're often very forward-thinking about the former. We spend four years in college to get that job, learn to use Excel or PowerPoint, read books on getting ahead. But eulogy values we tend to consider only in retrospect, rationalizing after the fact: *Yes, I'm a good person.* If you're ambitious (and since you're reading a book about success, you probably are), you don't need to worry too much about paying attention to the résumé values. You're *always* thinking about them. But to serve your longer-term career and life, you need to be forward-thinking about eulogy values too. That's where thinking about death a bit comes in.

Picture your funeral. The people who loved you have all gathered to pay their respects. They're going to praise the qualities that made you so special, that they will miss the most. What do you want them to say?

Taking the time to think about that can help you find your eulogy values, which will guide your decisions. In the famous commencement speech Steve Jobs gave at Stanford in 2005 he said, "Remembering that I'll be dead soon is the most important tool I've ever encountered to help me make the big choices in life."

While research in this arena is formally referred to by the utterly intimidating name "terror management theory," a study by the more endearing moniker of "The Scrooge Effect" shows that when you take a little time to think about death, you become more kind and generous to others. You put aside short-term goals for a moment and consider who you really want to be. It sounds morbid, but people who contemplate the end actually behave in healthier ways—and therefore may actually live longer. It also has been shown to increase self-esteem. You want to talk about "big picture" thinking? It doesn't get bigger than this. We're talking about stuff like fate and destiny.

We often confuse those two words as meaning the same thing. But UCLA professor Howard Suber clarifies the distinction. Fate is that thing we cannot avoid. It comes for us despite how we try to run from it. Destiny, on the other hand, is the thing we must chase, what *we* must bring to fruition. It's what we strive toward and make true. When bad things happen, the idea of fate makes us feel better, whereas taking the time to consider eulogy values helps us think more about destiny. Success doesn't come from shrugging off the bad as unchangeable and saying things are already "meant to be"; it's the result of chasing the good and writing our own future. Less fate, more destiny.

What if you have a story that isn't working? You think you know who you are and what's important, but you're not happy or getting where you want to be. It might be time to play screenwriter and take another pass at the script that is your life. Therapists help patients do this in a process aptly titled "story editing." University of Virginia professor Timothy Wilson did a study in which therapists helped underperforming students reinterpret their academic challenges from "I can't do this" to "I just need to learn the ropes." This helped them earn higher grades the next year and reduced dropout rates. Studies show this can work as well as antidepressant drugs and, in some cases, even better.

What do you do with this edited story once you have it? Play the part. A lot of psychological research shows that instead of behavior following our beliefs, often our beliefs come from our behaviors. As the old saw goes, "Actions speak louder than words." Wilson calls it the "do good, be good" method. When people do volunteer work, their self-perception changes. They begin to see themselves as the kind of people who do good things for others.

In Kurt Vonnegut's classic novel *Mother Night,* Howard W. Campbell Jr. is an American spy who poses as a Nazi propagandist during World War II. He becomes the "voice" of Nazi Germany on radio programs, ostensibly singing the praises of the Reich while in fact transmitting coded messages back to the United States. While his intentions are good, he comes to realize that his "fake" Nazi inspirational messages have more effect on motivating the enemy than his secret intelligence efforts do in assisting the allies. Vonnegut's moral is that "We are what we pretend to be, so we must be careful about what we pretend to be."

So instead of merely focusing on intentions, make sure that in your day-to-day actions you are being the main character in your perfect story. This way rather than ending up as Vonnegut's character did, you can go the way of a different fictional character: Don Quixote. The moral of Cervantes's story being "If you want to be a knight, act like a knight."

Meaning keeps us going when stark reality says "quit." Very often our stories are stronger than we are, and if they're meaningful ones, they can carry us through the tough times.

Viktor Frankl survived Auschwitz. He did not smoke his cigarettes or make a run for the wire. He lived to the ripe old age of ninety-two. He founded a new system of psychology that spread around the world. He shared the story that kept him alive, and it became one that keeps other people going as well.

We cannot help but tell stories. But which story are you telling yourself? And is it one that will get you where you want to go?

Grit isn't always this grim and serious. In fact, even in the most dire situations grit is sometimes nothing more than a game.

*

Joe Simpson, clad in mountain-climbing gear, sat at the bottom of a hundred-foot crevasse, shivering. It was so dark it was like the world had been dipped in ink. He was cold, but his hands trembled more out of fear.

"*Simon!*" he screamed desperately. There was no reply.

He could barely move without lightning bolts of pain flying up his body. One of his legs was shorter than the other, and it was positioned in a horrifyingly unnatural angle. His shin had been slammed upward through his knee joint and into his femur.

As he screamed again, it became increasingly clear he was all alone, that no help would be coming.

Two days earlier Joe and Simon had begun their ascent of Siula Grande in the Peruvian Andes. At 21,000 feet, it is the largest mountain in the southern hemisphere. Its 4500-foot western face had never been climbed, and they were the first to do it.

Elated, but exhausted, all they needed to do was get back down. But in mountain climbing, this is when 80 percent of accidents happen . . . On the morning of June 8, 1985, Joe stumbled and slid, shattering his leg. They still had far to go. Breaking a leg this high up on a mountain, with no rescue team available, meant it was only a matter of time. Joe would die. But they acted as if there was still a chance. Connected by rope, Simon was the anchor as he lowered Joe down the mountain. Then Joe, nearly immobile, waited as Simon followed. Their pace was excruciatingly slow. So much snow blew past them that Simon could not even see where he was lowering Joe.

This continued for hours until suddenly Joe slid off the edge of the mountain. Still connected by the rope, Simon was nearly pulled down himself. He dug his feet in, stopping his descent.

Joe was suspended in midair, hanging by the rope. He couldn't even touch the mountain. He looked up, but the wind was blowing so much snow, he couldn't see Simon. Hundreds of feet below the gaping maw of a crevasse stared at him. He was helpless, hanging, and still in horrible pain. Every few seconds the rope jerked in fits. Simon was struggling to prevent both men from plunging to their deaths.

And then Joe fell. Imagine a fifteen-story building. That's how far. But not to the base of the mountain. He kept dropping . . . into the dark crevasse.

Amazingly, he was not dead. He had landed on a pile of snow in the crevasse. Looking down with his flashlight, he could see he had landed on an ice bridge. The crevasse rose five hundred feet above him, and past the ice bridge it continued down into blackness. Had he landed just two feet to the right, well, he would not have landed. He would have kept falling into the abyss—who knows how far.

He was still attached to the rope. He pulled on it, the other end still connected to Simon . . . or Simon's corpse. But as Joe feverishly yanked on it, he felt the slack. It was too easy to pull. When the end of the rope was in his hand, he could see clearly: the end had been cut. Simon, assuming his climbing partner was dead, was not coming to save him.

Joe couldn't blame him. He was shocked to still be alive. Again and again he tried to climb, but each time his broken leg screamed at him and he seized in pain. There was no way to go up . . . which meant the only way was down.

His fingers black from frostbite, he could barely tie the knots for a descent. He could not bring himself to look down. He had no idea how deep the crevasse went, but what he did know was that the rope was only so long.

Normally climbers tie a knot at the end of the rope so if they reach the end it will act as a brake and they will not slide off. Joe didn't. This way, if he ran out of rope, his death would be quick. He descended slowly into the darkness. Time passed, and what he found shocked him.

Sunlight. A slope to his right led up and out of the crevasse. He was not in a pit. It was the first glimmer of hope he'd had. If he climbed the slope, he could get out of here. But it was 130 feet up and at a 45-degree angle. With the snow and his broken leg, it would be like crawling on sand. But the fact that there was a way out emboldened him.

Hours passed as he crawled like a toddler, but finally he was out of the crevasse. Sunlight washed over him and he was ecstatic, but only for a moment. Looking around at the base of the mountain, he realized he was still six miles from base camp. Simon was nowhere to be seen. His leg still pulsed with pain. Everything so far had been only a warm-up.

Like Seligman's dogs, Joe Simpson had no earthly reason to think he should or could keep fighting. But he did. How? In the most dangerous, high-stakes situation imaginable he did the craziest thing: he made it a game. He started setting goals: *Can I make it to that glacier in twenty minutes?* If he made it, he was ecstatic. If he didn't, he was frustrated, but it only made him more obsessive. "An excited tingle ran down my spine. I was committed. The game had taken over, and I could no longer choose to walk away from it."

Lifting his mangled body, he struggled to hop forward. Every misstep gave him a paralyzing jolt of pain . . . but he had only ten minutes left to get to that snowbank. He had to win his little game.

He struggled to find the best way to crawl. Their footprints from the ascent were still visible in the snow. Smiling, he followed them like breadcrumbs. But the wind whipped the snow across them, hiding them faster than he could move his tortured body. Despair overwhelmed him again. But he returned to the game: *Set the goal. Check the watch. Keep playing. Get to the next marker in time.* His pace was horribly slow, though he barely noticed until the snow he crawled across became rock. He was getting closer. But the snow had been forgiving. The dirt and rock would not be so kind when his leg inevitably hit them. The pain was unrelenting.

Keep playing the game. Next marker up ahead: the lake. They had made their camp near the lake. His brain was flooded with hope. *I can make it!* But would anyone still be there? It had been four days. Simon had cut the rope and surely thought Joe was dead. Wouldn't Simon already be gone? It would be night soon, and Joe had barely slept. He returned to the game. It was all he could do. At this point, his only goal was to not die alone. *Get to the lake in twenty minutes. Play the game.*

Night fell and he collapsed in a heap, utterly delirious. Maybe he slept. It was almost impossible to tell the difference between awake and asleep anymore. Then he was woken up by a terrible smell. It was . . . poop. He looked around. He was in the latrine area of the campsite. In an instant he was awake again and shouting, "*Simon!*"

Nothing. But then . . .

Lights bounced in the distance, heading his way. And voices. Joe cried. The lights grew closer and blinded him. Simon grabbed Joe by the shoulders and held him tight.

Joe Simpson had won his game.

It sounds silly that turning Joe Simpson's predicament into a game saved his life on Siula Grande, but after looking at the research and interviewing people, I heard similar things like this over and over again. Remember James Waters, the Navy SEAL? When I talked to him about getting through BUD/S, he said this: "Many people don't recognize that what they're doing at BUD/S is assessing your ability to handle a difficult circumstance and keep going. It's a game. You've got to have fun with it and you've got to keep your eye on the bigger picture."

When school classes and grading are structured like a game, students perform better. A professor at Rensselaer Polytechnic Institute redesigned his class to resemble World of Warcraft, and students studied harder, were more engaged, and even cheated less.

Which raises questions: Why are games, which can be taxing, frustrating, and an awful lot like work, so much fun while our jobs, well . . . suck? Why do kids hate homework that's repetitive and incredibly hard but they'll gleefully run away from homework to play games . . . which are repetitive and incredibly hard? Why are puzzles fun but doing your taxes is awful? What is it that makes something a game and not just a frustrating pain in the ass?

We've all experienced something malfunctioning and we just get frustrated and angry. But occasionally we're made curious by a problem and go down the rabbit hole of trying to solve it, and then this "inconvenience" becomes fun. It's like a detective solving a mystery.

Like Tyler Cowen's criticism that personal stories filter the messiness of life, games are merely a framework superimposed over a set of activities. With that structure, things that sound utterly boring on the surface can become incredibly fun and rewarding—even addictive.

So just a few elements can turn filling out your taxes into a fun-filled experience. One is "cognitive reappraisal," a fancy term for "telling yourself a different story about what is happening." You know how the baby who doesn't want to eat suddenly opens his or her mouth when the spoon is an airplane? Yeah, we adults really aren't that much different from toddlers. (Sorry.)

We've probably all heard about Walter Mischel's marshmallow

study but usually in terms of willpower. (Quick summary: kids were promised two marshmallows if they could resist eating one. The kids who resisted, demonstrating greater willpower, went on to be much more successful in life down the line.) But another interesting element of that study is how many of the resisters managed to avoid the temptation. Most didn't just bear down, grit their teeth, and exhibit superhuman willpower. They actually engaged in cognitive reappraisal. They looked at their situation through another lens or made it a game. Mischel explains: "When children transform marshmallows into puffy clouds floating in the air rather than thinking of them as delicious chewy treats, I have seen them sit in their chair with the treats and bell in front of them until my graduate students and I couldn't stand it anymore."

By engaging in cognitive reappraisal, and telling ourselves a different story about what is happening, we can subvert the entire willpower paradigm. Some research has shown that willpower is like a muscle, and it gets tired with overuse. But it only gets depleted if there's a struggle. Games change the struggle to something else. They make the process fun, and as Mischel showed in his research, we are able to persist far longer and without the same level of teeth-gritting willpower depletion.

Here's an example: What if I put a big ol' pile of cocaine in front of you? (I'll assume, for the sake of argument, you are not a cocaine addict.) Cocaine is pleasurable. You know that. People do it for a reason, right? But you'd likely reply, "No, thanks." Why? *Because it doesn't jibe with your story.* You just don't see yourself as the kind of person who does cocaine. You could come up with all kinds of reasons why. (What's a reason? A story.) Would you have to close your eyes and clench your fists and beg me to take the cocaine away? Probably not. You'd exert no willpower on this one.

But would the same be true with a juicy steak? Especially if you were hungry? Say you *are* the kind of person who indulges in steak. Now what happens? Struggle. Willpower depletion. Unless you are a vegetarian. Boom—another story. You'd say no and exert zero willpower. You'd have no trouble ignoring the steak. Change the story and you change your behavior. Games are another kind of story: a fun one.

All the fancy science is great, but let's talk about life. Why isn't your job fun? The answer is quite simple, really: work, as we know it today, is a *really* lousy game.

David Foster Wallace once said, "If you are immune to boredom, there is literally nothing you cannot accomplish." In many ways, this is very true. If you never got bored, you'd be a big step closer to being a computer. Computers do all kinds of boring things for us, and they do them quite well and very quickly. Computers don't need game mechanics. They don't get bored or unmotivated. Yet we are designing offices as if we were machines—but we're not. Jane McGonigal, a researcher and game designer, argues that by its very nature, efficiency entails removing game mechanics from the design of labor. In other words, we're taking the fun out of it.

Karl Marx was wrong about a lot of things in economics, but we're now realizing he was also right about some stuff. When you remove people's emotional connection to their labor and treat them merely as machines that produce effort, it's soul killing.

Can we put those emotional elements back? Sure. Frankly, it's not that hard. Yale University's Innovation Alignment Team (part of the student entrepreneurial society) wanted to see if they could increase the number of students who disinfect their hands after meals at one of the school cafeterias. Did they bombard students with information or lobby the administration to create rules to mandate it? Nope. They decided to make it fun.

They hooked up a few speakers and an iPod to the disinfectant dispenser. When someone used it, it would make a clever sound. The same kind video games make when a player scores. Before their setup, thirteen students used it. Afterward, ninety-one did. A silly tweak that made it "fun" increased usage by a factor of seven almost immediately.

We can apply game mechanics to our lives and turn dull moments into fun ones. Can this make us grittier at work and lead to success in life? Oh yeah. Work doesn't have to be a lousy game. So let's learn why work sucks, why games are awesome, and how we can turn the former into the latter. C'mon, let's "game the system."

Whiny neutered goats fly. Picture it in your mind. You've just learned what all good games have in common: WNGF. They're Winnable. They have Novel challenges and Goals, and provide Feedback.

Any time something feels frustrating, it's probably lacking at least one of the four. Let's break them down:

WINNABLE

Good games are winnable by design. They don't make games you can't win. Each game has clear rules. We intuitively know that and it makes us very positive about our chances if we persist. We've got good reason to be optimistic. Games turn us all into someone who can make it through BUD/S, like James Waters.

This "justifiable optimism" makes difficult things fun. Games are often harder than real life, but they are fun when they're hard and boring when they're easy. Nicole Lazarro's research showed that we fail at games 80 percent of the time. Jane McGonigal explains:

> Roughly four times out of five, gamers don't complete the mission, run out of time, don't solve the puzzle, lose the fight, fail to improve their score, crash and burn, or die. Which makes you wonder: do gamers actually enjoy failing? As it turns out, yes . . . When we're playing a well-designed game, failure doesn't disappoint us. It makes us happy in a very particular way: excited, interested, and most of all optimistic.

In this light, using a game frame at BUD/S makes perfect sense. BUD/S is winnable. People pass all the time. The same guy pulling the regulator out of your mouth in pool comp is there to save you if you really start drowning. Why do people fail it? Panic. They forget it's a game. They think they'll really die. Joe Simpson didn't know if he would survive the mountain, but he *could* get to that next rock in twenty minutes. That game was winnable and it kept him going.

As a corollary, you have control in a game. What you do is important. Your actions make a difference, so you know your time is well spent. Research shows that a feeling of control kills stress. Even when you just *feel* you have control, stress plummets.

On the other hand, the office often feels like a game that's not winnable. You don't feel you have control. You don't feel like what you do makes much of a difference. Who wants to play *that* game? Research by Dan Ariely showed that when we feel like what we do is futile or pointless, motivation and happiness plummet. We become like the dogs in Seligman's study.

But you can fix this. You may not be able to overhaul how your company does things, but like Joe Simpson, you can define a game for yourself that is winnable. Is your game to learn as much as possible at the office so you're ready for that promotion? Do you want to get better at giving presentations or acquire another skill set? All of these are winnable.

Now, what if your boss hates you? Or you're facing discrimination in the workplace? Those games really aren't winnable. Move on. Find a game you can win.

NOVEL CHALLENGES

Good games continually have new levels, new enemies, new achievements. Our brains love novelty, and good games make sure we're always stimulated by something just a little different, honing our attention.

Games engage us with challenges. They are designed to create what researcher Mihály Csikszentmihályi calls "flow," which is when we're immersed in something enough to forget the passage of time. We're never bored or overwhelmed because good games keep a perfect balance of hard but not too hard, easy but never too easy. And as we improve, games up the difficulty. We're always stretching our abilities just enough to keep us hooked. McGonigal explains:

> Csikszentmihályi's research showed that flow was most reliably and most efficiently produced by the specific combination of self-chosen goals, personally optimized obstacles, and continuous feedback that make up the essential structure of gameplay. "Games are an obvious source of flow," he wrote, "and play is the flow experience par excellence."

Joe Simpson had plenty of challenges: a broken leg, no food, little water. The mountain provided novelty as well: a crevasse, snow, rocks. Simpson kept facing new "levels," which added spice to his game.

Now think back to your first day at your job. That certainly wasn't boring. There was so much to learn, so many new and different things to master. Slightly overwhelming perhaps, but it was novel and challenging. Six months later I'm guessing that all stopped. It's now like playing the same level of a game ten hours a day, five days a week for years. That's not a fun game.

The workplace wants you to be good at your job, and that makes sense, but that's like a game you're too good at. It's dull. Good games have that 80 percent failure rate to inspire you to keep working, but the office doesn't like failure. Zero failure means zero fun. And there's so much busy work that offers no challenge at all. How is that engaging?

The good news is that this is partly in our hands. Research shows we often don't do what makes us happiest; we do what's easy. Like if we don't feel like going out with friends, we may make ourselves, and then we have fun. We think we want to rest, but what we really want is a different type of challenge.

We crave ease, but stimulation is what really makes us happy. We try to subtract at work, do less, check out. These are signs of burnout. We don't need to subtract; we need to add novel challenges to create engagement.

Here's a fun example from Duke professor Dan Ariely: Pillsbury started making instant cake mix in the 1940s, but it didn't sell very well, which didn't make any sense. The mix made things easier. The company then realized that making a cake is not mere drudgery. Cakes hold meaning; they show love. So when Pillsbury made the cake mix *less* simple—you had to add the eggs yourself—sales soared.

Therefore, to make work fun, add challenges. For something to have meaning, you ultimately have to make your mark, to be engaged. If your game is winnable, if you have control, if it challenges you—without being overwhelming—you'll enjoy it more.

GOALS

Whether it's Mario rescuing the princess or a Special Ops soldier killing all his enemies in the latest Call of Duty, good games are very clear about what you need to do to win. They serve to focus you and guide decision-making.

Joe Simpson set a time limit for himself of twenty minutes to get to the next marker. That was arbitrary, but it gave him a framework to evaluate success or failure in his game. Thinking back to what Tyler Cowen said, this turns the "mess" of life into a coherent story.

In an office environment, there are definite goals—but are they *your* goals? When the company gets what it wants, do you always get what you want? Um, not so much. You can't get what you want until you take the time to *decide* what you want. Goals can be intimidating. We don't want to fail, so often we don't set them. But if you make your game winnable, setting goals will be less scary. Failure is okay in a game. As Nicole Lazarro discovered, failure in a game just makes things more fun.

FEEDBACK

If you do something right, a game rewards you with points or abilities. If you do something wrong, you're penalized. And both of these happen *quickly*. Writer Aaron Dignan notes that you always know where you stand in a game, how you're doing, and what you need to do to perform better.

Research shows that the most motivating thing is progress in meaningful work.

Working in a call center can be drudgery. People hang up on you and are rude, and you have to keep reading the same script over and over despite the resistance. But Adam Grant (who you met in chapter 2) found a simple way to powerfully energize workers at a university call center. He brought in a student whose scholarship had been granted due to their efforts. The student told them how much their work meant and how grateful he was. The workers got feedback. They saw what they were doing was meaningful. The result? The amount of money they brought in after the visit *quintupled*.

The progress you see doesn't need to be big. As Harvard professor Teresa Amabile found, "Our research inside companies revealed that the best way to motivate people, day in and day out, is by facilitating progress—even small wins." In fact, the data shows that consistent small wins are even better at producing happiness than occasionally bagging an elephant: "Life satisfaction is 22 percent more likely for those with a steady stream of minor accomplishments than those who express interest only in major accomplishments."

Napoleon once said, "A soldier will fight long and hard for a bit of colored ribbon." The reward games provide is often nothing more than a cute badge or a simple animation, but those silly little things keep you playing.

Celebrating those "small wins" is something that gritty survivors all have in common. And it's one of the reasons Alcoholics Anonymous is successful. Staying sober one day at a time is a small win. And as a paper in *American Psychologist* showed, "Once a small win has been accomplished, forces are set in motion that favor another small win."

Good games keep you going by giving frequent, immediate feedback. But what about your job? You get a review *annually*. As Jane

McGonigal reports in her book, studies show many C-level executives play computer games at work. Why? *To feel more productive.* Oh, the irony.

So you need a better way to score your work game. Amabile recommends taking a moment at the end of every day to ask yourself, "What one thing can I do to make progress on important work tomorrow?" It gives you a goal to shoot for. Give yourself a clear idea of how to measure or achieve that, like Joe Simpson's twenty minutes, and you're on your way to a motivating system.

If your goal is a raise or a promotion, seek feedback. Communicate with your boss on a consistent basis and see how you're doing. As you saw in chapter 2 with the work of Jeffrey Pfeffer, ass kissing helps. But you can be sincere and score points with *El Jefe* by regularly asking how you're doing and how you can do better. If you were the boss, and an employee regularly said, "How can I make your life easier?" what would your reaction be? Exactly.

Making work a game is quite simple; you don't have to change what you're doing all that much, you just have to change your perspective. But therein lies the reason many of us don't do it: it feels kinda silly.

Games may seem childish and trivial, but when you take the time to look at how many games are already secretly hidden in the things you do so passionately, the power of this perspective seems far less immature. Do you walk a lot more because of your Fitbit? Does Fantasy Football become an enjoyable part-time job for you? I had a friend who flew back from Japan to California in the "wrong" direction deliberately because he absolutely *had* to get Executive Platinum frequent flier status and this was the quickest way to do it.

Games become addictive. If you craft your work into one, you can find success and happiness at the same time with a positive feedback loop. As McGonigal says, "Clearly, this is a game that you win even if you lose." You can use a game frame perspective to "level up" in other areas of your life as well. Being a spouse, parent, friend, and neighbor can all benefit from WNGF—doing what is winnable, has novel challenges and goals, and provides feedback. Plus, games are always more fun when played with other people.

Joe Simpson did the impossible. During his travails on the mountain, he faced unbelievable hardship. By the time he was reunited with Simon, he weighed only 100 pounds. His leg would require six surgeries. But Joe returned to climbing. That's grit.

Whether it's optimism, meaning, or a simple game, the story in your head is always the answer to perseverance. Yet before we close the case on grit, we need to look at the other side of the coin.

As W. C. Fields once said, "If at first you don't succeed, try, try again . . . then give up. There's no use being a damn fool about it."

We've seen the benefits of grit. Time to look at the upside of quitting.

*

Spencer Glendon is a very impressive guy. He was a Fulbright Scholar, earned a Ph.D. in economics from Harvard, helped charities on the South Side of Chicago, and is currently a partner at one of the biggest money management funds in Massachusetts. But that's not what's most impressive about him.

What's truly mind-blowing is that while doing these things he was almost always extremely ill. In high school, Spencer suffered from chronic ulcerative colitis. This led to serious progressive liver problems. He eventually needed a transplant, which he got from a good friend. But organ transplants mean immunosuppressive therapy. Basically, he has no immune system. Colds that would give you and I a stuffy nose left him bedridden for a week.

When most of us feel under the weather, we push on through with coffee and willpower, but for Spencer there was no negotiating with his body. It would fail him and he would be bedridden again. Sounds awful, huh? But this is exactly what made Spencer awesome.

As he likes to say, "I've had what I think of as the good fortune to be physically compromised almost through my entire life."

You're probably thinking the same thing I am: *Huh?*

When he was in high school and seriously ill, he went to see a therapist. He wanted to do the things all young people want to do: go to parties, date, play sports. Often they just weren't realistic options. And it was heartbreaking.

His therapist couldn't lie to him. Spencer couldn't live a life like his peers. But that didn't mean he had to be miserable. The therapist told him to focus on accomplishing one thing a day. If he could do just that one thing, he could feel good about himself. His energy was limited, but if he focused on just one thing, he could still do some of what he wanted. So that's what he did.

Sometimes it was just making dinner. If he could cook dinner that night he would have accomplished something. He had to quit a lot of activities, but he could still achieve one thing.

He would do the one thing that day, and one thing the next, and the next. Now, when he's at his sickest, he still makes dinner. (Unsurprisingly, he's also become a great cook.)

Coming to terms with his illness taught him something that almost all of us overlook: Everything we do in life is a trade-off. Choosing to do one thing means not doing something else. There was no way for Spencer to say "I want to do this" without also saying "And I'm willing to give *that* up to do it."

There was no small irony that an economics Ph.D. got such a profound lesson in what is formally known as "opportunity cost." As Henry David Thoreau said, "The price of anything is the amount of life you exchange for it."

We don't like to think about limits, but we all have them. While grit is often about stories, quitting is often an issue of limits—pushing them, optimizing them, and most of all, knowing them. Spencer could not deny or ignore his. He was forced to acknowledge trade-offs and focus his little energy on the things that mattered—and to quit doing everything else.

Many successful people take this perspective. One study of Olympians quoted an athlete as saying, "Everything is opportunity/cost. If I go out to a movie instead of going hiking as my leisure activity, what is the cost of that? If I go to the movies instead of a hike, does that help or hurt my paddling? I've got to judge that."

"Quit" doesn't have to be the opposite of "grit." This is where "strategic quitting" comes in. Once you've found something you're passionate about, quitting secondary things can be an advantage, because it frees up time to do that number-one thing. Whenever you wish you had more time, more money, etc., strategic quitting is the answer. And if you're very busy, this may be the only answer.

We all quit, but we often don't make an explicit, intentional decision to quit. We wait for graduation or Mom to tell us to stop or we get bored. We fear missing opportunities, but the irony is by not quitting unproductive things ASAP we are missing the opportunity to do more of what matters or try more things that might.

We have all said that we should have quit that job or ended that relationship sooner. If you quit the stuff you know isn't working for you, you free up time for things that might. We're bombarded by stories of persistence leading to success, but we don't hear as much about the benefits of quitting. No one wants to be the skydiver who pulled the rip cord too late.

They say time equals money, but they're wrong. When researchers Gal Zauberman and John Lynch asked people to think about how much time and how much money they'd have in the future, the results didn't add up. We're consistently conservative about predicting how much extra cash we'll have in our wallets, but when it comes to time, we always think there will be more tomorrow. Or next week. Or next year.

That's one of the reasons we all feel so rushed, so tired, and like we're not getting enough done or making enough progress. We all have only twenty-four hours in a day. Every day. If we use an hour for this, we're not using it for that. But we act like there are no limits. When we choose an extra hour at work, we are, in effect, choosing one less hour with our kids. We can't do it all and do it well. And there will not be more time later. Time does not equal money, because we can get more money.

We hear story after story of the great and powerful who persisted and won. Not too many stories get passed along about the great quitters of history. If persistence works so well, do successful people in the real world ever quit?

Mihály Csikszentmihályi was putting together a study of some of the most creative successful people around: 275 Nobel Prize winners, National Book Award winners, and other people clearly at the top of their fields. It was a major study by a renowned researcher that would be well publicized. It was incredibly flattering just to be invited. So what happened?

Over a third said no. Many more didn't even reply. They had their own work to do. Csikszentmihályi invited Peter Drucker and received this in response:

> I hope you will not think me presumptuous or rude if I say that one of the secrets of productivity . . . is to have a *very big* waste paper basket to take care of *all* invitations such as yours.

Csikszentmihályi probably should have seen this coming. The reason Drucker was invited to join the study was because he was a world-renowned expert on being effective and getting things done. Drucker thought that time was the most precious resource. And the first line of defense he recommended to people wasn't better scheduling; it was getting rid of everything that wasn't moving the needle when it came to achieving their goals.

In Drucker's book *The Effective Executive,* he explains: "The executive who wants to be effective and who wants his organization to be effective polices all programs, all activities, all tasks. He always asks: 'Is this still worth doing?' And if it isn't, he gets rid of it so as to be able to concentrate on the few tasks that, if done with excellence, will really make a difference in the results of his own job and in the performance of his organization."

Jim Collins, author of *Good to Great,* did an exhaustive study of companies that turned themselves around and went from disappointments to huge successes. What he found was that most of the big changes they made weren't about new initiatives but about the bad things they needed to *stop* doing.

When we hear about the ten thousand hours of deliberate practice that experts perform to become great, that number seems overwhelming. But it all starts to click once you realize how many other activities successful people are discarding in order to free up more time for improvement. It's no surprise that hours matter.

Merely knowing how many hours a student spent studying in college is predictive of how much money they make later in life. That's not a huge surprise, but they could have been partying, they could have been doing extracurricular activities. They made a choice, conscious or not.

Once you get into the working world, it's not all that different. As I'm sure you've suspected, successful people do work a lot of hours. When Harvard professor John Kotter studied top business leaders, he found they put in an average of sixty to sixty-five hours per week.

If you practice something one hour a day, that's 27.4 years to reach the ten-thousand-hour mark of expertise. But what if you quit a few less important things and made it four hours a day? Now it's 6.8 years. That's the difference between starting something at twenty and being an expert when you're forty-seven and starting at twenty and being world-class at twenty-seven. Famed researcher Walter Mischel credits his success to a Yiddish word his grandmother taught him: *sitzfleisch*. It means "buttocks." As in "Put your butt in that chair and work on what's important."

So what's the first step? Know your number-one priority. Then start quitting stuff that isn't as important and see what happens. You'll learn really fast if something really is more essential than you thought.

Spencer's feeling pretty good now. His body is treating him much better, but his attitude toward his time hasn't changed. Opportunity/cost. Trade-offs. He does what is important. (Frankly, I'm flattered to have made the cut, because otherwise you wouldn't be reading about him.)

Why are we so quick to quit some things? We beat ourselves up saying we're lazy or weak, and maybe that's true, but often it's not. Everybody can't be a supermodel or play in the NBA. Many of the things we desire are simply unattainable. Research shows that when we choose to quit pursuing unattainable goals, we're happier, less stressed, and get sick less often. Which people are the most stressed out? Those who wouldn't quit what wasn't working.

Grit can't exist without quit. Spencer explained the downside of grit: "I know plenty of people for whom grit is a liability because it allows them to stick with something that makes them or others miserable and towards no long-term good aim. The alternative of which is the thing that you would most like to do that would bring you the most joy and might bring other people the most joy or be the most productive."

We always think we need more: more help, more motivation, more energy. But in our current world the answer is often the exact opposite: *we need less*. Fewer distractions, fewer goals, fewer responsibilities. Is that so we can watch more TV? No. We need less of those things so we can go all in on our priorities. The question is what are you going to do less of? What are you going to quit or say no to in order to make time for what matters most?

Imagine you were Spencer at his lowest point. What would you do if you were ill and could manage only one task per day? Congratulations. You now know what matters to you most, what should get the most hours, what should be done first. You know where you should apply grit, and by the same token, what you should quit. As the old saying goes, "You can do anything once you stop trying to do everything."

You may ask "But if I just keep quitting things, won't I turn into a total flake?" Actually, being a flake is another powerful secret to success.

*

Growing up in Topeka, Kansas, Matt Polly was the classic ninety-eight-pound weakling. Just like every schoolyard punching bag, he dreamed of becoming the Baddest Man in the World. A superhero.

A tough guy. For most kids, this dream stays just that, a dream. But Matt didn't let it go.

And so at age nineteen he did something totally crazy: he decided to drop out of Princeton and moved to China to find the Shaolin Temple and master kung fu.

His parents were furious. He was supposed to be on his way to medical school, not to being Chuck Norris. It was nuts . . . but he knew he could go back to school. He knew his parents would forgive him. He wasn't married with a kid and a mortgage. He could give this crazy idea a shot and see what happened.

This was 1992, before the Internet, before Google Maps and Yelp reviews of kung fu monasteries. He'd studied Mandarin in school, but the bulk of what he knew about Asian culture came from the Wu-Tang Clan. He didn't even know where the Shaolin Temple *was*.

But why not give it a shot? He'd figure it out, right? And that's how a nineteen-year-old, six-foot-three white guy ended up wandering around Tiananmen Square in the cold with an upside-down map asking people how to find the Shaolin Temple.

Eventually, he found it. Those who ran the temple seemed more like used car salesmen than Zen masters, but for $1,300 a month, they were willing to let the crazy guy from Kansas train with the monks.

The culture shock was huge. An upper-middle-class American kid who had every privilege was now living in a village with one telephone line where people went to bed hungry at night. He was a pampered outsider, a *laowai*. But he knew if he really wanted to learn, if he wanted to become the Baddest Man in the World, he'd have to be accepted as one of them. But how?

He'd have to "eat bitter," Chinese slang for "to suffer." The monks trained in kung fu five hours a day. So he did seven. Each night he went to bed exhausted and woke up sore. He had bruises in places where some people didn't have places. This was no vacation. But the monks noticed his hard work, and his kung fu improved by leaps and bounds.

He told his parents he'd be gone for only a year. But a year came and went and he wasn't a badass yet, so he stayed. And his parents cut him off. But he continued to train.

Injuries. Dysentery. Getting hit in the head again and again and again. Eventually his coach took him aside. The Zhengzhou International Shaolin Wushu Festival was coming up. Martial artists from all over the world would be competing, and he wanted Matt to represent the Shaolin Temple. Him. The schoolyard punching bag. The crazy *laowai* who couldn't live without his precious Coca-Cola. Matt didn't think he'd last a single round with ranked fighters who had spent the better part of a decade training, but his coach believed in him. And so he accepted.

The next eight months passed in the blink of a black eye. He nervously entered a stadium of ten thousand people, but he handily won his first match. The 149-pound westerner beat a Korean fighter, pulling off a crowd-pleasing head kick.

But that was the *first fight*. This was a tournament. He had multiple matches in *one day*, and his next bout would be against the reigning champ of the festival. Matt and his friend went to watch the champ's first fight.

Their jaws simultaneously dropped as the champ smashed his opponent's nose with a knee to the face, winning by a knockout. The Russian fighter was carried away on a stretcher.

Matt's friend turned to him: "Don't worry. They won't carry you out on a stretcher."

"No?"

"You are too tall for Chinese stretchers. They will leave you on the platform instead."

Matt turned pale with that same fear from the playground. He ran to the bathroom, quivering. What had he gotten himself into? There was no chance he could beat this monster. Maybe he wouldn't be the Baddest Man in the World.

But maybe that was okay too. It was a crazy experiment. If he could just go the distance with the champ, it would be worth it. He just needed to *not die*.

Which might not be easy considering as he walked out to his

match, the crowd was shouting *"Da si laowai!"*—*Beat the foreigner to death!*

Seconds later he was in a world of pain. He was being trounced. But he didn't quit. He had come here to find his courage and, like Rocky, his only goal was to go the distance . . . and to not need that extra-long stretcher.

Matt lost every round. He lost the fight. But he was still standing at the end of the match. And his smile was twice as big as the champ's when he won the silver medal.

Then, just like with Princeton, he quit.

He had lost the big fight, but he had won the battle with himself. Matt realized he would never be the Baddest Man in the World. There would always be someone tougher. But he had tried something really cool, found his courage, and achieved his goal. It was time to return home. As he'd thought, his parents forgave him. And not too long after, Princeton diploma in hand, he headed off to Oxford to be a Rhodes Scholar.

So this wild little detour, had it been just youthful craziness? No. It ended up changing his life. Years later, Matt wrote a book. *American Shaolin* got rave reviews. He was on NPR. A movie studio optioned the rights and got Jackie Chan interested. His experiment ended up launching his career as a writer.

The hallowed halls of Princeton and Oxford didn't make his future. A crazy thing he did at nineteen did. So maybe it wasn't that crazy after all.

Some might say "Matt Polly becoming a successful author after that was just dumb luck." But here's the thing: there's a *science* to luck.

Richard Wiseman, a professor at the University of Hertfordshire, did a study of lucky and unlucky people to see if it was just random chance, spooky magic . . . or if there were real differences that caused such different results in life. It turns out luck isn't just serendipity or due to the paranormal. A lot of it is about the choices people make.

Studying over a thousand subjects, Wiseman found that lucky

people maximize opportunities. The study showed they are more open to new experiences, more extroverted, and less neurotic. They listen to their hunches. Most of all, Wiseman says, lucky people *just try stuff.* It makes intuitive sense: if you lock yourself in your house, how many exciting, new, cool things are going to happen to you? Not many.

Is this some genetic gift? Hardly. After seeing that luck was largely a function of choices, Wiseman tried another experiment: Luck School. If he got unlucky people to behave more like lucky people, would they get the same results? Turns out they did. Afterward, 80 percent of Luck School graduates felt their luck had increased. And they weren't just luckier; they also came away happier.

Doesn't trying all these things mean more bad things happen to lucky people too? Sure. But the old saying is true: "You regret most the things you did not do." Thomas Gilovich of Cornell University found that people are twice as likely to regret a failure to act. Why? We rationalize our failures, but we can't rationalize away the stuff we never tried at all. As we get older we also tend to remember the good things and forget the bad. So simply doing more means greater happiness when we're older (and cooler stories for the grand-kids).

Lucky people don't dwell on failure; they see the good side of the bad and often learn from it. They have an optimistic explanatory style much like the positive-minded baseball teams. A lot of research bears this out. A study cleverly titled "Keep Your Fingers Crossed!" showed "activating good-luck-related superstitions via a common saying or action (e.g., "break a leg," keeping one's fingers crossed) or a lucky charm improves subsequent performance in golfing, motor dexterity, memory, and anagram games." But it's not because of magic. These actions gives people confidence, which helps them perform better. (So wish your friends luck. It really does help.) This optimism also makes lucky people grittier and more likely to keep trying new things, which over time means even more good stuff happens to them. As long as what they do isn't too risky and they rationalize the occasional bad stuff, it's an upward spiral. Eventually something hits.

So keep trying new things. It makes you luckier. If you do what you've always done, you'll get what you've always gotten. When there's no clear path to success, no relevant model for what you're trying to achieve, trying crazy things may be the *only* way to solve the issue.

Here's an example. It's called the Spaghetti Problem. It's a pretty simple challenge: build the tallest structure you can that will support a marshmallow. It has to be freestanding and your team gets eighteen minutes to do it. You get these tools:

- 20 pieces of dry spaghetti
- 1 meter of tape
- 1 piece of string
- 1 marshmallow

Peter Skillman (who has the awesome title of General Manager of Smart Things at Microsoft) designed it as a creativity exercise. He ran the challenge for over five years, testing more than seven hundred people, including groups of engineers, managers, and MBA students. You know who outperformed everyone? Kindergarteners. Yes, six-year-olds beat everyone. (In fact, the MBA students were the lowest performing group.) Did the tykes do more planning? Nope. Did they have some special knowledge about Italian food or the consistency of marshmallows? Nope. What was their secret? They just jumped in. Like Wiseman's lucky people: they just tried more stuff. They started failing immediately—and learning quickly.

This was their system: prototype and test, prototype and test, prototype and test—until the time was up. When there is no set path, this system wins. It's an old Silicon Valley mantra: Fail fast and fail cheap. Research shows this method of trying lots of little experiments to see what works best also works for people over four feet tall. Like you and me.

So why don't we? It's simple, really. Often we're afraid of failure, but does being afraid of failure really make all that much sense?

To answer that question, we need to look at something else kindergarteners think a lot about: becoming Batman. Now, becoming Batman certainly isn't easy, but you know what would be involved: mostly studying martial arts relentlessly like Matt did. A far more interesting question, which relates to success, is: How do you *stay* Batman? This will give us the answer to why we're so afraid of failure.

The Caped Crusader is among the most relatable of superheroes. He doesn't possess any superpowers. Being a billionaire and having a collection of cool gadgets helps, but it doesn't change the one overriding problem with staying Batman: he can never lose a fight. While a professional boxer with a record of thirty wins and one loss is extremely impressive, for the Dark Knight it means death. The villains of Gotham don't let referees stop the bouts. So to be Batman means never losing. Ever. You cannot afford to fail. So if you did everything it takes to become the Dark Knight, how long could you maintain that perfect record? Luckily, we can draw on research. Yes, this has been studied. (God, I love science.)

E. Paul Zehr, a professor at the University of Victoria, looked at comparable athletes to get a rough idea. He studied the records of top boxers, MMA fighters, and NFL running backs. How long could they stay undefeated and without a crippling injury? How long could you stay Batman?

Three years. Yup, that's it.

Let's hope Gotham's criminal element consists of more jaywalkers and fewer evil masterminds, because after your decade-plus of training, you're not going to have a lot of time to clean up the city.

Luckily, you're not trying to be Batman. But all too often you and I *act like we are*. We think we always have to be perfect. One failure and it's all over. But you're not Batman. You can fail and quit and learn. In fact, that's the only way you *can* learn.

Comedians know this. That's why the biggest threat to their success these days is in your pocket right now. It's your smartphone.

In fact, Dave Chappelle bans phones at his performances. Let me explain.

Chris Rock doesn't think of those amazing jokes on the fly. His HBO special isn't an hour of improvisation. It's more like a full year of experiments. In the book *Little Bets,* former venture-capitalist-turned-writer Peter Sims explains the comedian's process. Rock goes to a local comedy club, unannounced, with a yellow pad, and just tries stuff. Then he notes the reactions. The vast majority of jokes fail miserably, earning only groans and silence. Then he makes notes on his pad and tries more stuff. But a few things click. The audience roars. He makes a note and moves on.

The audience thinks this is him bombing, but it's not. It's him *testing.* Trying things. Keeping what works, quitting what doesn't. After six months to a year of doing this five nights a week, you get to watch the brilliant hour-long special that is nonstop laughs. In an interview, Rock said, "There are a few guys good enough to write a perfect act and get onstage, but everybody else workshops it and workshops it, and it can get real messy . . . if you think you don't have room to make mistakes, it's going to lead to safer, gooier stand-up."

So when audiences whip out their smartphones and record these experiments, comedians get shortchanged. And the fans who watch those videos on YouTube get shortchanged, because those aren't performances; they're tests. Comedians need to see what fails so they can cut it. They need to know what to "quit." When comedians can't fail, they can't succeed. Here's Chris Rock again: "Comedians need a place where we can work on that stuff . . . No comedian's ever done a joke that bombs all the time and kept doing it. Nobody in the history of stand-up. Not one guy."

Sometimes Chris Rock is wrong in a good way. Some jokes he thinks will fail inexplicably turn out to earn big laughs. Democratically, he trusts the audience's judgment over his own. There's plenty of precedent for this as well. Viagra started as a treatment for angina. Then the drug's developers noticed an interesting, um, side effect.

Peter Sims says, "Most successful entrepreneurs don't begin with brilliant ideas—they discover them . . . They do things to discover what they should do."

So what happens if you fail at something? You won't die like Batman, so you shouldn't act like you're Batman. Try being more like a comedian or a kindergartener. Try things. Quit what fails. *Then* apply grit.

The research lines up with what the comedians and the kindergarteners already know. Steven Johnson notes that historical studies of patent records reveal that "sheer quantity ultimately leads to quality." Trying more stuff. Just like the old saying "The harder I work, the luckier I get."

What's all this leading to? You need to combine strategic quitting with your own personal R&D division.

Okay, some of you are probably angry with me right now. *First you told me about opportunity/cost and quitting stuff to free up time to focus on the one thing that matters. Now you're telling me to do lots of different stuff. What gives?*

The answer is simple: If you don't know what to be gritty at yet, you need to try lots of things—knowing you'll quit most of them—to find the answer. Once you discover your focus, devote 5 to 10 percent of your time to little experiments to make sure you keep learning and growing.

This gives you the best of both worlds. Use trying and quitting as a deliberate strategy to find out what is worth *not* quitting. You're not being a total flake but someone who strategically tests the waters.

The things you should opportunity/cost quit, à la Spencer, are things you do every day or week that produce no value. What we're talking about here are limited duration *experiments*. Giving something a shot. Taking a yoga class—but not signing up for a yearlong membership just yet. This is what spurs new opportunities and creates good luck. As Ralph Waldo Emerson said, "All life is an experiment.

The more experiments you make the better." In other words: Fail fast, fail cheap.

Ironically, even the most noted researcher in the field of grit, Angela Duckworth, agrees with this. In her paper "Grit: Perseverance and Passion for Long-Term Goals," she says, "A strong desire for novelty and a low threshold for frustration may be adaptive earlier in life: Moving on from dead-end pursuits is essential to the discovery of more promising paths."

Take that 5 to 10 percent of your time and treat it the way a venture capital firm handles money. VC firms invest in things that have a comparatively low chance of success but, if successful, could turn into something really, really big. They put money in ten companies expecting seven to go bust, two to break even, and one to be the next Google or Facebook.

Does this work for people like you and me in the real world? Yes. For example, job hopping, especially early on in your career, can be a path to more money, your true calling, and a coveted CEO title. Economist Henry Siu said, "People who switch jobs more frequently early in their careers tend to have higher wages and incomes in their prime-working years. Job-hopping is actually correlated with higher incomes, because people have found better matches—their true calling."

And changing roles is far more likely to get you to a leadership position:

> Lazear analyzed the number of prior jobs held by 5,000 respondents in a 1997 survey of 12,500 GSB alumni. Among those with at least fifteen years of work experience, respondents who have had two or fewer roles had only a 2 percent chance of eventually becoming a C-level leader, while those who have held at least five positions had an 18% chance of reaching the top.

What about doing more things outside your career, akin to Matt's journey to China? It turns out that trying stuff outside your field of expertise is correlated with big achievements. The average scientist is about as likely to have a hobby as any member of the public. However, eminent scientists (members of the Royal Society or National Academy of Sciences) are nearly twice as likely to have one. Nobel Prize–winning scientists? Almost three times as likely. Steven Johnson found the same thing holds true for geniuses of the past, like Benjamin Franklin and Charles Darwin. These guys had a *lot* of hobbies. Facing different challenges in different contexts allowed them to look at things differently, to challenge assumptions, and to realize breakthroughs. Getting lots of different ideas crashing together turns out to be one of the keys to creativity.

The same is true for successful companies. They don't just try new things; they often completely reinvent themselves when their little bets bear fruit. YouTube started out as a dating site, of all things. eBay was originally focused on selling PEZ dispensers. Google began as a project to organize library book searches.

So don't be afraid to do some experiments, and quit the ones that don't work. It can lead to great things. You need to quit some things to find out what to be gritty at. And you need to try stuff knowing you might quit some of it to open yourself up to the luck and opportunities that can make you successful.

Matt's still trying crazy experiments—to say the least. A few years ago, his then-girlfriend's family asked him, as a former Shaolin kung fu student, how he'd fare in the UFC. Now in his midthirties and nearly 100 pounds heavier than he'd been in China, he didn't think he'd do that well.

But he needed an idea for his next book. And he was always itching to try something new. And guys will go a *long* way to impress a girl. So the old gunfighter put his spurs back on. Matt spent the next two years training with UFC champions in New York and Las Vegas. Of course, it wasn't easy. More punches to the head, more "eating bitter." It took time to get those skills back. (His coach fined him $20 every time he dropped his hands in training, leaving his face exposed. After six months, Matt owed him $580.)

And in 2011, at the ripe age of thirty-eight, he fought his first MMA match in front of a crowd of three hundred. His opponent was sixteen years younger than him. In the second round, one of his contact lenses got knocked out. He fought half blind. But this wasn't time for quit—it was time for grit. Matt kept swinging.

When it was time for the third round, the ref shook his head. TKO. His opponent could not continue. Matt won.

And he wrote a book about it. And married his girlfriend. (He'd had to delay the wedding for a year because he needed a lot more training than he'd thought, but just like his parents, she forgave him . . . eventually.) We're all curious to see what Matt's next experiment will be. Wrestling polar bears at age sixty? Who knows?

Spending 5 percent of your time trying new things, knowing you will quit most of them, can lead to great opportunities. (And not all of them need to involve concussions.)

You now know there are good times to show grit and good times to quit. Both can lead to success. The tricky part is how to tell the difference. How do you know *when* you should quit something? "Should I stay or should I go?" as the song says. Let's look at that next. We'll start by getting the answer to a question we have all faced: When is the perfect time to stop dating and get married? Yup, science has an answer.

*

Again, we face the issue of limits. With dating, you know you need to quit at some point, but when? Some would say "When I meet the right person." But how do you know the next person won't be even better? Is the more realistic answer "When I meet a pretty good person and I'm tired of this crap"?

Here's what's fascinating: mathematicians have solved this problem. There's an easy formula that gives you an exact answer for how many dates to go on and how to pick the right person. It's what math folks call an "optimal stopping problem."

How many people do you need to date to find the perfect match? Matt Parker explains in his book *Things to Make and Do in the*

Fourth Dimension. First, take a guess at the number of different people you might go out with. A rough guess will do. Obviously you have to sleep, you probably won't go on a date every night, and you'd like to be married before you're 112, so the number isn't as big as you might think. To make it simple, we'll say it's 100.

We need the square root of that number. (Yes, the calculator app on your smartphone can help you find true love.) In our example, it's 10.

Now go out on dates with 10 people and politely tell them "No, thanks," but make sure to note who was the best of the bunch. Keep dating until you find somebody who rocks your world more than that person did. Mathematically speaking, this person is your match. (No, you aren't obligated to invite me to the wedding, but it was very kind of you to ask.) How accurate is this? Pretty darn accurate. Parker says with 100 potential spouses, it's about 90 percent likely to give you the best of the bunch.

Fascinating, right? But let's face it: you're not going to do this. This is about as unromantic as you can get. In the end, you're going to go by feel. That's just how humans are.

Many people are attached to the idea of "soulmates"—that perfect person just for you who will be kind and perfect, thoughtful and forgiving, shower you with kindness and gifts, and never forgetting to take out the trash. But if soulmates exist, what is the likelihood you'll actually meet yours? Randall Munroe, creator of the webcomic *XKCD* and a former NASA roboticist, ran the numbers. They're not pretty. Your chance to run into that one perfect person would happen in "one lifetime out of ten thousand."

Ouch. I know, that's sad. But it's actually very helpful information, because a study by Andrea Lockhart shows that people who expect a fairy-tale relationship experience a lot more disappointment than those who don't.

What's the problem here? We're dreaming but we're not taking reality into consideration. We're not thinking about the obstacles that life presents so that we can assemble a solid plan for finding and staying with that special someone. When you think you and your partner are "made for each other," it's easy to assume you don't have to work at the relationship. And in an era when divorce is easy and options seem plentiful, it's not surprising that divorce—the relationship equivalent of quitting—is so common. You wouldn't say "I got my dream job. Whew, now I can stop working," but people frequently do something akin to this with relationships because it's "meant to be." Until it turns out it wasn't.

What's the answer? It's helpful to look at the opposite extreme: arranged marriages. Hold on now. I'm not telling you to marry a stranger. Stick with me for a second. Early on, "love marriages" are happier than arranged marriages, scoring a 70 out of 91 on an academic "love scale" vs. 58 out of 91. No surprise, right? But later something happens. A decade in, arranged marriages score a 68 and the ones based on love a lowly 40.

What's going on? A lot, certainly. One key factor is that in an arranged marriage you need to deal with reality a bit more from day one. You're not saying "We're soulmates!" and then later on becoming disappointed when the universe doesn't hand you wedded bliss on a silver platter. You're saying "I'm handcuffed to a stranger and *I* need to make this work." So with time, you often do. And as anyone who has actually been married can tell you, it's going to take some work.

Dreams aren't bad, but we need a little more than that to achieve success at anything, be it relationships or career. We have to face life's challenges head-on and not take the ostrich route of head-in-the-sand delusion. The research bears this out; while fairy tales predict problems, seeing love as a "journey" is quite healthy: "It may be romantic for lovers to think they were made for each other, but it backfires when conflicts arise and reality pokes the bubble of perfect unity. Instead, thinking about love as a journey, often involving twists and turns but ultimately moving toward a destination, takes away some of the repercussions of relational conflicts."

What's a system that will work whenever you're trying to turn dreams into reality? How do you know what to quit and what to stick with? One researcher came up with a shockingly easy system. It's called WOOP.

Gabriele Oettingen was skeptical. As a professor of psychology at New York University, she just wasn't buying all this stuff that said merely dreaming about what you want could passively deliver happiness to your doorstep in a FedEx box.

So she did some studies, and it turned out she was right. Actually, she was more than right. Not only did dreaming not bring you your desires; it actually *hurt* your chances of getting what you want. No, folks, *The Secret* doesn't work.

It turns out that your brain isn't very good at telling fantasy from reality. (This is why movies are so thrilling.) When you dream, that grey matter feels you already have what you want and so it doesn't marshal the resources you need to motivate yourself and achieve. Instead, it relaxes. And you do less, you accomplish less, and those dreams stay mere dreams. Positive thinking, by itself, doesn't work.

Are you dreaming about how svelte you'll look in that swimsuit after the diet you're planning? Women who did that lost twenty-four fewer pounds than those who didn't. Fantasizing about getting that perfect job? Those who dwelled on it sent out fewer applications and ended up getting fewer offers. Students who imagined a big A for the semester spent less time studying and got lower grades.

If dreaming is so bad, why do we do it? Because it's the mental equivalent of getting drunk: it feels really good right now but doesn't lead to good things later. That's exactly what Oettingen's research showed: while dreaming, we feel good. But dreaming ends up increasing depression later on. Fantasizing gives us the reward before we've accomplished the task and saps the energy we need to realize it. More dreams now mean less achievement later.

While positive self-talk and optimism can definitely help us not quit, by themselves they don't guarantee we'll achieve our goals. Now, dreaming isn't inherently bad—but it's just the first step. Next comes facing that awful buzzkill called "reality" and its ever-present obstacles.

After you dream, think, *What's getting in the way of my fantasy?*

And what will I do to overcome that? The fancy psych term is "implementation intentions." You and I can just call it "a plan."

In one study, Peter Gollwitzer and Veronika Brandstätter found that just planning out some basics, like when to do something, where, and how, made students almost 40 percent more likely to follow through with goals.

The two magic words are "if" and "then." For any obstacle, just thinking, *If X happens, I'll handle it by doing Y* makes a huge difference. How powerful are these two simple words? They even work for people who have very serious behavioral problems: drug addicts going through withdrawal. With no if-then implementation intentions, zero people followed through on putting a résumé together. But when the two magic words were used ahead of time, 80 percent of the people were ready to apply for a job.

What's so powerful here? You're getting your non-conscious mind involved. Instead of waiting until problems arise, you're giving your brain a habitual response to enact on autopilot.

You can find the roots of this method at work everywhere, from ancient philosophy to modern elite military units. The Stoics used an idea called *premeditatio malorum* ("premeditation of evils") to prepare. It's asking yourself, "What's the worst that could happen?" By considering the awful possibilities, you make sure you're ready for them. U.S. Army Special Forces units take time before every mission to use a variant of if-then. Author Dan Coyle explains: "They spend the entire morning going over every possible mistake or disaster that could happen during the mission. Every possible screwup is mercilessly examined, and linked to an appropriate response: *if the helicopter crash-lands, we'll do X. If we are dropped off at the wrong spot, we'll do Y. If we are outnumbered, we'll do Z.*"

Oettingen pulled together a simple system for you to do this called WOOP. (Yeah, the formal term is "mental contrasting" but, c'mon. Who wouldn't rather say "WOOP"?) WOOP—wish, outcome, obstacle, plan—is applicable to most any of your goals, from career to relationships to exercise and weight loss.

First, you get to dream. What's the thing you *wish* for? What are you fantasizing about? *(I want an awesome job.)* Really crystalize it in your mind and see the *outcome* you desire. *(I want to work as a VP at Google.)* Then it's time to face reality. What obstacle is in the way? *(I don't know how to get an interview there.)* Then address it. What's your plan? *(I'm going to check LinkedIn and see if I know anyone who works there and can connect me with HR.)*

Pretty straightforward, right? The cool thing is that this process doesn't sap your drive the way just fantasizing does. But there's an even bigger benefit to WOOP, one that's key when you're thinking about grit and quit. Ironically, this added advantage is that WOOP *doesn't* work for everyone, and whether it works isn't random. In her research, Oettingen found that mental contrasting gives a motivational boost when your goal is something you can achieve but it doesn't when your goal is outside the realm of possibility. It's like a personal litmus test for feasibility. When what you want is something reasonable (*I'm a qualified candidate who wants a job at Google but isn't sure about the next step*) WOOP will give you a plan and the energy to carry it out. But when your goal is more unrealistic (*I want to be the emperor of Australia by Thursday*) you will find yourself less energized and you'll know it.

So instead of just saying "We're soulmates!" you might want to step back for just a second. What's your wish? *A perfect marriage.* And what would that outcome be? *A happy home life with no fighting.* And what's a likely obstacle? *We keep arguing about what to buy at IKEA.* So what's your plan? *If we start arguing over which color Grönkulla to buy, I'm going to listen to what my spouse has to say and really consider their opinion.* If this energizes you to go on a Swedish shopping spree with the one you love, you're in good shape. If you feel even less motivated to work things out with your spouse, well, science may have just saved you a few years in a relationship that isn't going to work. Not only does it tell you when goals are unrealistic and it might be time to quit vs. grit, spending the time to walk through the mental exercise helps you disengage from an unattainable desire and experience less regret when you put it aside.

WOOP can tell you what needs grit and help you muster the

drive to soldier on. But it also can tell you what to quit and help you handle that transition less painfully. I'm not sure if mathematicians familiar with the optimal stopping problem have happier marriages, but you can WOOP your way to answers regarding grit and quit.

Okay, we've covered a lot: Shaolin temples, stand-up comedians, liver disease, and arranged marriages. Let's tie this all together so we know where to start, when to quit, when to show grit, and how to ultimately get where we want to go.

*

We all need role models. I say be a Toronto raccoon.

Their ability to get into trash cans shows a level of grit and resourcefulness that is almost beyond compare. These little scoundrels have turned the residents of the Canadian city into a collective of victims.

Suzanne MacDonald, a researcher who studies raccoon behavior at York University, says, "Raccoons in the city are extraordinary, not only in their ability to approach things, but they have no fear, and they stick with it, they will spend hours trying to get food out of something."

Every attempt to hold them back has failed. They do not quit and routinely surmount any attempt to stop them. The people of Toronto have tried everything from strapping down the lids of trash cans to concealing the bins and nothing has been effective. "We've devised all sorts of ways of protecting our garbage, which all fail," says Michael Pettit, a local professor of psychology.

This is no minor problem. The city government has been trying to cope with the scourge for well over a decade. As *The Wall Street Journal* reports, in 2002 Toronto went so far as to finance the development of "raccoon-proof" trash cans. How well did they work? Well, let's just say that in 2015 the city spent an additional $31 million dollars to create a new, redesigned "raccoon-proof" trash can. Not a good sign, folks.

How do these puckish bandits do it? Despite having smaller brains, they exhibit many of the principles we've discussed in this chapter. Their optimism cannot be questioned. Perhaps it's a fun game for them. Spencer Glendon and Peter Drucker would be proud of their extreme focus. And these knaves always try different things when encountering the newfangled attempts to stymie them. Clearly their "little bets" are paying off.

Has all this effort by the people of Toronto shown negative effects on Mother Nature's mischief-makers? Hardly. A piece on the American Psychological Association's website explains, "Raccoons had attracted interest because they flourished, rather than receded, in the face of human expansion." Not only are the pint-size thieves thriving, but all these challenges have *actually made the raccoons smarter.* Suzanne MacDonald studied the difference in problem-solving ability between Toronto's urban raccoons and their brethren in the wild. She found that the "urbanites trump their country cousins in both intelligence and ability." And MacDonald isn't just a raccoon researcher; she's a victim. One little bugger managed to open her garage to get to her own trash bins.

Instead of fighting them, perhaps it's time to learn from them. Instead of seeing insurmountable problems, you can be like a Toronto raccoon and see how the challenges to be overcome will make you smarter and more successful.

That said, the city of Toronto isn't giving up on their decades-long quest. Mayor John Tory told members of the press, "The members of Raccoon Nation are smart, they're hungry, and they're determined . . . Defeat is not an option."

I can almost see the raccoons of Toronto rubbing their little paws together in anticipation of that next challenge to be overcome. "What's that you say, hairless apes? 'Raccoon-proof'? All right. *Bring it.*"

Let's round up the research and make it fun—make it a *game,* even. Answer the following questions and we'll take it from there.

A. Yes!
B. I'm not sure, but I have a few hunches.
C. What was the question? I got distracted.

If you answered *a*, skip right on down to the next question.

If you answered *b*, it's time to WOOP. Take each of those hunches and run them through the wish-outcome-obstacle-plan process. The one that energizes you the most should get serious consideration. The ones that leave you *meh* get the boot.

If you answered *c*, it's time for some "little bets." You need to try more stuff until something excites you. Whatever strikes a chord, give it a WOOP.

2. ARE YOU OPTIMISTIC?

A. Absolutely!
B. We're all going to die lonely and without anything good to watch on TV.

If you answered *a*, you're rockin' and rollin'. Head to question 3.

If you answered *b*, it's time to look at your explanatory style. The real dilemma with pessimism is that it's actually more accurate. Yes, the cynics are often right. But as we learned in the first chapter, always playing the odds can be a prescription for mediocrity—especially when the thing you're betting on is yourself. This is why Martin Seligman developed a great balance so you don't go full-on delusional. He calls it "flexible optimism." Being a little pessimistic at times keeps us honest. But when the risks are very low (which is true, frankly, for most things) or when the payoffs are very high (such as a career you might want to devote your life to) optimism is the way to go. It's a balance. A balance that with practice you can find.

With the little things, show optimism. What have you got to lose? And with the big things that can change your life, optimism is the fuel to push yourself past the odds. When things seem high risk and low reward, pessimism is a tool you can dust off to make sure you don't go all Pollyanna.

Want to be gritty like an awesome insurance salesperson? Sorry, that's not terribly sexy. Okay, let's try again: Want to be gritty like a Navy SEAL? You need to remember Seligman's three Ps; don't see bad things as permanent, pervasive, or personal.

3. DO YOU HAVE A MEANINGFUL STORY?

A. Viktor Frankl would be proud of me.
B. I borrowed my story from a Bill Murray film.

Did you answer *a*? On to the next question. You're doing great.

If you answered *b,* it might be time to think about that eulogy. Who do you want to be remembered as? What qualities do you want your friends and loved ones to prize and miss? They remind you who you are when things get hard. Stories don't have to be 100 percent true. The goal is to use them as a springboard to make them true with time and hard work.

And stories are personal. They can come from the most serious things, like religion, patriotism, parenthood, or career goals, but they don't have to. They're just about something meaningful to you that drives you to reach outside yourself. Research shows that thinking about superheroes can make you physically stronger in the gym. But only if you feel a connection to superheroes. Stories affect the muscles in your body and also the willpower inside your head.

When the story you tell yourself says "This is worth it" you will work harder and stick through the greatest challenges, like Viktor Frankl did. Sometimes the stories are true, sometimes they're not, but they keep us going. For an extra boost, try writing your story down. Research shows it can make you 11 percent happier with your life.

A. Call me Mario.

B. I'm still waiting for my annual review.

Did you answer *a*? Ignore me and keep on playing. Head to the next question.

If you related more to *b*, remember that whiny neutered goats fly. You need winnable games, novel challenges, goals, and feedback to feel engaged in whatever it is you do.

Ever wonder why it's so easy to help other people with their problems but often so hard to deal with your own? That distance you feel with your friend's issues shifts them from emotionally fraught problems to fun challenges. They go from stress grenades to cool puzzles. Reframing problems as game-like challenges increases resilience and reduces stress.

Freakonomics did a fascinating experiment. They looked at the number of *Dilbert* comics in offices and juxtaposed them with the company's level of morale. The more *Dilbert* comics hanging on cubicle farm walls predicted just how unengaged the employees felt. Remember, it's *your* game. Don't wait for others to make your job or your life exciting. Apply WNGF and take the reins. Many hear the story of Joe Simpson and wonder why anyone would want to do something as dangerous as mountain climbing in the first place. Good question. But his answer was simple: climbing is fun.

5. YOU ARE A GRIT MACHINE.
ARE YOU THINKING LIKE A SICK PERSON?

A. I know what my most important thing is and I'm focusing on that.

B. Can't answer right now. I've got three hundred things on my to-do list.

If you answered *a,* you know what to do.

If you answered *b,* what old activities and routines take up a bunch of your time but provide little value? Andy Rooney found himself being a bit of a pack rat and decided to do something about it. He added up how much his house was costing him per month by calculating mortgage, utilities, taxes, etc. Then he divided by the amount of square footage. That told him how much "rent" per square foot any item in his house should be paying to stay there. Was the refrigerator worth it? Yeah, it provided a lot of value. How about that old rusty exercise machine in the basement he never used? Nope. So he got rid of it. You can do a similar rough calculation with your time. Get rid of the activities that provide little value and don't serve your goals. Then add those hours to fuel progress toward the big things that matter.

You can't do it all and do it well. Kill the activities that don't produce results and double down on what does.

6. YOU'RE ALMOST THERE.
HAVE YOU ADDED SOME "LITTLE BETS"?

A. I've packed my bags for the Shaolin temple.
B. I don't even try new television channels because who knows what could be on there?

Did you answer *a?* Why are you still reading this? Go conquer the world.

Did you answer *b?* Stop being Batman. Stop trying to be perfect at everything. Try, fail, and learn like those crazy kindergarteners who smoked the competition in the Spaghetti Problem. And I do mean literally; a study showed that we're more creative when we think like a kid.

We don't like to admit it, but often we really don't know what we want. Research shows that "only 6 percent of people work in the profession they aspired to in childhood" and a third of people end up in a career that has nothing to do with their college major. So you need to get out there and try more stuff, like Richard Wiseman's lucky people did. You don't need to quit Princeton and move to China—but it's not always a terrible idea either.

Stories and limits—that's what grit and quit come down to. Focus on those two and you can be as unstoppable as a Toronto raccoon—but so successful that you'll never have to eat out of a trash can.

So you know what to be gritty at, or at least how to find it. But you'll need help reaching success, right? Or maybe you just need to tell everyone to go away and then work hard? Which is it? Next up: Is success about who you know or what you know? Let's get to it.

CHAPTER 4

It's Not What You Know, It's Who You Know (Unless It Really Is What You Know)

What We Can Learn About the Power of Networks from Hostage Negotiators, Top Comedians, and the Smartest Man Who Ever Lived

The day Paul Erdös was born both his sisters, ages three and five, died from scarlet fever. His mother was so scared something would happen to him too that she didn't let him go to school. Or leave the house. He had no friends.

Erdös said, "Numbers became my best friends."

The child of two mathematics teachers, he spent most of his time home alone surrounded by math books. He quickly proved himself to be a prodigy. By age three, he could multiply triple digit numbers. By age four, he could hear a person's age and calculate how many seconds they'd been alive. He achieved a Ph.D. in math by the time he was twenty-one.

As an adult, fueled by amphetamines, he would put in nineteen-hour days doing the only thing he loved: math. He was inhumanly productive. Some years he would produce more than fifty academic papers—a number most mathematicians would be happy to complete in an entire lifetime.

But as Spider-Man always reminds us, "With great power comes great responsibility," and with great math skills comes, well . . . great *oddity*. There's no two ways about it: Erdös was weird. *Time* magazine would even do a piece on him titled "The Oddball's Oddball."

If you were Erdös's friend, he might show up at your house in the middle of the night wanting to do math and announce, "My brain is open." And suddenly you had a houseguest for a few days. He wouldn't do laundry. You had to do it for him. If he wanted to work on a theorem at five A.M., he'd bang pots and pans until you came downstairs. This is a guy who referred to children as "epsilon" because in mathematics epsilon is the Greek letter used for "small number."

He worked obsessively. As colleague Paul Winkler explained, "Erdös came to my twins' bar mitzvah, notebook in hand . . . my mother-in-law tried to throw him out. She thought he was some guy who wandered in off the street, in a rumpled suit, carrying a pad under his arm. It is entirely possible that he proved a theorem or two during the ceremony." In fact, he did little else. He hadn't read a novel since the 1940s or seen a movie since the 1950s. Life was math. Full stop.

He was certainly successful. Erdös produced more papers during his life than any other mathematician—ever. Some were even published posthumously, meaning Erdös, technically, kept publishing seven years after his death. He received at least fifteen honorary doctorates.

But his accomplishments are not why he's remembered. It's more about what he did with others. More specifically, the effect he had on others. Unlike the stereotypical mathematician, not leaving his office, hunched over a proof, Erdös was the amphetamine-powered itinerant networker of math. He loved to collaborate. He lived out of a suitcase and routinely traveled to twenty-five countries, eventually working with more than five hundred other mathematicians around the globe. He collaborated with so many different people sometimes he couldn't remember them all:

On one occasion, Erdös met a mathematician and asked him where he was from. "Vancouver," the mathematician replied.

"Oh, then you must know my good friend Elliot Mendelson," Erdös said. The reply was "I *am* your good friend Elliot Mendelson."

Yes, he was brilliant, but this is not why so many tolerated his eccentric personality. To use the terminology of Adam Grant, Erdös was a Giver. He wanted to make you better. He encouraged you, helped you. Having him show up on your doorstep in the middle of the night was the mathematical equivalent of having Yoda appear and tell you he wanted to make you a great Jedi Knight . . . of math.

As Erdös knew better than anyone, math was a lonely game, but he made it a quest. A quest you could go on with friends. As if crisscrossing the world, supporting and collaborating with mathematicians wasn't enough, he also spurred them on with awards. Like a mob boss putting out a hit on someone, Erdös offered cash prizes out of his own pocket—sometimes as much as ten thousand dollars—for solving this difficult problem or that intractable theorem, giving a public incentive to the lonely work of mathematics.

The Fields Medal is the highest honor a mathematician can receive. Paul Erdös never won it. But a number of the people he helped did, and that leads us to what Erdös is best known for: the "Erdös number." No, it was not a theorem or a mathematical tool. It was simply a measure of how close you were to working with Paul Erdös. (Think of it like Six Degrees of Kevin Bacon—but for nerds.) If you collaborated with Erdös on a paper, you had an Erdös number of one. If you collaborated with someone who collaborated with Erdös, your Erdös number was two, and so on. Paul Erdös was so influential and helped so many people that mathematicians rank themselves by how close they were to working with him.

Research has shown that, on average, how close your connection to Erdös is predicts how good a mathematician you are. Two Nobel Prize winners in physics have an Erdös number of two. Fourteen have an Erdös number of three. Erdös made people great.

On September 20, 1996, Paul Erdös died at the age of eighty-three. (Or, in his own idiosyncratic vocabulary, he "left." He said people "died" when they had stopped doing math.) Technically, Erdös's number was zero. That might feel like a lonely or distressing number, but I like to think it makes sense. That zero symbolizes how Erdös gave everything to the people around him. It wasn't about his own number. It was about how many others he gave numbers to.

The boy who grew up with no friends created the greatest network in math, perhaps the greatest that ever will be. The number that bears his name is an enduring legacy by which all mathematicians are measured. He had more friends than anyone in math, more people who remain indebted to him, who miss him and loved him . . . and even after his death, that group continues to grow. Looking at Erdös numbers, it is currently estimated he influenced over two hundred thousand mathematicians.

It would seem success really is about connections, right? Who you know, not what you know. But if success really hinges on connections, should you be like Paul Erdös? Are extroverts more successful? Let's find out.

My mom told me to be a "people person." (Full disclosure: I'm not. C'mon, I'm here, alone, writing this book.)

Everyone enjoys the company of close friends and everyone needs some alone time. That's not terribly insightful. The key question is how do you recharge your batteries? Is your idea of fun a party or reading a book? Do you prefer to be one-on-one with close friends or "the more the merrier"?

Introversion–extroversion is one of the most established categories in psychology, but many specifics about it are still debated. We're really only concerned with the social part here and there's not too much debate about that: extroverts get more "reward value" from social activities and from being the center of attention.

Some theorize that introverts simply have more going on in their heads. Not that extroverts are vapid (some of what's going on in introverts' heads can be negative, like anxiety), but this means that loud, busy places quickly tip an introvert into overstimulation, whereas extroverts devoid of a stimulating environment get bored.

For example, I'm quite the introvert. In grad school I had a girlfriend who loved to go to bars and parties, the louder the better. To her that was exciting. To me it was auditory waterboarding. When she and I would go on long drives, I'd play podcasts in the car and be fascinated. She'd be asleep in thirty seconds. (I'm sure you're shocked to find out we're not together anymore.)

Now, there's a reason mom said "Be a people person," and there are many reasons why it's good to be an extrovert. Dealing with other people is a huge part of what most of us do, and how we get along with others is often key to success. As we saw in chapter 2, Adam Grant and Jeffrey Pfeffer may take different stances on the best way to deal with others, but nobody disputes that dealing with others is often an important component of getting ahead.

Well, this is a book about success, so let's get down to dollars and cents: the research pretty consistently shows extroverts make more money. Stanford did a twenty-year study of its MBA grads and found most of them to be classic extroverts.

This is traceable all the way back to childhood. Another study found that "childhood extraversion positively predicted . . . extrinsic success." Moving someone from the bottom fifth of popularity in their high school class to the top fifth equals a 10 percent boost in income during adulthood.

But success isn't just about money. Wanna get promoted? One study says, "extraversion was positively related to career satisfaction, salary level, and the number of promotions received over one's entire career."

Even the *bad* habits of extroverts reveal the secrets of their financial success. If you're the type who likes to drink and smoke, do you earn more cash? Drinkers make more money. Smokers don't. Drinkers make 10 percent more than abstainers. And males that hit a bar at least once a month make another 7 percent on top of that. Why does liquor make you richer? Unlike smoking, drinking is primarily a *social* activity. The authors of the study speculate that increased drinking leads to increased "social capital": you're probably out bonding with others and making connections.

Most people think of leaders as extroverts. That perception becomes a self-fulfilling prophecy. Want to be CEO? Wanna be top dog? In a study of four thousand managers, people who scored "very high" on extroversion were disproportionately represented. And the higher up the ladder, the more common they were. Of the general population, 16 percent scored "very high" on extroversion, while 60 percent of top executives did.

Why might this be the case? The answer is a bit frightening, actually. Research shows that you don't actually need to know more to be seen as a leader. Merely by speaking first and speaking often— very extroverted behavior—people come to be seen as *El Jefe*. Meanwhile, other studies show that those who initially act shy in groups are perceived as less intelligent. As Pfeffer pointed out, to get ahead you need to self-promote. This comes naturally to extroverts and is actually more important than competence when it comes to being seen as a leader.

But what if you're between jobs or looking to move on to greener pastures? Again, the extroverts have the edge. Mark Granovetter's groundbreaking work on the importance of "weak ties" showed that you don't usually find out about that next great opportunity from close friends. You tend to hear about the same things they do. People who have more peripheral acquaintances are more plugged in and learn about emerging possibilities. Having a big network also pays off when you get that job. One study found, "Multilevel analyses showed that networking is related to concurrent salary and that it is related to the growth rate of salary over time."

In fact, one can argue that companies would be smart to make the size of someone's network a key element in determining whom they hire, because it can affect the bottom line. MIT research showed "The more socially connected the IBM employees were, the better they performed. They could even quantify the difference: On average, every email contact was worth an added $948 in revenue."

It's quite hard to underestimate the value of a big network. For instance, let's have some fun and think about the most lucrative business there is—and one where the stakes are incredibly high: drug dealing. Big upside, ginormous downside.

Yup, research shows having a big network is even important for careers on the wrong side of the law. Funny that the advice most drug dealers live by is "keep things small" in order to avoid arrest. But research from Simon Fraser University showed that by having a large network dealers earned more money and were more likely to stay out of jail. The size of the criminal organization had no effect. Being a street-corner dealer or a lieutenant in the Cali cartel didn't matter. What did have an effect was how many people the dealer knew in the business:

> The results of these studies were clear: offenders who were better at building and managing their criminal network earned significantly more money from crime than others . . . the size of a dealer's core criminal network was significantly associated with survival. Network size also emerges as a protective factor: the larger the size of a dealer's network, the longer the survival.

Strong friendships kept the dealers out of jail, while "weak ties" provided them with business opportunities.

So it's pretty clear which side is winning the introversion–extroversion death match. But what about when we step outside the workplace and look at life in general?

Remember when we talked about Richard Wiseman's research on luck? Guess what: he also found that extroverts are luckier. A big part of the science of luck was about encountering new opportunities. In the same way that having a large network opens you up to job opportunities, it exposes you to *all kinds* of other new possibilities. That's why those rich, extroverted stock traders are always on the phone.

The introverts are against the ropes and getting battered. Time to deliver the coup de grâce. Extroverts are *happier* than introverts. And this is no small detail: "The relationship between extraversion and happiness or subjective well-being (SWB) is one of the most consistently replicated and robust findings in the SWB literature." In fact, extroverts are even happier than introverts when *alone,* and one study showed that when introverts pretend to be extroverts, they were happier too.

Ouch.

Extroverts make more money, get more promotions, are more likely to become leaders, find new jobs faster, and are both luckier and happier. That's pretty damning evidence. After all that, one question looms: *Why in the world would anybody want to be an introvert?*

*

All right, let's talk introversion. (It's okay. The extroverts probably stopped reading after chapter 2 to go hang out with friends.) As the old saying goes, "It's the quiet ones you have to watch."

We learned about Paul Erdös, who made his reputation by knowing everyone and their sister in the world of math. But can a scientist succeed by knowing almost *no one*? Actually, yes. We just don't give Isaac Newton enough credit. This guy rewrote the rules of our universe. And he did it almost completely on his own.

Aristotle, Kepler, Galileo . . . yeah, yeah, yeah. They made their contributions, but Newton gave us a coherent, integrated road map to how the world works. He brought us from magic to science. Before him, predicting how things would move was more a matter of guess than math. After him, we knew the universe worked by *rules*. James Gleick described Newton as the "chief architect of the modern world."

Nobody would have such an impact until Einstein, nearly *two hundred years later*. And while Einstein certainly overturned how scientists thought about the rules of the universe, he didn't change the way the average person sees the world they inhabit day to day. Newton was a game changer for all of us.

Even the term "paradigm shift" feels a bit underpowered. Einstein struggled and ultimately failed to come up with his unified field theory, which would explain how all the ideas of physics could be meshed into one coherent whole. Newton pretty much said, "Here's how the world works" and unraveled a nearly complete system.

He developed calculus, optics, and gravity while still in his twenties. And there was no fancy technology to help him. To develop insights on optics, this guy deliberately jammed a needle in his eye. And how about gravity? Before Newton, we didn't really understand it. People knew things fell to Earth and Galileo had been dropping stuff off the Tower of Pisa, but it wasn't an obvious rule. Galileo understood how acceleration worked—but he had no idea *why* it worked.

Plus, Newton did all this almost entirely on his own. He did say, "If I have seen further, it is by standing on the shoulders of giants," but the truth was he had amazingly little contact with anyone, big or small, during much of his life.

If anyone created the stereotype of the absent-minded professor, it was probably Newton. Sometimes he wouldn't leave his bedroom for days. He mumbled to himself and drew equations in the dirt with a stick while on his solitary walks. The lone genius? It's hard to think of a better example. He didn't have the mathematical tools to unravel how the world worked, so he *created* them. The calculus we all struggled with in high school? He invented it. By himself. He had few friends, and correspondence by letter was often the only way he communicated with others. He never married. In fact, many suspect he died a virgin.

We all know the apple-hitting-his-head story of gravity, but that story probably isn't true. If anything, he was probably at home, alone, with the door locked, when it happened. One can easily imagine Newton as that crazy neighbor shouting at the kids to get off his lawn. But Newton never even knew his neighbors. When he left Trinity in 1696, it wasn't hard. Despite having lived in the city for thirty-five years, he didn't have any friends there.

As James Gleick writes in his biography *Isaac Newton*, "He was born into a world of darkness, obscurity, and magic; led a strangely pure and obsessive life, lacking parents, lovers, and friends; quarreled bitterly with great men who crossed his path; veered at least once to the brink of madness; cloaked his work in secrecy; and yet discovered more of the essential core of human knowledge than anyone before or after."

If you forced someone to work the way Newton did it would easily qualify as inhumane. But this was self-administered solitary confinement, and he didn't seem to regard it that way. Pascal once said, "All the unhappiness of man stems from one thing only: That he is incapable of staying quietly in his room." Sir Isaac Newton seems to be proof positive of this.

If you were Paul Erdös's boss, you'd try to surround him with as many smart people as possible and you'd give him an unlimited travel budget. If you were Newton's boss, it might be a good idea to give him more funding or equipment, but the primary rule you'd live by to make sure this genius kept cranking out incredible, world-changing developments is obvious: *just leave him the hell alone.*

No doubt, Newton is in the running for the title of Smartest Person Who Ever Lived. When you're that incomprehensibly smart, who needs help? The rest of us troglodytes will only slow you down. But putting aside the sheer brilliance of the man, is there something else we can take away from the life of Newton, as extreme as it was?

Remember that ten-thousand-hour theory of expertise? Well, without anybody bothering you, you have a lot of time to get really good at stuff. In this age of constant distractions, we can all learn something from Newton. Yes, extroverts can draw on the resources of an incredible network, but that doesn't leave a lot of time for something important: hard, lonely work in the trenches. You see, the superpower of introverts is that they are far more likely to become experts in their field.

How much more likely? Here's a quote from a study for you: "Extraversion was negatively related to individual proficiency." What's that mean in English? *The more extroverted you are, the worse you are at your job.* As we saw, having lots of friends has clear benefits . . . but can also be an enormous distraction.

When you think *athlete* you might envision the popular captain of the football team in high school. Or maybe the charismatic baseball player telling you to buy razors in that commercial. It's only natural to think they're all hard-partying extroverts. You couldn't be more wrong. Author (and Olympic gold medalist) David Hemery reports that almost nine out of ten top athletes identify as introverts. "A remarkably distinguishing feature is that a large proportion, 89 percent of these sports achievers, classed themselves as introverts . . . Only 6 percent of the sports achievers felt that they were extroverts and the remaining 5 percent felt that they were 'middle of the road.'"

Team athletes may spend a lot of time surrounded by people, but that's rarely what makes them great. It's the lonely hours in the batting cage. Taking three-point shot after three-point shot until you can't lift your arms. Missing the party to do a few more sprints after the sun goes down.

Elite musicians? Same thing. When K. Anders Ericsson asked top violinists what daily activity was most relevant to improving their skills, 90 percent replied, "Practice alone." What was the best predictor of skill for top chess players? "Serious study alone." In fact, among older tournament-ranked players, it was the *only* statistically significant predictor.

Want to know who will do best in school or who will actually have more knowledge? Don't bet on IQ. Being an introvert is more predictive of good grades than intelligence. In her book *Quiet*, Susan Cain reports:

> At the university level, introversion predicts academic performance better than cognitive ability. One study tested 141 college students' knowledge of twenty different subjects, from art to astronomy to statistics, and found that introverts knew more than the extroverts about every single one of them. Introverts receive disproportionate numbers of graduate degrees, National Merit Scholarship finalist positions, and Phi Beta Kappa keys.

Want to know who is going to be the creative genius later in life? Pick the unpopular nerd:

> . . . the single-minded focus on what would turn out to be a lifelong passion, is typical for highly creative people. According to the psychologist Mihály Csikszentmihályi, who between 1990 and 1995 studied the lives of ninety-one exceptionally creative people in the arts, sciences, business, and government, many of his subjects were on the social margins during adolescence, partly because "intense curiosity or focused interest seems odd to their peers." Teens who are too gregarious to spend time alone often fail to cultivate their talents "because practicing music or studying math requires a solitude they dread."

Best investment bankers? Emotionally stable introverts. In other professions, like computer programming and professional tennis, being downright *disagreeable* is tied with higher earnings.

Research reveals that introverts also succeed in areas where we always assume extroverts typically rule. Much like with pro athletes, we assume leaders should be people-loving extroverts. And, as we saw in the previous section, research shows that extroverts are more likely to become leaders and to be *perceived* as effective. But are they really effective? When Adam Grant (whom we met in chapter 2) looked at leadership, he found something really interesting. Whether an introvert or an extrovert is the better leader depends on whom they are leading. When employees are passive, the social, energetic extroverts really shine. However, when you're dealing with very motivated workers, introverts do better because they know how to listen, help, and get out of the way.

And while extroverts are more likely to stand out as leadership material initially, with their more talkative nature and social dominance, studies show this often doesn't last long. Extroverts' weakness in listening skills become apparent after they assume a leadership role and they often lose status among coworkers in team situations.

So, in some areas, we give extroverts too much credit. In fact, there are plenty of downsides associated with extroversion that we don't hear much about. Before you start praying that your sons and daughters are all outgoing, consider that extroversion is tied to crime, infidelity, car accidents, overconfidence, and financial risk taking. This may come as a shock. We're always told it's good to be a "people person."

Why haven't we heard anything about the downside of extroversion? Frankly, it's a marketing issue. There are a lot more extroverts than introverts, and the extroverts have more friends and talk more. As Susan Cain points out, an extrovert bias has crept into our workplaces, schools, and culture, especially in the United States.

So there are successful extroverts and introverts and the world definitely needs both, but chances are, you're not really either one. Yes, one-third of people are die-hard introverts or 24/7 extroverts, but the remaining two-thirds are what are called ambiverts. They're somewhere in between. It's a spectrum.

And just because you're in the middle doesn't mean you don't get a superpower too. Oddly enough, ambiverts make the best salespeople. Extroverts, who you might think would have the edge here, can be too talky or overbearing. Introverts are good listeners but may lack the social drive. When Adam Grant studied salepeople he found the top performers clustered in the middle of the introversion–extroversion spectrum.

This is where the real lesson for most of us comes in. If you can't stand a moment alone, sure, get that MBA and chase that leadership position over a passive workforce. You're built for it. If people drive you crazy, dive deep into your passion, earn those ten thousand hours, and be renowned as the best in your field. But the bulk of us need to know when to turn on our extrovert side and build that network and when to close the door and develop those skills. As Adam Grant told *The Wall Street Journal,* "Read each situation more carefully and ask yourself, 'What do I need to do right now to be most happy or successful?'"

The introvert side is pretty straightforward: *put in the hours.* But introverts and ambiverts alike struggle with the best way to network. Even the verb has a negative connotation about it, like it's insincere and phony, used by glad-handing politicians and sleazy used-car salesmen.

Here's the good news: while extroverts may have a natural talent for networking, it's a skill any of us can develop, and it doesn't have to feel gross or fake. As you saw in the research, whether you're looking for a legit job or trying to sell kilos of cocaine, having a network is something you need.

*

It seemed the bombing would never end. As World War II raged on, the UK was being pounded by the planes of Hitler's Luftwaffe. But the UK was developing a secret weapon that had the power to turn the tide: a new type of radar.

There had already been much back and forth in terms of radar development. The Germans navigated their UK bombing attacks with radar, and in response, the British had developed increasingly sophisticated ways to jam the signals. This technological one-upmanship has been called "The Battle of the Beams."

And now the UK had made a breakthrough, called the "cavity magnetron." That might sound like the name of Optimus Prime's dentist, but it was something most of us have in our kitchen today: a microwave. Using microwave radar would allow the machines to be dramatically smaller. Instead of being housed in a huge tower, they could conceivably be placed on every UK plane.

While the UK had cracked the problem of creating the tech, manufacturing it at a large enough scale and fast enough to save their country would be impossible. Under relentless Nazi bombardment, there just wasn't the capacity to produce thousands upon thousands of microwave radar devices in short order.

But there was another way. Radar technology had already benefited from collaboration between the Allied powers; maybe once again collaboration would save Great Britain. In 1940, UK military leaders took the cavity magnetron to the United States and showed what it could do. The Americans were blown away and committed to turning the development and manufacturing resources of their country toward making the dream a reality.

The Radiation Laboratory at MIT headed up the project. (The name was deliberately made vague to conceal the purpose of their mission. It was later given the much cooler nickname of the "Rad Lab.") Thirty-five hundred people were employed at the lab, including some of the most brilliant minds of that generation. Nine would later go on to win a Nobel Prize for other work.

The advancements they made were spectacular. One of their systems would be used to direct UK antiaircraft fire and was responsible for taking out 85 percent of the German V-1 bombs, which had been tearing London apart. Another type of radar was so sensitive it could detect the periscopes on Nazi submarines, allowing the Allies to gain the edge in naval warfare.

But before these tremendous successes would be realized on the battlefield, the Rad Lab faced one enormous problem: the damn device didn't work. At least not consistently. Testing the new radar off the Charles River in Cambridge, they kept experiencing failures. Again and again, when it seemed they knew the science in and out, when they had tracked down every bug, every problem, the radar would utterly fail. It was inexplicable. It felt like God did not want them to succeed, like some great power was actively working against them.

They were *right*. But it wasn't God. It was Harvard.

Unbeknownst to MIT, the Radio Research Laboratory at Harvard University had received millions of dollars from the U.S. government to secretly develop radar *jamming* technology, which they were testing on the other side of the Charles River. (The Americans should have taken a few tips on the power of collaboration from their friends in the UK.) Harvard's efforts were so effective they once brought down all communications for the Boston Police Department, accidentally jamming the radios in squad cars for the entire city.

Luckily, before the MIT researchers had been driven absolutely insane, the presence of their unintentional "enemies" across the Charles River was made known to them, and then a new type of powerful collaboration began: a healthy rivalry.

MIT redoubled their efforts to overcome Harvard's jamming technologies and Harvard fought back with better ways of beating MIT's radar. The resulting progress from the two academic giants was stunning.

With Harvard's "help," MIT's radar became devastating:

In November 1942, U-boats claimed 117 Allied ships. Less than a year later, in the two-month period of September to October 1943, only 9 Allied ships were sunk, while a total of 25 U-boats were destroyed by aircraft equipped with ASV radars.

And with MIT's "assistance," Harvard's jamming technology drove the Nazis into a panic:

So effective was the Allies' jamming system—it reduced German anti-aircraft efficiency by 75 percent—that by the end of the war almost 90 percent of Germany's high-frequency radio experts, some 7,000 men, were diverted from other urgent work to the single job of finding a way to prevent jamming of German radar.

Many now believe that radar was what won the war.

When we collaborate—including in healthy rivalries—the gains can be exponential. But when we don't communicate, we can end up not only missing those benefits but also getting our efforts "jammed" by our friends.

We've established the payoff to networking is huge. But it can feel sleazy. Research from Francesca Gino shows that when we try to meet someone just to get something from them, it makes us feel immoral. The people who feel least sleazy about networking are powerful people. But those who need to network the most—the least powerful—are the most likely to feel bad about it. We like networking better when it's serendipitous, when it feels like an accident, not deliberate and Machiavellian.

This presents a big problem for introverts, who aren't as inclined toward making random acquaintances. It even creates difficulties for extroverts, who may make connections easily but not ones that can necessarily advance their careers.

Since you need to have a network to be successful, can you build one and still feel good about yourself? Even if you're an introvert?

To answer these questions, let's take a look at Adam Rifkin. In 2011, *Fortune* magazine named him the best networker in Silicon Valley. Guess what? Adam's a shy introvert. He's also the nicest guy you'll ever meet. In fact, he goes by the nickname "Panda."

What's Panda's secret to networking? Be a friend. Yeah, it's that simple. Networking isn't just a skill anybody can learn. *It's a skill you already know.* Make friends.

In Adam Grant's terminology, Panda is a Giver. Grant wrote about Panda in his bestseller *Give and Take.* (I'd say it was odd that both Grant and I know Panda, but then again, Panda knows *everybody.*) When I asked Panda about networking he said this:

> It is better to give than to receive. Look for opportunities to do something for the other person, such as sharing knowledge or offering an introduction to someone that person might not know but would be interested in knowing. Do not be transactional about networking. Do not offer something because you want something in return. Instead, show a genuine interest in something you and the other person have in common.

Harvard and MIT didn't communicate and that caused them both a mess of problems. It's good to know your neighbors. It's good to make friends. But when it comes to friends in business, we use the awful word "networking," and it really makes us feel icky. If you focus on making friends, the problem goes away. It's all about the perspective you take going in.

Other big networkers agree. Bestselling author Ramit Sethi told me:

> We all have friends who are just cool to be around. They're always sending you awesome stuff. "Hey, check out this book," "Oh, you've got to see this video I just watched. Here, here's a copy." That is actually networking, because they're serving you first. Now, one day if they came to you and said, "Hey man, I know you have a friend who works at X company. I'm actually trying to get connected there. Do you think you can introduce me?" Of course you would say yes. Networking is about a personal relationship.

So if slimy networking is like the mistrustful situation we saw in Moldova, what's the opposite? Iceland. It's one of the happiest places in the world, and part of this is due to the fact that it's tightly knit. The population is so connected that they run into friends wherever they go. This is so common in Iceland that saying "I ran into friends" is an acceptable excuse for being late to work.

What's going on here? We have this huge distinction between work and personal. Guess what? Your brain doesn't. Early humans spent the vast majority of their existence in small tribes where everyone knew everyone, they all worked together, and most people were blood relatives. The work/personal distinction is new, alien, and arbitrary to our mammalian brains. This is why "networking" sounds sleazy but "family" sounds good.

One of the main reasons humans have been so successful, as Israeli researcher Yuval Noah Harari points out, is due to what is called "fictive kinship." Most species hang out only with family. Everybody else is a potential enemy. Good ol' Homo sapiens have been so successful because we've extended the definition of family by using mutually agreed upon stories. Families are not merely blood relatives. We're in many families: We're Americans. We're IBM employees. We're on the same softball team. Most simply, we're friends. Friends are just family we choose. This allows us to collaborate on a scale that's impossible for other animals. This is the secret to our success as a species. It's also the secret to your success as an individual: friendship.

This is all pretty intuitive, but you still might feel awkward about going up to that person who could be important to your career with what feels like the thin veneer of "friendship." We still prefer that organic clicking. But that's a false distinction too. One of the primary things every couple has in common is not magic or *je ne sais quoi;* it's proximity. It's really hard to fall in love when you never encounter each other.

This is true of other relationships as well. You become good friends with your neighbors first and foremost because they live near you. Now, you don't have to go bowling with them every week or swear a blood oath, but right now you have plenty of friendships— lesser or greater—based on proximity, whether it's neighbors, the woman in the next cubicle, or the UPS guy, and those connections are not evil or unnatural. Often it's just a matter of trying to be friends. Mr. Rogers sang, "Won't you be my neighbor?" He didn't ask you to move in or anything. Just be a good neighbor.

You make friends all the time based on rather shallow things like geography, but it feels different in business. It's like when someone asks you if you lead with your left foot or right foot when you walk, for a second you can't move, because when you try to do something deliberately that you normally do unconsciously, it gets awkward.

There's no need to be afraid of networking. The truth is, we often underestimate by as much as 50 percent how much others are willing to help us when asked. As we talked about in chapter 2, being mistrustful or assuming others are selfish can be self-fulfilling prophecies. Remember, the rule of thumb is simple when making friends: be socially optimistic. Assume other people will like you and they probably will.

Robert Fulghum had a huge bestseller in the 1980s titled *All I Really Need to Know I Learned in Kindergarten.* So get out your crayons 'cause we're going back to kindergarten. Let's review some of the fundamentals of friendship, which are intuitive but also backed by science.

YOU LIKE IRON MAN? I LIKE IRON MAN TOO.

See that boy playing with the same toys you like to play with? Introduce yourself. We all choose to be friends with people who are like us.

Frankly, it's downright scary how powerful similarity is. Research shows you like names better when they are similar to yours. You prefer brands that merely share your initials. Birthdays are easier to remember when they are closer to yours. You even prefer people who move the way you do. Why do news anchors and actors need to be so good looking? Because we assume attractive people are more similar to us. (We're such narcissists, ain't we?)

Even similarity of stuff you *don't* like helps you bond with others. Research shows that shared complaints make us feel closer to others. Do you both dislike the same person? That might be the path to your new BFF. You know the old saying "The enemy of my enemy is my friend"? A study titled "I Feel Like I Know You: Sharing Negative Attitudes of Others Promotes Feelings of Familiarity" showed that's true.

So look around the school playground for similarity. That kid is more inclined to like you and you're more inclined to like them. Don't see anybody who has obvious similarities? Well, this is where the next fundamental comes in . . .

LISTEN AND ENCOURAGE OTHER TODDLERS

Want to find out how you're similar to another kid in kindergarten? Ask them questions and listen. You're likely to hear something you can connect over. Beyond that, listening is vital to bonding—and it's something most of us are terrible at.

Neuroscientist Diana Tamir found that your brain gets more

pleasure from you talking about yourself than it does from food or money. This is why you should stop doing it and let others do it as much as possible around you. Arthur Aron's research has demonstrated that asking people questions about themselves can create a bond as strong as a lifelong friendship in a surprisingly short amount of time.

FBI behavioral expert Robin Dreeke said the most important thing to do is to "seek someone else's thoughts and opinions without judging them." Stop thinking about what you're going to say next and focus on what they're saying right now.

Found something you both have in common? Great. Don't be afraid to pay the person a sincere compliment. Research shows we like compliments more than sex or money. What is key here, according to influence expert Robert Cialdini, is the sincere part. You don't want to feel slimy and they don't want you to be slimy. Just say whatever positive thing honestly comes to mind. Studies show that even obvious, insincere flattery has incredible effects—but we're not selling insurance, so keep it real.

Don't try to play it cool or impress, which can backfire. We all prefer warmth to competence. In fact, research shows we'd rather work with a kind fool than a competent jerk when given the option. And don't offer advice or tell them how they're wrong. Asking for advice, however, can really help others warm to you.

Dreeke loves to ask about what challenges people face. We all love to complain a little about the things that stress us out. That leads to the next fundamental.

BE A GIVER. SHARE YOUR TWINKIES.

Offer to help people. Do like Adam Grant, Panda, and Paul Erdös, and be a Giver. When people say they're having trouble with something, try to find a way you can help.

You don't want to be a phony transactional networker. You want this to become an organic, serendipitous, natural friendship, right? Friends do each other favors. They don't have a goal or payoff in mind. So rely on karma. There's plenty of research showing that trying to make others in your network happy makes the happiness come back to you. Happy friends make you 15 percent more likely to be happy too. Even if a *friend of a friend of a friend* becomes happier, there is a 6 percent chance you will become happier. So don't worry about the payoff and don't ask for anything. This makes them feel good about you, and you feel good about yourself. You're just being a friend. And if you do offer some help, follow through.

(Warning: If you follow through with all of this, you may accidentally wind up becoming a good person.)

Okay, you're done with the idea of uncomfortable networking and you're focusing on making friends. You've got the attitude. But how do you actually get started? There are a number of great techniques that can make the process easier, less time consuming, and not so intimidating:

START WITH THE FRIENDS YOU ALREADY HAVE

Research shows that one of the quickest and easiest ways to boost your network isn't to pass your business card out on street corners; it's to just reconnect with old friends. And there's no sleazy element to it at all—they're *already* your friends. You just haven't caught up with them in a year. It's a great place to start and not the least bit intimidating. Go through your Facebook friends list, your LinkedIn connections, or your address book, and send a few emails every week, asking "What's up?" Research shows that those dormant friendships can actually be bigger boosters to your career than any new connections you make. Also, University of Chicago neuroscientist John Cacioppo found that when we leverage Facebook to set up face-to-face meetings, it boosts our happiness. When we use it as a substitute, however, it increases loneliness.

One warning, though: don't think that being friends merely on social media sites really counts as networking. Again, return to kindergarten. Having "friends" stacked like books in a digital library on a network is not the same as actually talking to people and spending time with them. That's not a relationship; that's virtual stamp collecting.

FIND YOUR "SUPERCONNECTORS"

All people in a network are not created equal, contact-wise. Brian Uzzi and Sharon Dunlap did research and found that there's an 80/20 rule of sorts in networking. You probably met the vast majority of your friends through a handful of "superfriends"—the buddies of yours who are most like Panda. So when it comes to trying to expand your network and make new friends, do what works. If you look at your Facebook friends or address book contacts, you'll find that you met many of them through a small group of people. Reaching out to these "superfriends" and saying, "Whom do you know that I should meet?" will produce disproportionate results.

MAKE THE TIME—AND THE BUDGET

People say they want to increase their network but few really make it enough of a priority, dedicate time for it, or commit something specific to it, such as "I'm gonna allocate an extra fifty dollars a week to coffees and lunches in which I connect with people." Bestselling author Ben Casnocha saw that top networkers pre-committed a certain amount of time and money to their networking goal so that when opportunities came up they didn't hesitate. College students know that Friday and Saturday nights (and maybe a few other nights) are for parties and they don't have trouble making new friends. Take a similar approach.

Academic studies show that the biggest source of conflict between friends is making the time to see each other. Like we saw with Spencer Glendon, time is limited and valuable. Making time is the most fundamental way to show someone is important to you and that you care. So allocate an amount in advance to make sure networking goes from something you'd "like to do" to something that actually gets done. And there's a lot of debate over whether or not money can really buy happiness, but research is conclusive in one area: money definitely brings happiness when we spend it on the people we love. So text a friend and buy them coffee.

JOIN GROUPS

No, not some corny "networking group." Again, that's awkward and borderline gross. Just throwing a party is nice but probably too infrequent to produce consistent results. Do you know a bunch of friends who have lunch every week? How about a group who watches football every Sunday? A book club at work? These are fun, passive ways to make sure you stay in the mix and connect with others organically. Research shows that the best teams are a mix of old friends and new blood, and that's also an advantage in networking. Plus, by being in a few of these groups you can easily increase that scientific form of "luck" Richard Wiseman talked about, engineering serendipity in your life while having a good time with people you like.

This isn't just some wonky theory I read about in a dusty academic journal. When I'm in Los Angeles, I never miss my friend Andy Walker's weekly Friday lunch. When I'm visiting San Francisco I make sure to hit Panda's 106 Miles get-togethers for Silicon Valley entrepreneurs. I fly out to Boston a few times a year just for Gautam Mukunda's "interesting people" dinners, for which he gathers a handful of fascinating folks in his network for an evening of wine and conversation. And I'd rather sacrifice a kidney than miss my friend James Clear's annual blogger meet-up. None of these are transactional, icky affairs. They're a chance for me to see my best friends and make new friends in a relaxed environment.

Get-togethers like these are also passive ways to change yourself for the better. Remember how Mom said to stay away from that kid who kept getting detention? Or she told you "Why can't you hang out with that nice girl who gets all A's?" Mom was right. In his excellent book *The Power of Habit*, Charles Duhigg referenced a 1994

Harvard study of people who had dramatically changed their lives. Often their secret wasn't momentous upheaval. It was just joining a group that consisted of the type of people they wanted to become.

So choose those groups wisely. The Terman Study followed over a thousand people from youth until death. Here's what the researchers had to say about whom to hang out with: "The groups you associate with often determine the type of person you become. For people who want improved health, association with other healthy people is usually the strongest and most direct path of change."

Research also shows that being a part of a number of social groups versus just one increases your resilience and helps you overcome stress. If you don't know of any awesome groups like these, the easy solution is to *start one and be the hub of the network*. All those other friends of yours looking for a regular time to hang out and network in a non-slimy way will thank you.

ALWAYS FOLLOW UP

We all meet people but we rarely take the time to follow up and actually begin a friendship. Analyzing eight million phone calls between two million people, researchers at Notre Dame found that what makes close friendships endure is simply staying in touch every two weeks. Now, you don't need to connect with people that often if they're not close friends, but the principle still stands: checking in every now and then matters.

This doesn't need to take a lot of time. Sending a handful of emails every week can make a big difference over time. Panda's network is gargantuan, but he spends a surprisingly small amount of time maintaining it. Mostly he just looks for small favors or introductions he can make via email every week. By just doing favors, he helps people out and maintains relationships naturally at the same time. (This is also quite healthy. Longitudinal studies show the people who live the longest aren't the ones who get the most help; they're the ones who *give* the most help.)

And what about forming friendships with coworkers? This is another excellent idea. You can't rely on HR team-bonding exercises; studies show they're only effective at building distrust.

Research also shows the best predictor of work team success is how the team members feel about one another. What's something that improves team communication and effectiveness that you won't read about in most formal manuals? Joking around with your coworkers.

To know who the top performers at work are, look at lunch tables. This is what Ben Waber's research uncovered: "We found that the people who sat at the larger tables had substantially higher performance." They had bigger networks and knew more about what their colleagues were up to.

Having a diverse group of friends at the office pays big dividends too: "Those who bridge relatively disconnected pockets of a network are promoted earlier and are more mobile in their careers because they hear about opportunities before others do . . . Having an epiphany is no big deal unless you can motivate others to believe in it and act on it."

Yeah, I know. Some people you work with are jerks. (My boss can be a total idiot at times and I'm self-employed.) There are people at the office you don't get along with. I get it. But when I spoke to Stanford Graduate School of Business professor Jeffrey Pfeffer, I asked him what was the number-one mistake people made when trying to get ahead at the office. His answer? Opting out of the social dynamics of the company. Saying "Yeah, I know relationships help you get ahead but I refuse to play that game." Clinical psychologist and workplace consultant Al Bernstein says, "You can't not play politics; you can only play them badly . . . the only place where relationships don't matter is on a desert island far away from the rest of the world." Harvard researcher Shawn Achor found that the workers least likely to develop workplace friendships were also the least likely to get promoted. (Feel free to read that sentence a few hundred more times so it sinks in.)

Office gossip can be the bane of your existence, but it pays to be a part of the grapevine. Research shows 70 to 90 percent of workplace gossip is true, and that information won't be in the weekly company email. You need to know what's going on if you want to get ahead.

If you're a leader at your organization, it's very important you go out of your way to foster good relationships between your employees. When workers have at least one close talented friend at a company their effort and productivity go up 10 percent. How's that for motivating?

It seems most of us need a kick in the pants here. In the study "Social Isolation in America: Changes in Core Discussion Networks over Two Decades," the authors found that in 1985 most people reported having three confidants in their lives. In 2004, the most common response was *zero:* "The number of people saying there is no one with whom they discuss important matters nearly tripled." And having few friends is more dangerous than obesity and is the equivalent health risk of smoking fifteen cigarettes a day.

I think that says it all. Harvard and MIT should have shared their Twinkies—and some info on what they were working on. It would have made their lives a lot easier and their work more productive, and, hey, it's even nice for colleges to have friends, right?

Maybe you already have a solid network. However, there's one special type of networking relationship we *all* need to be successful. And it deserves special attention.

*

We all want to be funny. In the 1980s, when Judd Apatow was young, he shoved poison ivy up his nose to make friends laugh, which, as you might imagine, was a very bad idea. His dad always played comedy albums when he was young and it inspired him. When he grew up, he knew he wanted to be a comedian.

He'd watch *Saturday Night Live,* record the episodes on a video cassette recorder, transcribe the tapes by hand, and study the jokes. He scoured *TV Guide* every week to see which comedians were going to be on the talk shows. He wrote a thirty-page paper on the Marx brothers when he was in the fifth grade. Not for school, just for himself.

You need a passion like this when you're a lonely kid. When you're picked on. When your parents are going through an acrimonious divorce. But it was also lonely to have a passion nobody else understood.

So how do you learn comedy when you're still living at home and spending most of your time doing geometry homework? (This was long before the Internet.) Apatow's friend had been interviewing bands for the high school radio station, WKWZ 88.5 FM. What if he did the same thing with professional comedians?

Little did Apatow know, at this point comedians weren't that big a deal. No one wanted to interview them. And so when he called the publicists, hoping they wouldn't just laugh and hang up, they thought the same thing young Apatow did: *Why not?* (It probably helped that Apatow didn't mention they would be on a high school radio station and that he was fifteen.) Almost every comedian he asked agreed.

Yes, many were quite surprised when he showed up on their doorstep, pimply faced and with the big Syosset High School AV department recorder in hand, but this is how a lonely, comedy-obsessed kid managed to interview the biggest names in the field, from Jay Leno to Garry Shandling to *The Simpsons* cocreator James Brooks. He visited his grandmother in Los Angeles so he could interview Jerry Seinfeld. He traveled to Poughkeepsie to talk to "Weird Al" Yankovic.

From them, he learned how to write a joke, how to get stage time, how to use personal experiences in his act, how to adapt material to different crowds. But most of all, he learned he was not alone. There were a lot of people out there just like him.

So he started writing. When he had put some stuff together he was happy with, he offered to sell the material to Jay Leno. Leno didn't buy it, but he gave feedback and encouragement—just as George Carlin had done for Leno so many years before.

And six years after Apatow interviewed him, Garry Shandling hired Apatow to write jokes for the Oscars and then brought him on as a staff writer on *The Larry Sanders Show*. Apatow wrote for Roseanne Barr and Tom Arnold. Jay Leno kept bringing him on *The*

Tonight Show when, frankly, there was no reason to. Until one day there was . . .

Judd Apatow is now the acclaimed director of *The 40-Year-Old Virgin* and *Knocked Up*. He couldn't have gotten there without his mentors. We all need mentors to succeed. (But, luckily, we don't need to stick poison ivy up our noses.)

All right, you wanna be a real ramblin' earth shaker? Somebody who changes the world and gets recognized in the history books? K. Anders Ericsson, the guy who created that ten-thousand-hour theory of expertise, says there ain't no two ways about it; you're gonna need a mentor: "These findings are consistent with a study of internationally successful athletes, scientists, and artists, where [Benjamin] Bloom (1985) found that, virtually without exception, each individual had been trained by a master teacher, who had trained earlier students to reach an international level."

Remember Mihály Csikszentmihályi, the researcher who interviewed over ninety-one of the most creative people in the world? What did he find those big-timers have in common? Yup, by the time they were college age, almost every one of them had an important mentor.

Gerard Roche surveyed 1,250 top executives and found two-thirds had had a mentor, and those who did, made more money and were happier with their careers: "The average increase in salary of executives who have had a mentor is 28.8 percent, combined with an average 65.9 percent increase in bonus, for an overall 29.0 percent rise in total cash compensation." And, ladies, this is even more important for you. Every single one of the successful female executives in the study turned out to have had a mentor.

Even if you're starting your own company and don't have a boss, it's still vital. In Shane Snow's great read *Smartcuts,* he points to research showing entrepreneurs with mentors raise seven times as much money and their businesses experience three and a half times as much growth.

Why are mentors so important? You don't have time to make

all the mistakes yourself, and of course making those mistakes can mean failure. It's better to let others make those mistakes and you can learn from them. Great mentors and great teachers help you learn faster. Even in high school, the right teacher makes a huge difference. Stanford economist Eric Hanushek says that bad teachers cover six months of material in one year. Great teachers cover a year and a half. That math isn't hard to decode, folks. He says you're way better off with an awesome teacher in a lousy school than vice versa.

But there's another, less acknowledged boost that good mentors give. I've talked a lot about that ten-thousand-hour theory of expertise and why anyone would want to spend that much time painfully improving at something. In chapter 1, you saw that one of the reasons was a touch of craziness and obsession. But that's not the whole story. Mentors make learning fun. They add a relationship to the stress and help you overcome the frustration while pushing you to be your best. Adam Grant says mentors can be what leads you down the path to grit and deliberate practice:

> It turns out that actually most of these world-class performers had a first coach, or a first teacher, who made the activity fun. If you excel at something, and you experience mastery, it often does make it more fun and enjoyable to do it. We've overlooked the reverse effect, which is that often interest precedes the development of talent. It's having a coach or teacher who really makes something exciting to be involved in that leads you to often put in the practice necessary to become an expert at it.

Fun doesn't usually get lumped into that category with "hard work" and "expertise" and "being the best." Fun is emotional. That emotional component is critical. Not only should you care about your mentors; the mentors who really make you succeed need to care about *you*.

Judd Apatow had some amazing mentors, but one of the subtle yet vital reasons things worked out for him the way they did is because of that personal connection. He realized they too had been lonely kids who loved comedy. Feeling that connection isn't just nice to have; it's essential. Researchers Penelope Lockwood and Ziva Kunda found that the difference between being inspired by a role model and being demoralized by one comes down to two things: relevance and attainability. When you relate to someone you look up to, you get motivated. And when that person makes you feel you can do that too, bang—that produces real results.

Which is why your employer's mentorship program, while well meaning, doesn't help. Christina Underhill looked at the past two decades of mentorship research and found a striking division. Yeah, formal mentoring made a small improvement, but the real results came from informal mentors—the kind you find on your own. Shane Snow reports, "When students and mentors came together on their own and formed personal relationships, the mentored did significantly better, as measured by future income, tenure, number of promotions, job satisfaction, work stress, and self-esteem."

So we agree this is important, and we agree most everybody has this wrong, that you need to find a mentor informally. But how do you find the *right* one?

Approaching a mentor is a little different from networking in general. You want somebody top-notch, which by definition means this person is gonna be busy. A lot of people want their time. They're going to picky. They have to be. As with Spencer Glendon, they can't waste time. They have a lot of opportunities but only twenty-four hours in a day.

So how do you get an amazing mentor who is right for you? Here are five principles:

BE A WORTHY PUPIL, GRASSHOPPER

There is an old saying: "When the student is ready, the teacher appears." If you're doing everything you can to advance your career, getting a mentor won't be too hard. Why? Because if you're doing awesome work, people more successful than you will notice and want to help you. Talented, resourceful self-starters are rare. If people don't notice, you're doing something wrong. You're either not working hard enough or not doing enough outreach.

There's that old chicken-and-egg dilemma of "How do I get a job without experience but how do I get experience without a job?" Lazy people will argue this is the same thing: "You're telling me I need to be successful to get a mentor but I need a mentor to make me successful." Wrong.

Many people want a mentor because they are too lazy to do the hard work themselves. Neuroscience research shows that when an expert speaks, parts of your brain actually *shut down:*

> In a 2009 study, Emory University School of Medicine scientists led by Gregory Berns, M.D., a professor of neuroeconomics and psychiatry at Emory, found that people will actually stop thinking for themselves when a person they perceive as an expert offers them advice or direction . . . "The brain activation results suggest that the offloading of decision-making was driven by trust in the expert."

This kind of reaction is fine for your teachers at school—they're getting paid. You, on the other hand, are asking for the time of a very busy, very accomplished person *for free.* Brain activity shutting down is not what any mentor wants. He or she wants to give you enough info to light a fire under your butt, not to be seen as a walking textbook.

What makes a mentor want to go the extra mile for you? When you demonstrate you have explored every conceivable avenue and can go no further without the mentor's help. Seeing that you have done everything in your power shows you're smart, you won't waste their time, and you're resourceful. Most mentors see themselves that way too, so the two of you now have something very important in common.

Instead of thinking about what you need, remember what they're probably thinking: *I'm the best in my field and I'm busy. Who do I want to help for free in my very limited time?*

STUDY THEM. NO, *REALLY* STUDY THEM.

If they're at the top of their field, there will certainly be info about them on the interwebz. Spend the time. To be intimately familiar with someone's work is rare and quite flattering.

But flattering a person is far from the only reason to do that research. As we established, you need to know this person is the right mentor *for you*. Seeing a pretty face from a distance might be enough to make you want to go on a date with someone, but it's not enough to make you want to marry them. (It better not be, for your sake.) And have no illusions, dear reader: this is a marriage, not a one-night stand.

You want to know the person really is the best. And you want to know he or she is not a jerk. Also, Dan Coyle, bestselling author of *The Talent Code,* says you want someone who scares you a bit. Yeah, they need to know their stuff, but they also need to be able to motivate you.

And once they do get to know you, that research pays off, because it's very good for you if they think you're smarter than the average bear. Robert Rosenthal and Lenore Jacobson did a classic study in which teachers were told that certain students were "academic spurters" and had very high potential. At the end of the school year, those kids were tested and had gained an average of 22 IQ points. Here's the kicker: the "academic spurters" were chosen at random. They weren't special. But the teacher *believing* they were special made it a self-fulfilling prophecy. The teachers didn't spend more time with these kids. Rosenthal "thinks the teachers were more excited about teaching these students . . . And they must have subtly communicated respect for and enthusiasm about these students, so that the students themselves felt more capable of understanding and anticipated better performance from themselves."

WASTING A MENTOR'S TIME IS A MORTAL SIN

Yes, it will annoy them, but more importantly it shows you lack basic skills. It screams to a mentor, "This person isn't ready for my help."

Writing a multi-page email to a very busy person doesn't show you're serious—it shows you're insane. So respect their time and start small.

Asking great questions is a perfect way to build a relationship. But the key word here is "great" questions. *Never ask a mentor a question Google can easily answer for you.* Carve this in stone. Scrawl it in blood above your desk. Get a tattoo of it. You can learn the basics of any subject on Khan Academy. And you should have already done all that work.

Asking your mentor a question is like a power up in a video game. Don't waste them. Use them when they'll really count.

FOLLOW UP

Early on, don't mention the M word: mentor. You wouldn't ask someone to marry you on the first date, would you? You're trying to start a relationship, not close a sale. It's going to take time, and that's okay. But you're going to need to follow up. You're the one asking them for something.

Bestselling author Ryan Holiday has benefited from having a number of mentors, like writer Robert Greene. Holiday has this to say:

Stay in the picture. You are easily forgotten by busy people, remember that. The key then is to find ways to stay relevant and fresh. Drop emails and questions at an interval that straddles the fine line between bothersome and buzzworthy. It's easier to keep something alive than it is to revive the deceased . . . but it's on you to keep the blood flowing, not the mentor.

You need to consistently hit them with a conversation defibrillator to keep the relationship alive but without being a nuisance. Do what they said, get results, and let them know they made a difference. This is what mentors want. If they engage, you can follow up with "I [did my homework] and figured [really impressive next steps] would be [fill in the blank], but I'd love your insight. Do you think [well-thought-out strategy one] or [well-thought-out strategy two] is better?"

You want these interactions to become conversational back-and-forths, not one-offs.

MAKE THEM PROUD

It's like those old Black Belt Theater movies: "Do not bring dishonor upon the Ancient Order of the Ninja!" No mentor wants to feel they wasted their time helping you. In the end, your goal and your mentor's goals should be aligned: to make you awesome. But there's a secondary goal here too: to make them look good.

Dean Keith Simonton, the expert on eminence, says that being seen as a great mentor is impressive in itself. And how do you know who is a great mentor? By the success of their students, of course.

So think about your career, but think about theirs too. As we've discussed, many experts are not known for their people skills. But reaching the top in their field *and* being someone who can teach others is very impressive. For senior executives, being a renowned shaper of talent who can groom future leaders adds a lot to their résumé and may be their ticket to a CEO position.

Maybe you find a mentor who really helps you improve your skills, but they're clueless when it comes to navigating office politics. This is very common—and not a problem. The solution? Get a second mentor. You see, mentors are like potato chips: you can't have just one. In Roche's studies of executives, the average number of mentors was two and among females it was three. Dean Keith Simonton explains:

> Prospective pupils should draw upon many mentors rather than just one. The same advice has been given in choice of models, and for the same reason. With many mentors on which to base their personal growth, talented youths are less likely to follow the suicidal path toward mere replication. In-

stead, they will be obliged to synthesize the diversity represented by their training. A synthesis of techniques or styles or ideas may be a pupil's key to fame.

Before we round this out, there's one more common objection I need to address. Maybe you're fairly accomplished already. Maybe you feel you're far enough along that you don't need a mentor. You're wrong.

Atul Gawande is an endocrine surgeon. And a professor at Harvard Medical School. And a staff writer for the *New Yorker*. And he's written four bestselling books. And he won a Rhodes Scholarship and a MacArthur "Genius" Grant. And he's married with three kids. (Every time I look at his résumé I think, *Jeez, and what the heck have I been doing with* my *time?*) So in 2011, what did he think the next thing he absolutely needed to do was? Get a coach. Someone who could make him better.

You can say it's ironic (or the act of a workaholic) that someone so accomplished felt they needed help to improve, but that's not how Gawande sees it. Professional athletes all have coaches. They often hire multiple experts to help with fitness, diet, and particular aspects of the game. So if someone whose job it is to throw a ball for a living takes their work seriously enough to enlist professional guidance, um, maybe a surgeon who cuts people open every day should too? And what happened when renowned surgeon Robert Osteen agreed to come out of retirement and stand behind Gawande in the OR, notepad in hand? What happened when this MacArthur "Genius" humbly submitted to being told, in fine detail, all the minor errors he was making? The number of postsurgical complications that Gawande's patients experienced went down. The already great surgeon was getting even better.

We all have stuff we can learn from someone else. And it's great to make a lifelong friend in the process. Judd Apatow was a lonely kid with a passion. So he took a little bet, reached out to potential mentors, and reaped tremendous rewards. He also made lifelong friends . . . But it doesn't end there. Apatow now pays it forward:

People were nice to me, like Garry Shandling and James Brooks, and they really taught me everything that I know when I worked on their shows. To me, it's the natural part of this, where you always need help. So if I am working on a show like *Freaks and Geeks,* I need a staff. And sometimes I have young writers on the staff and they're really talented, but they don't know how to do it yet and part of my job is to teach them how to do it. So it makes my job easier. So mentorship is something that pays off for them, but it makes my life easier.

Where did he learn the value of paying it forward? From a mentor, of course. Garry Shandling told him, "When I see talent, I want them to be all they can be. I really want to help—and by doing so, I am helped as well. Whenever I mentor, I notice I'm learning something myself."

The research backs Shandling up. Yoda lived that long and was so chill for a reason: mentoring makes you happy. Mentoring a young person is four times more predictive of happiness than your health or how much money you make. So if you've got the skills, don't just think about who can help you. Think about whom you can help.

So you know how to network and get a mentor and click with people. But sometimes people are difficult. Sometimes they're downright angry. How do you deal with hard situations? Time to bring out the big guns.

Let's learn from the people who know how to connect with the most difficult folks imaginable in the worst situations with the highest stakes: hostage negotiators.

*

At the 1972 Olympics, members of the Palestinian terrorist group Black September took eleven Israeli athletes hostage. The tragedy finally came to a close with a standoff between police and the terrorists. But when the smoke cleared, all eleven Israelis were dead, as were five of the terrorists and one German police officer. As terrorist attacks and other crisis situations escalated in the '70s, law enforcement came to realize they needed a better way to handle these problems.

Up until this time, crisis negotiation was almost unheard of. When police responded to incidents with barricaded criminals it was often up to the responding officer, with no formal training, to try to deal with the suspect. Storming the location often seemed to be the only way to resolve the problem, despite its poor record for results. But two cops thought there might be a better way.

Harvey Schlossberg was an anomaly: a police detective with a Ph.D. in psychology. Frank Bolz was a streetwise veteran of the New York Police Department. They believed that talking to hostage takers was the path to fewer casualties and more successful resolution of these intense problems. Nobody had ever tried this, and their methods met with resistance from many who felt that using force was the only option. They put together a playbook that the NYPD could use to handle these incidents, but would it work when real lives were at stake? Their system was put to the test far sooner than they had ever guessed.

On January 19, 1973, four members of an extremist Muslim group entered John and Al's, a sporting goods store in the Williamsburg neighborhood of Brooklyn, taking twelve people hostage. A three-hour shootout with NYPD ensued. One officer was killed, and two policemen and one of the gunmen were wounded. The hostage takers swore they would fight to the death. There was good reason to take them seriously—the store they were in didn't just sell basketballs and tennis racquets; it was also a veritable armory, stocked with guns and ammunition for sale to hunters and sportsmen.

Despite this tremendous threat, instead of a SWAT team leading the response, a "think tank" was established. The NYPD would not fire another shot. The only weapon they would employ would be psychology. Bolz and Schlossberg arrived on the scene and gave their simple advice: talk and wait. So the talking began. It would continue for a near record forty-seven hours.

A Muslim minister was allowed entry into the store. He returned with bad news: "They are willing to die for Allah." And if that wasn't enough, pressure was on the police from an unexpected source: the neighborhood. The hostage takers were black, and the responding law enforcement was overwhelmingly white. Racial tension had already been high in Williamsburg, and the officers understandably feared community sympathy would shift to the perpetrators as time stretched on. But the NYPD stuck by their plan and continued to talk.

The gunmen released a hostage with a message: they wanted food, cigarettes, and medical treatment for their wounded comrade. In exchange for another hostage, a doctor was provided.

The second night came and a torrent of shots was unleashed from the store, but the NYPD did not return fire. Then something unexpected happened. With the gunmen distracted by the negotiations, the nine remaining hostages managed to escape. Breaking through a plasterboard wall, they made their way to the rooftop, where they were rescued by Emergency Services personnel. Panicked that they had lost their leverage, the hostage takers fired wildly at the surrounding police presence. The NYPD could finally assault the store with no fear of civilian casualties. But they didn't. Instead, they brought members of the gunmen's families to speak to them. Four hours later, Salih Ali Abdullah, Shulab Abdula Raheem, Dawd A. Rahman, and the wounded Yusef Abdullah Almussudig emerged from the store, surrendering. It was over.

The hostage takers had let loose hundreds more rounds since the initial shootout, but the NYPD had responded with only words. And no one else had been harmed.

The NYPD sent their negotiation playbook to the FBI for review. It wasn't merely approved; before the year was out the Feds started their own hostage negotiation program at Quantico. Today approximately 70 percent of police negotiators are trained using the FBI program. While assaults lead to a 78 percent casualty rate, data from the FBI shows that negotiation during hostage situations results in a 95 percent success rate.

You know what the motto of the NYPD Hostage Negotiation Team is to this day? "Talk to me."

Many people, when they hear about hostage negotiation, shake their heads and say, "Why don't they just shoot the guy?" But those people don't know the stats. When police launch an assault during a hostage situation, it's the police who suffer the bulk of the casualties. Fighting may end things quickly, but the research shows it doesn't end things well.

You and I do the same thing in our personal relationships. Things go sideways and often our first response is to fight. Not physical violence, but yelling and arguing vs. discussing and negotiating. Why is this? Philosopher Daniel Dennett says it's because a "war metaphor" is wired into our brains when it comes to disagreement. When there's a war, someone is conquered. It's not a discussion of facts and logic; it's a fight to the death. No matter who is really right, if you win, I lose. In almost every conversation, status is on the line. Nobody wants to look stupid. So, as Dennett explains, we set up a situation where learning is equivalent to losing.

Even if you have rock-solid evidence and impeccable logic, and you back the other person into a corner, what happens? They might concede—but they definitely hate you. When we make it win-or-lose, everyone loses.

Al Bernstein, a clinical psychologist, agrees. He calls it the "Godzilla vs. Rodan" effect. When the other person starts yelling and you start yelling and you both follow the war metaphor, buildings gets knocked down, Tokyo gets leveled, but very little gets accomplished. You might think, "I'm just trying to explain . . ." But Bernstein says this is a trap. Explaining is almost always veiled dominance. You're not trying to educate; you're still trying to win. The subtext is, "Here's why I am right and you are wrong." And that is exactly what the other side will hear no matter what you say.

Research from neuroscience confirms this. When people are riled up about something and you show them evidence that conflicts with what they believe, what does an MRI scan show? The areas of their brain associated with logic literally *shut down*. The regions associated with aggression light up. As far as their brain is concerned, it's not a rational discussion—it's war. The brain can't process what you're saying; it's just trying to win. Your head works the same way unless you make an effort to control it.

I'm sure some die-hard arguers are disagreeing. Can't fighting ever work? Sure it can. Research shows if you have power and the other person doesn't, intimidation can be very effective—in the short term. If your boss shouts, you probably back down. But what does this mean for the relationship? Bosses who do this too often aren't going to have much luck retaining A-player employees with options. And it's not enough to be the five-hundred-pound gorilla; you have to *stay* the five-hundred-pound gorilla. When you bully people they remember it. And if you later lose power and they gain it, expect revenge.

The NYPD was smart enough not to fall into this trap during the Williamsburg crisis. Even after the hostages escaped, they didn't resort to fighting. It wasn't the optimal solution. Some would have said the police should have gone in with guns blazing, but we know the numbers on how that works out for the officers.

Law enforcement *is* dealing with life and death. Regular people like you and me are not, but we act like it. Our "dinosaur brain" assumes every dispute is an existential threat: "This argument over who should take out the trash is a matter of life and death." Yes, very rational. But even when life is on the line, smart hostage negotiators like the NYPD choose talk over war. After the 1970s, crisis negotiators focused on a bargaining model. No violence. "You give me the hostages, I'll give you the money." Sounds better, right? But that had problems too.

This style underwent a seismic shift in the 1980s. Police realized that while talking was having great success, the model of a business-style quid pro quo just wasn't applicable to many of the incidents they were encountering. The 1970s had seen a rise in high-profile, terrorist-led hijackings of planes with clear demands. But 97 percent of what police were seeing in the field in the 1980s were incidents involving emotionally disturbed individuals who didn't want money and didn't have a political agenda.

So a second generation of negotiating principles was developed.

With fighting and bargaining both coming up short, what did crisis negotiators and heavily armed law enforcement dealing with violent criminals realize was the best solution? *Empathy*. Domestic disputes and suicidal individuals don't respond well to people who sound like salesmen. Being sincere and focusing on emotions, however, leads to effective resolutions.

In his research on the subject, Michael McMains found that police made three big mistakes when it came to dealing with crisis incidents: they made everything black and white, they wanted to solve things immediately, and they didn't focus on emotions.

You and I make the same mistakes. Granted, we're not dealing with emotionally disturbed people. Actually, hold on. Often we *are* dealing with emotionally disturbed people; we just call them coworkers and family members. They're not terrorists making demands (although sometimes it seems like that too). Usually they're just upset. They just want to be heard.

Hostage negotiators are dealing with the most intense situations imaginable but the attitude they take from beginning to end during a crisis is one of acceptance, caring, and patience. Again, we're back to friendship. Much like war, friendship is something we instinctively understand. Acceptance, caring, and patience are great to focus on because in many situations with the people we love, sadly, nothing concrete is going to get resolved.

Relationship researcher John Gottman found that 69 percent of romantic couples problems are perpetual. They don't get fixed. This is why a bargaining approach doesn't work. We need to listen and relate and understand, and despite these things not working, marriages can thrive. When we just focus on the concrete bargaining and not the feelings, that's when things fall apart.

We've all experienced the power of feelings. Being in a bad mood can make you a totally different person. Like when you get "hangry," then you eat something and boom—all is right in the world again and you're much more pleasant to deal with. One study showed food is an effective persuasion tool: "The consumption of proffered food induces a momentary mood of compliance toward the donor that is strongest at the time the food is being consumed and that decreases in strength rapidly after the food has been consumed." We have a cheeseburger, we feel better, and we're more likely to be in the right mood to close a deal.

Emotions get people to change their behavior. On his show *Crowd Control,* Dan Pink tried to get people to stop illegally using handicapped parking spots. When Dan's team changed the handicapped signs so they had a picture of a person in a wheelchair on them, illegal parking in the spots didn't go down—it stopped altogether. Seeing a person's face, thinking about how someone else might feel, made all the difference.

Is this applicable in office disputes? In hard-nosed negotiations? Yes. Remember what Harvard professor Deepak Malhotra tells his students is the most important part of a salary negotiation: they have to like you.

Why is friendship such a powerful model for dealing with people, even in business? It comes down to what negotiators call "value creation." When we're stuck in bargaining mode we're always calculating costs and benefits in the short term. Without the loyalty and trust of friendship, the model is competitive by nature. We don't want the other person to get more than we do. But when we treat the relationship like a friendship, we exchange more information and can explore new ways to meet each other's needs. Something that's cheap for you might be expensive for them, and vice versa. Instead of trying to get a bigger slice of a set pie, we can expand the pie for everyone. Research shows that many elements of friendship are conducive to good negotiations: happy people are better negotiators. When people feel positive about the deal-making process they're more likely to close a deal and both parties are happier with the results. And when we joke around like friends do, it builds trust.

Resolving difficult conversations means we need less Moldova and more Iceland. Here are four quick steps adapted from hostage negotiation and clinical psychology that can help you turn wars into friendly discussions:

KEEP CALM AND SLOW IT DOWN

Don't get angry. How do you control your anger? Al Bernstein recommends pretending you are talking to a child. You wouldn't try to rationalize with a screaming child, and you wouldn't get angry with them for yelling. You'd just dismiss the hysterics and deal with the underlying problem. Remember the Godzilla vs. Rodan effect. The NYPD teaches its hostage negotiators that their behavior is contagious.

Slow it down. The other person's anger will subside with time if you don't aggravate them by yelling back. Rushing things leads to pressure, and that only intensifies emotional decision-making, as opposed to rational decision-making. Al Bernstein likes to say "Please speak more slowly. I'd like to help."

USE ACTIVE LISTENING

Active listening means you are listening and you are letting them know you're listening. Don't make statements. Former FBI lead international hostage negotiator Chris Voss says you want to ask them open-ended questions. Ones that start with "what" or "how" are best because it's very hard to answer them with just yes or no.

Don't judge anything they say. Just listen and acknowledge. Every now and then paraphrase back to them what you're hearing. Your goal is for them to reply "Exactly." If you can repeat back to them the gist of what they're saying, they can't shout "You just don't get it! You don't understand!" See it as a game. Play detective.

Sounds simple, but it can be tricky. You need to resist the urge to open your mouth when they say something you disagree with. Also, your attention can wander. We can hear and understand seven hundred words a minute, but people only speak about one hundred words a minute. This lag can cause your mind to wander. Focus.

Just listening and acknowledging can make a huge difference. What did relationship expert John Gottman say the number-one thing for improving a romantic relationship was? Learn to be a good listener. And the number-one reason people leave their jobs? They didn't feel their boss listened to them.

LABEL EMOTIONS

Remember, you want to focus on feelings. Respond to their emotions by saying "Sounds like you're angry" or "Sounds like this really upsets you." Hostage negotiators use this to show understanding and to cool hot emotions. And neuroscience research shows that giving a name to feelings helps reduce their intensity.

MAKE THEM THINK

We want to calm the rage monster in their head by bringing the thinking part of their brain back online. Again, use questions, not statements. Al Bernstein likes to ask "What would you like me to do?" This forces them to consider options and think instead of just vent.

Pretend to be Socrates. Don't solve their problem and tell them what to do. That puts you back in a war metaphor. Help them solve their own problem by asking questions, feeding their responses back to them, and subtly helping them consider whether what they're saying makes sense.

If they come up with a solution, they're more likely to follow through with it. They don't have to concede defeat and say "You're right." They'll be less defensive if they solve their own problem.

When the hostage takers in Williamsburg lost their captives, the NYPD could have stormed the place. They didn't. They brought in the gunmen's families to talk. Empathy. Communication. And it worked out for the best.

Fighting only works when you're by far the biggest and the strongest and will be certain to stay that way. (Which is much more rare than we tend to think.) When fighting looks like the only solution, it's usually better to just walk away. The war model doesn't work best for people in the "war" business, like law enforcement, and it won't work for you. The best results come from being a friend, listening, and asking questions.

So we know how to defuse conflict and keep a relationship alive. What's the most important thing that makes people want to stay friends with you over the long haul? A little thing called gratitude.

*

Whatever success you've had so far in your life, how many people helped make it possible? Family, friends, teachers, mentors? How many people assisted you, advised you, consoled you, or gave you hope when you needed it? None of us—not even Newton—can do it all on our own.

Have you taken the time to sincerely thank all of them? Of course not. You're busy.

When we're young, we take things for granted. Sometimes we don't realize how important someone's help was until years later. And thanking someone, really thanking them, can be awkward, especially when some time has passed. But we often regret not saying those words. Especially when it's no longer possible to do so. As Harriet Beecher Stowe once said, "The bitterest tears shed over graves are for words left unsaid and deeds left undone."

But one guy did thank nearly *every* one of the people who helped him. His name is Walter Green.

Walter valued his relationships more than anything, but like many of us, for much of his life he was a little too busy. He'd been quite successful as chairman and CEO of the company he built, which had grown to over fourteen hundred employees. Later in life he sold his business and retired comfortably. It would have been easy to just spend all his time on the golf course. But something nagged at him. He'd never got to thank his parents the way he wanted to.

You can't really blame him—sadly, his father passed away from a heart attack when Walter was just seventeen. So now, with plenty of free time, Walter decided to do the next best thing. He was going to thank all the people who had made his success possible.

"Counting your blessings" is not just good advice your grand-mother gave you; it's also one of the most scientifically proven ways to increase your happiness. Just writing down good things that happened to you before going to bed has repeatedly been shown to increase happiness.

And so Walter sat down and counted all the people who had helped him become a success. He would call them "my forty-four." Forty-four people. There were the buddies who helped him find himself in college, the big brother who had looked out for him after their father died, the family doctor who saw that his kids were always healthy, the mentors who had advised him, the mentees who had made him proud, the colleagues who had given support, his assistant of twenty-five years, his children, and the love of his life, his wife, Lola. They ranged in age from twenty-eight to eighty-seven. Forty-four may sound like a big number, but if you dig in your memory deep enough, you'll probably find it's not that hard to come up with a similar number of people who helped shape you over the years. It just goes to show how easy it can be to forget how many others have influenced your life.

Walter developed his gratitude plan. Kinda like a lifetime achievement award, but an award given instead of received. Eulogies are so much more valuable when we do them before someone's gone.

He was going to tell all of his forty-four how much they meant. Sweet, right? But there's a twist . . .

He wasn't going to send a text. Or an email. Or even make a phone call. Walter was *serious* about saying thanks. So he got on a plane—actually, a lot of planes—and visited every single one of his forty-four to express his gratitude face-to-face. He would crisscross the country and even fly as far as Kenya. It would take a year of his life by the time he was done.

The first step was to call each of them and schedule a time, telling them what he had planned. What was the most common response?

"Walter, are you *okay*?"

Just goes to show how rare true gratitude is. Then he'd explain further. And they'd reply, "Are you *sure* you're okay?"

He prepared for each meeting, asking himself, "What difference did this person make in my life?"

And so began Walter's yearlong gratitude quest. He met them in their homes or hotel rooms or their offices or a restaurant to have a meal. With each one he talked about how they met. (With some of these relationships stretching back more than forty years, sometimes they couldn't remember.) They shared memories. And Walter offered a sincere thank you, tailored to each individual, for the contribution they had made to his life.

The last thing he did was ask them for their perspective on who he was. This wasn't narcissistic. Collectively, these people had known him for over *one thousand years*. How better to get an honest look in the mirror and see who he had been and who he had become? They could give him an answer to the eternal questions that keep us all up at night: *"Who am I?" "Am I doing the right things? Am I doing enough?"*

(Walter's also a big hugger, so no meeting was without a warm embrace.)

He didn't take notes while they talked. He wanted to give every person his full attention. But he audio-recorded each conversation. After the year ended he sent each a CD of their conversation. It was gift wrapped with a photo of the two of them he'd had taken at the meeting and included a letter about what he experienced on his year of gratitude.

Expressing his gratitude didn't just help Walter. Many of his forty-four were inspired to reflect and give thanks to those who had helped them. One even started a program to educate children on the value of honoring relationships. There are many scientifically tested ways to make ourselves feel good, but what makes gratitude so special is it can't help but make two people happy.

When the year was over, a friend asked Walter, "What did you get from this?" He realized he hadn't really thought about that. He blurted out the first idea in his head: *peace of mind.*

After that, while on a cruise with his wife, he had chest pain. The ship's doctor said his EKG was abnormal. His blood pressure was elevated by 50 percent. He knew his dad had died from a heart attack. This could be the end . . .

But Walter found he was far calmer than he expected. He was at peace. He had expressed his gratitude. His life felt complete.

Turned out it wasn't a heart attack. Just a benign muscular issue in his chest. But there was no greater proof that his year of gratitude had changed him in the most fundamental way. As William Arthur Ward once said, "Feeling gratitude and not expressing it is like wrapping a present and not giving it." Walter had given the present. He had found peace and love. And those things are so much better when you've still got years ahead of you to enjoy them. And share them.

You and I made a lot of friends in this chapter—Paul Erdös, Isaac Newton, Judd Apatow, Walter Green—and we even learned how to network a little bit smarter than Harvard or MIT. Let's give thanks with a few takeaways, shall we?

KNOW WHO YOU ARE

Why fight uphill? Just like knowing whether you're a filtered or unfiltered leader can put you on the fast track, so does knowing whether you're an introvert, an extrovert, or an ambivert and making sure everything is aligned with that so you can best leverage your natural superpowers. In chapter 1 it was "pick the right pond"; here it's "pick the right role." Natural schmoozers shouldn't pursue laboratory research and bookworms might wanna dodge that sales job. Of course, the answers are clearest at the extremes, so ambiverts need to test the waters a bit to see where they get the most from their introverted side and the best of their extroverted side.

IN THE END, IT'S ALL ABOUT FRIENDSHIP

Please stop using the word "networking." From mentors to co-workers, our brains don't really process "contacts" very well. And that's where things get slimy. However, we're really good with "us" and "them", "friend" and "enemy." So think back to kindergarten and make friends. Almost all of the principles of influence are based around friendship. Using these techniques isn't insincere if you're actually trying to make a pal.

THE MOST SUCCESSFUL ARE ALWAYS GETTING AND GIVING

Atul Gawande's accomplishments make me cry myself to sleep at night, yet this guy still felt he needed to get advice from a mentor. And by constantly giving to others, Panda built the biggest network in Silicon Valley. These aren't two separate lessons; they're one. If you're not always giving and getting you'll never be making all the progress you could. Ask for help from those above you, share your Twinkies with those below you, and you shall go far, grasshopper.

YOUR NETWORK INFLUENCES YOU, LIKE IT OR NOT.
MAKE SURE IT'S A GOOD ONE.

Over and over we've seen that the people around you affect you. They can make you happier, healthier, and more successful—or the opposite. Most of this influence is passive and gradual. You won't notice it. Mom told you not to hang out with the bad kids, and she was right. Research by Nicholas Christakis at Yale shows a network amplifies anything in it, good or bad. So surround yourself with the people you want to be.

Remember, the first step in networking is maintaining the relationships you already have. And how do you do that? Research from the journal *Cognition and Emotion* shows that gratitude is the quality that makes people want to spend more time with you. Gratitude is the tactical nuke of happiness and the cornerstone of long-lasting relationships.

If it's that simple—just taking time to say thanks—why don't we all do it? Researchers call it "hedonic adaptation." I call it "taking things for granted." When you first get your new house, it's the greatest thing that ever happened to you. A year later, it's that money pit that needs a new roof. The joy of the new never lasts. And this happens with everything.

Best example? Tim Kreider got stabbed in the throat while on vacation. The knife sunk in two millimeters from his carotid artery, which he describes as the difference between being "flown home in the cargo hold instead of in coach." He lived. And for the next year nothing could upset him. He just felt so lucky to be alive. Being stabbed in the throat turned the volume down on everything negative. "That's supposed to bother me? I've been stabbed in the throat!"

Then hedonic adaptation set in. He found himself getting frustrated by little things again—traffic, computer problems. Once again, he took being alive for granted. Just like we all do.

Tim then came up with a little solution. He makes sure to celebrate his "stabbiversary" every year, to remind himself how lucky he is. And that's what you need to do. Making time to feel gratitude for what you have undoes the "hedonic adaptation." And what's the best way to do this? Thank the people around you. Relationships are the key to happiness, and taking the time to say "thanks" renews that feeling of being blessed.

So my final recommendation is to be like Walter Green: do a gratitude visit. This isn't just some cute idea. Research by Martin

Seligman at the University of Pennsylvania shows that doing a gratitude visit is one of the most powerful ways to feel happier and to make someone else happy in the process.

It's quite simple. Seligman says to write a letter of gratitude to someone. Make it concrete; say what they did for you and how it affected your life. Then set a time to sit down with them, but don't say why. When you meet, read them the letter. Here's my little addition: make sure to bring tissues. They're probably going to cry and so may you. And both of you will be happier for it.

You may not have the travel budget that Walter did. An email or text is fine too. Studies show gratitude gives our friendships a "booster shot" and predicts relationship satisfaction. Gratitude doesn't just help friendships. It also improves work relationships. One study showed that while we say "thanks" regularly to family, only 15 percent show gratitude at work. And 35 percent of those surveyed said their boss never says it.

You're not too busy—and neither are they—for a brief show of sincere gratitude. You may think they already know how you feel, but showing it is where the real magic is. (I'm gonna say thank you for reading this book right now, because if I came to your house and did that, it'd be a little weird.)

So we've covered the what you know vs. who you know question. But what about the attitude we take toward people and our careers? Everyone is always saying we need to be confident. Confidence is undeniably powerful and has huge effects on us and how others see us, but it's also the biggest double-edged sword you and I will talk about in this book.

Should you always be confident and optimistic no matter what? Or is that what deluded people who read too many self-help books do? To determine the answers, let's look at what happens when one of the sharpest people in the world deals with confidence so extreme no human being on Earth can match it.

CHAPTER 5

Believe in Yourself . . . Sometimes

What We Can Learn About Walking the Tightrope
Between Confidence and Delusion from Chess Masters,
Secret Military Units, Kung Fu Con Artists, and People
Who Cannot Feel Fear

It didn't make any sense to him. Why would the computer do that?

He eyed the clock. He didn't want to waste too much time on a single move, but this was really bothering him.

It was 1997 and Garry Kasparov, the greatest chess master in the world, was playing against Deep Blue, an IBM supercomputer, as the world watched. It wasn't merely a friendly game of chess; this match had been blown up into an epic debate—which is smarter: man or machine?

This was a rematch, actually. Kasparov had won the competition last year handily, losing only one of six games. As chess grandmaster Maurice Ashley described him in the documentary *The Man vs. The Machine:*

> This was the most dominant player of his generation. He had been world champion already for twelve years. He was the highest ranked player in history . . . When he walked into a tournament, people thought about being in second place, not about first place. They knew it was just a foregone conclusion this guy was going to smash everybody else.

But Deep Blue was no slouch either. Despite losing the overall match to Kasparov last year, it had won the first of the six games.

And IBM's well-funded team of engineers had learned from that loss and spent the past year honing Deep Blue's software.

Regardless, Kasparov was confident. As IBM's chess consultant, Joel Benjamin, said, "He definitely has a healthy ego, and that is generally something that is a positive factor for champions. It's better to be too confident than not confident enough."

But at this moment the machine had given Kasparov pause. It was the forty-fourth move of the first game and Deep Blue had shifted its rook from D5 to D1. For the life of him, Kasparov could not figure out why it would want to do that.

Kasparov's mind went over it again and again. The clock was ticking.

Could it have made an error? That question was dangerous. For Kasparov to assume his opponent screwed up every time he didn't understand a move was egotistical and lazy. It would be too easy to underestimate the machine merely because he had beaten it last year.

He was the greatest chess master alive. If he couldn't figure out what the computer was doing, nobody could. While Deep Blue had access to all of Kasparov's previous matches and knew what he was capable of, Kasparov had very little knowledge of what the machine could do. What if it was smarter than he thought? What if instead of being able to think five or ten moves ahead it was capable of thinking twenty moves ahead?

Maybe it's doing something I'm not smart enough to see.

That forty-fourth move didn't end up affecting the game. Kasparov won anyway—but he was still visibly shaken.

In the second game, Deep Blue made another inexplicable move. It "should" have advanced its queen, but instead it moved a pawn. This was good for Kasparov, but again *it didn't make any sense . . .* unless the machine was smarter than he was. He shifted uncomfortably in his chair. After only a few more moves, it was visible to all watching that the human champ couldn't win, but he might be able to get a draw. Yet Kasparov extended his hand to Deep Blue's human representative. He gave up.

In the remaining games Kasparov's play style shifted dramatically. He became defensive instead of aggressive. Games three, four, and five would all end in draws. And in game six he made a rookie error and fell prey to a common trap. He should have known better. But Kasparov was intimidated. And it would be his downfall. He lost the sixth game and, with it, the match.

Machine had finally beaten man. But was it really a genius computer? Could it really think twenty moves ahead and use strategies the grandmaster could not uncover?

Nope. In fact, the exact opposite was true. The inexplicable rook move in the first game? It was due to a software bug. An error in the code.

IBM had programmed in a failsafe for just this type of event. To prevent the machine from wasting too much time during a "hiccup," it would make a totally random move. So that's what it did.

Of course, Kasparov didn't know this. He saw the move and figured Deep Blue knew what it was doing—and that he didn't. And this got under his skin. He read the computer's random move as genius, as brazen confidence, evidence it was smarter than he was. And Kasparov's resulting loss of confidence became his undoing.

As commentators later proved, Kasparov *could* have achieved a draw in the second game, but he felt he was already beaten and resigned. He was not confident in his own abilities and assumed the machine knew better.

Normally Kasparov could look into the eyes of his opponent and try to read him. *Is he bluffing?* But Deep Blue never flinched. Deep Blue wasn't even capable of flinching. It shook Kasparov's confidence all the same.

Sometimes the mere *appearance* of confidence can be the difference between winning and losing.

Let's cut to the chase: yup, successful people are confident. And the more successful people become, often the more confident they are. Marshall Goldsmith, one of the top business thought leaders according to *The Economist,* said this:

Successful people consistently over-rate themselves relative to their peers. I have asked over 50,000 participants in my training programs to rate themselves in terms of their performance relative to their professional peers—80 to 85 percent rank themselves in the top 20 percent of their peer group—and about 70 percent rank themselves in the top 10 percent. The numbers get even more ridiculous among professionals with higher perceived social status, such as physicians, pilots, and investment bankers.

There's definitely no shortage of confidence among top performers. Nikola Tesla, the famous developer of the system of electricity that keeps your house lit, was known to sign things not with his name but with the letters "GI." (That stood for "Great Inventor.") Humility was not his strong suit.

On the flip side, a study titled "Self-Esteem and Earnings" showed that your level of confidence is *at least* as important as how smart you are when it comes to how much money you end up making.

Ever wonder if good-looking people are more successful? They are. Beautiful women bring in 4 percent more money and handsome men claim an extra 3 percent. That may not sound like much, but for the average worker that's more than $230,000 over the course of a career. Meanwhile, unattractive women earn 3 percent less and unattractive men take home a whopping 22 percent less. Here's the kicker: the gorgeous don't rake in the dough because we like looking at them. Studies show it's because those pretty mugs make them more confident.

And more confidence provides more benefits. Studies show overconfidence increases productivity and causes you to choose more challenging tasks, which make you shine in the workplace. Overconfident people are more likely to be promoted than those who have actually accomplished more. As we talked about earlier, just speaking first and often—very confident behavior—makes others perceive you as a leader.

Can being overly confident make you deluded? Absolutely. But that can be good too. Again, here's Marshall Goldsmith:

> In a positive way, successful people are "delusional." They tend to see their previous history as a validation of who they are and what they have done. This positive interpretation of the past leads to increased optimism towards the future and increases the likelihood of future success.

According to one study, "Self-deception has been associated with stress reduction, a positive self-bias, and increased pain tolerance, all of which could enhance motivation and performance during competitive tasks."

Most of us already have these positive illusions about ourselves to some degree. In 1997, *U.S. News and World Report* did a survey asking people who was most likely to get into heaven when they died. President Bill Clinton scored 52 percent, Michael Jordan got 65 percent, and Mother Teresa received 79 percent. But who scored the highest? Who did people answering the survey feel was 87 percent likely to get into heaven? "Me." People filling it out thought *they* were the most likely to stroll through the pearly gates.

Which leads us to the issue of arrogance. Doesn't all this confidence turn you into a jerk? Sadly, there are some positives on that front too. Narcissists, the despicable kings and queens of confidence, score better in job interviews. One of that study's authors said, "We don't necessarily want to hire narcissists but might end up doing so because they come off as being self-confident and capable." Plus, they're more likely to reach leadership positions. Overconfidence has been shown to even raise output among teams, while underconfidence harms it.

Why is confidence so powerful? It gives us a feeling of control. Marshall Goldsmith explains:

> People who believe they can succeed see opportunities, where others see threats. They are not afraid of uncertainty or am-

biguity, they embrace it. They take more risks and achieve greater returns. Given the choice, they bet on themselves. Successful people have a high "internal locus of control." In other words, they do not feel like victims of fate. They see their success as a function of their own motivation and ability—not luck, random chance, or fate. They carry this belief even when luck does play a crucial role in success.

Kasparov didn't understand why Deep Blue would move its rook, but he thought the machine must have had a good reason, and that made him feel he wasn't in control. Without that control, he lost his confidence and ultimately the match.

If confidence is so powerful, should we simply pretend to have it when we don't?

*

The Americans were sloppy. If they kept this up, the Germans were sure to win the war. It was 1944 and the Nazis had already occupied France for four years. They had spies everywhere. The Americans thought their preparations weren't being noticed, but the Germans had been following their every move and were way ahead of them.

A group of U.S. soldiers had stolen a case of wine from a local merchant. Little did the Americans realize, the proprietor was a Nazi collaborator and part of the German spy network. Others had noticed U.S. soldiers in pubs and bars. Even when they weren't wearing the patches that indicated which units they were with, German intelligence had so effectively studied the American divisions they could often identify them merely by the songs they preferred to sing while drunk.

The Nazis were not just passively collecting this information. They put it to good use. Based on which units had been spotted in which cities, where the jeeps of U.S. generals (identifiable by stars on the bumpers) had been seen, and pictures from the air showing U.S. artillery movements, the Germans had adjusted their plans for certain victory. Knowing the Americans had an armored division headed his way, Nazi general Ramcke shifted dozens of 88 mm anti-tank guns to make sure the United States had a surprise waiting for them upon arrival.

But the real surprise was waiting for Germany. Because so much of the intelligence their spies had gathered was utterly and totally *fake*.

The Americans knew the bar owner was a Nazi collaborator. And they knew he'd angrily report the wine theft to the Germans, revealing their presence. Yes, there were Americans drinking in bars, but only ten of them, wearing patches from different units singing various units' songs. They went from bar to bar, switching their patches and changing their songs, creating the illusion of a formidable U.S. presence where there was none. Nor was it hard to make it look like U.S. generals had been coming to town. They just painted the identifying stars on an average jeep and had a run-of-the-mill major wear a general's uniform while acting arrogant.

These weren't the antics of a bunch of practical jokers. This was all done by the 23rd Headquarters Special Troops, nicknamed the "Ghost Army." In 1943 Ralph Ingersoll and Billy Harris assembled a team whose sole purpose was to deceive the enemy, to make them think American forces were where they weren't so they could better surprise the Germans when attacking and make them put weapons and resources where they would not be useful. Ingersoll referred to the unit as "my con artists." They executed twenty-one different missions between June 1944 and March 1945.

Wearing patches and singing songs was just the tip of the iceberg. The unit was made up of three divisions: sonic, radio, and visual. The sonic group had 145 men, who recorded the sounds of tanks, artillery, and soldiers on the move and had five-hundred-pound speakers that could project that audio out nearly fifteen miles, making the enemy think a division was on the way. The 296 men in the radio group knew the Germans listened to American transmissions, so they perfectly imitated the idiosyncrasies of the different units and provided misinformation as to where U.S. forces were and where they were not. The 379 men of the visual group, consisting largely of artists, was responsible for making it seem like there was an army where there wasn't one. The most used tool in their arsenal were ninety-three-pound inflatable tanks. At a distance or from the air, they looked like the real thing. And with a bulldozer to make the appropriate tread marks, the sonic team's recordings, and the radio group talking of the armored division's movements, the illusion was near complete. (The occasionally flaccid barrel of an inflatable tank could be remedied with a thin rope to lift it.)

Yeah, warfare trickery was nothing new, but before World War II there had never been a unit dedicated to it, a unit so specialized it could produce the look, sound, and communications of an army so realistically.

There was no rulebook for the group to follow. They were seen as a bunch of crazies and oddballs—artists instead of killers; guys who sketched instead of played cards when they had downtime. And many saw the unit's job as a suicide mission. Here was a relatively small group of men with few weapons that was *deliberately* trying to get the enemy's attention. They were fewer than a thousand soldiers pretending to be thirty thousand. Their fakery often succeeded in drawing the enemy in, which helped the United States cause as a whole, but if push came to shove, they had no real tanks, little firepower, and would be easily torn to shreds should their illusion be shattered.

The Ghost Army's biggest test and most critical mission was Operation Bettembourg. The Americans had driven the Nazis back to the Rhine River. German forces were expected to make a last stand, and they swore the river would "run red with American blood." And this wasn't bluster. Turns out there was a seventy-mile hole in the line of advancing U.S. forces, and if the Nazis discovered and exploited it, it could be very bad for the Allies. So the Ghost Army was sent in to fill the gap. Their mission was to pretend to be an intimidating division of twenty thousand men and fool the enemy into attacking the Americans at a point farther south, where U.S. forces would be ready for them.

What the Ghost Army did not expect was they would have to

keep up their deception for seven full days. They'd never had to sustain an illusion that long. Tensions ran high by the end of the week, but when the Germans were finally beaten, captured maps showed the Nazis had been fooled; the gap in U.S. forces that the Ghost Army covered had been marked as heavily guarded and a poor point of attack. The success at Bettembourg alone more than justified the Ghost Army's existence.

While the Ghost Army performed admirably when it mattered, they weren't perfect by any means. One time two Frenchmen managed to get past a security perimeter and were treated to the sight of four American GIs lifting what appeared to be a forty-ton Sherman tank. Utterly stunned, they turned to a nearby soldier. He deadpanned, "The Americans are *very* strong."

You can fake strength. You can fake confidence. Sometimes, like the Ghost Army, you can also get away with it. So when it comes to confidence, should you "fake it until you make it"?

A study from the University of California at Berkeley found that displaying overconfidence makes others feel you're both competent and higher in status. (On a lighter note, another study showed that wearing glasses does make people think you're smarter—though less attractive.)

When it comes to leadership, researcher Chiara Amati puts it bluntly: "Faking it seems, to a degree, to just be part of good people management." Jeffrey Pfeffer agrees: "The secret of leadership was the ability to play a role, to pretend, to be skilled in the theatrical arts . . . To come across effectively, we need to master how to convey power."

Many studies show faking it also has positive effects on you. In Richard Wiseman's book *The As If Principle*, he details a significant amount of research showing that smiling when you're sad can make you feel happy, and moving like you're powerful actually makes you more resistant to pain. Other studies show that a feeling of control reduces stress—even if you're *not* in control. The perception is all that matters.

But are you really going to be able to keep up the illusion 24/7? That sounds exhausting. Looking at narcissists, you'll find even they can't keep it up forever. They make excellent first impressions in both work and romance, but data shows that after weeks on a job they're regarded as untrustworthy, and a few months into dating, relationship satisfaction tanks. Faking it is like moving to Moldova. Trust is very fragile—easy to lose, hard to regain.

Let's assume you're an amazing actor. Oscar worthy. Maybe you're so good you fool even yourself. But there's a big problem here. Warren Buffett once said, "The CEO who misleads others in public may eventually mislead himself in private." And there's good reason to believe he's right.

Dan Ariely did a study in which people were given the opportunity to cheat on a test. (They didn't know the researchers administering the test would be able to tell.) Of course, those who exploited this performed better, but here's what's interesting: when surveyed about how they thought they'd do on another test, the cheaters rated themselves higher than non-cheaters. In other words, despite having succeeded due to deception, they attributed their success to being smarter. In deceiving others they ended up *deceiving themselves.*

That's dangerous. It's like pretending to fly a plane while in reality someone else is manning the controls, and the next time you walk into a cockpit believing you're actually a good pilot. As Nathaniel Hawthorne once wrote, "No man, for any considerable period, can wear one face to himself, and another to the multitude, without finally getting bewildered as to which may be the true." Faking it can be a very bad strategy, because when you fool others you can end up fooling yourself.

That leads us to the *downsides* of confidence.

*

In his multi-decade martial arts career, George Dillman has taught Muhammad Ali and Bruce Lee, among others. He's a ninth-degree black belt and was National Karate Champion for four consecutive years. In National Geographic's television program *Is It Real?* he demonstrated an incredible martial arts technique for which he has become famous: by focusing his body's internal chi energy, he can knock out opponents *without even touching them*.

In fact, he can do it even through a barrier, when he can't see his adversary. On camera he was able to knock out challengers from ten feet away with a sheet suspended between the two of them to obscure visibility. Dillman said this kind of intense use of chi drains him. The skill has rarely been seen because it takes decades to learn.

Skeptical? I understand. So let's see this no-touch knockout put to the most realistic test there is.

Like Dillman, Master Yanagi Ryuken can knock people out without touching them. In fact, using this technique he is able to take on more than a dozen adversaries. The video of this is stunning. Students run toward him, sometimes three at a time. With a flick of his wrist they drop as if punched in the face. In seconds he has dispatched all of his opponents.

To demonstrate just how real his incredible ability is, Yanagi faced off against an outsider, martial arts expert Iwakura Goh. And a bet was placed: five thousand dollars to the winner. So here we have a *real* test that can prove the power of the no-touch knockout. A referee stood between the two men and called for the fight to begin. Yanagi lifted his hands, focused his chi at his opponent . . .

And Iwakura beat the living crap out of him.

Whole fight lasted under a minute. Were you skeptical? You were right to be. Yes, extreme confidence in your abilities is very powerful, but not powerful enough to warp the laws of physics or physiology.

What about George Dillman? He has consistently refused to be tested. So Dillman is probably just a big ol' faker.

But if Yanagi is a faker, why submit to testing? Why get his butt kicked, lose five grand, and be embarrassed for all to see on the Internet? He obviously didn't think he was a phony. He was confident he *really* had this ability. His students believed too. Why else did they fall down in response to magic voodoo "punches" that didn't really work?

Writer and neuroscience Ph.D. Sam Harris said this:

It's a little hard to see how Yanagi's delusion got up and running, but once everyone began falling all over themselves, it is easy to see how it was maintained. Imagine it from his point of view: if you thought you might be able to knock people down at a distance, and then your students complied and fell down on cue, year after year, you might begin to believe that you really had these powers.

It's not just martial artists that experience this. CEOs do. And maybe you too. Confidence can improve performance and success. It can make others believe in you. But confidence can also be extremely dangerous. It can lead to delusion and hubris. And when your overconfidence meets reality, just like Yanagi's did, you too can get your ass kicked.

As the old saying goes, "There are no 'pretty good' alligator wrestlers." That's an arena where overconfidence gets you killed.

We all have a touch of delusion (everybody's kids seem to be above average and not many people admit to being a bad driver), but when that goes beyond normal thresholds, things get problematic. Unfortunately, we don't talk about this problem much. Everybody wants to increase self-confidence. That's because confidence feels good. Confidence makes us feel powerful. But plenty of research shows that when we feel powerful it can be a slippery slope to denial and hubris. Remember Ashlyn, the girl who didn't feel pain? On the surface, no pain sounds like a really nice deal, but you saw how problematic it can be. Feeling sure of yourself is really nice unless you're too sure—and when reality doesn't happen to agree with you.

This is a huge problem on the path to success in the business world. Richard Tedlow, professor emeritus at Harvard Business School, had this to say:

I have been teaching and writing about business history for four decades, and what is striking about the dozens of companies and CEOs I have studied is the large number of them who have made mistakes that could and should have been avoided, not just with the benefit of hindsight, but on the basis of information available to decision makers right then and there, in real time. These mistakes resulted from individuals denying reality.

We all spend a lot of time complaining about incompetence, but as Malcolm Gladwell pointed out in a talk he gave at High Point University, overconfidence is the far bigger problem. Why? Incompetence is a problem that inexperienced people have, and all things being equal, we don't entrust inexperienced people with all that much power or authority. Overconfidence is usually the mistake of experts, and we *do* give them a lot of power and authority. Plain and simple, incompetence is frustrating, but the people guilty of it usually can't screw things up that bad. The people guilty of overconfidence can do much more damage.

This hubris doesn't just lead to delusional thinking; it leads to real-world problems. Want to know which CEOs will run their company into the ground? Count how many times they use the word "I" in their annual letter to shareholders. This is what financial analyst Laura Rittenhouse discovered when she evaluated leaders and how their companies performed. Me, me, me means death, death, death for corporations. But when hubris takes over and you're self-absorbed, you can't see straight. What's worse is you're not aware of it. You're blind to your own blindness.

This effect explains why if you got the most confident people all together they'd be a very strange group. Adjusting for baseline confidence, it would consist of both the most competent and the *least* competent. Academics call this the "Dunning-Kruger effect."

Think of small children. They can be absurdly confident about things that are impossible, like fighting ghosts in the basement. They don't understand the world that well, and because they don't know the "rules," they can have outsized estimates of their abilities. This isn't just true of tykes. People who aren't that experienced in a field don't have the knowledge to properly evaluate how easy or hard something in that arena might be. It's why magicians applaud at different tricks than you or I might, and why comedians laugh at different jokes than we do. Their insight into the domain allows them to appreciate the nuances of how difficult achieving something really is.

The Dunning-Kruger effect is this odd phenomenon of people with the least experience being the most confident because they don't have the experience to judge just how challenging something is. We've all had a taste of this. Watching someone hold a particular yoga pose is quite easy; doing it yourself often proves far more difficult. Same with looking at a painting and saying "I could do that."

Even if our confidence starts out justified, we often fall down that slippery slope and begin to think we're skilled beyond our little domain. It's not that we're dumb; it's just that the story we tell ourselves makes us feel too powerful and we get sloppy.

And that's how you end up losing five grand and getting a bloody nose at the hands of a martial artist who doesn't believe in no-touch knockouts. But let's give you the benefit of the doubt. Maybe you do stay in touch with reality. The power that comes with confidence has another big negative that presents a roadblock on the highway to success: it can turn you into a jerk.

Across a staggering number of studies, feelings of power have very negative effects on a person's character. Power reduces empathy, makes us hypocritical, and causes us to dehumanize others. To a degree, there's a good reason for this: people in powerful positions need to make hard decisions that may be bad in the short term but good in the long term. Generals need to send soldiers into harm's way to win a war. If they felt paralyzing guilt over every loss of life, there'd be no way they could do the right thing. But as we saw with denial, this same emotional distance can quickly spiral out of control.

Studies show feelings of power cause us to be more selfish and more likely to commit infidelity. And we don't just lie more; that power also makes us *better* liars. Feeling like number one means we don't stress out about hurting others so we don't experience stress when we fib. Without those stress cues it's harder for others to detect our deceptions. We succeed because we don't care about other people.

You can imagine the effects this has at the office. While charismatic leaders can have positive effects on employees, leaders who feel powerful often have a negative impact on teamwork. One study says, "We argue that a leader's experience of heightened power produces verbal dominance, which reduces perceptions of leader openness and team open communication. Consequently, there is a negative effect of leader power on team performance."

Denial and being a jerk can derail your road to success. Confidence is good but with too much you can end up as a "pretty good" alligator wrestler. That said, the solution can't possibly be to walk around lacking confidence all the time . . . or can it?

*

They call her SM-046. Few know her real name. She lives a pretty normal life—she's the mother of three boys—but she feels no fear.

When asked by researchers to describe what fear is or to draw what a scared face might look like, she can't do it. When they tried to scare the heck out of her, showing her clips from horror movies, she was excited but never scared. In fact she asked for the name of one of the films so she could rent it.

They took her to an exotic pet store and let her handle snakes. She said, "This is so cool!" SM-046 asked to handle the bigger, deadly snakes, but the guy at the store said it wasn't safe. So she asked again. And again. And again. She asked fifteen times. She reached out to touch a tarantula and they had to stop her.

They took her to "the most haunted hospital in the world."

Waverly Hills Sanatorium has been featured on *Ghost Hunters* and half a dozen other shows about the paranormal. In the early twentieth century it was a hospital for tuberculosis patients and plenty of people have died there. Every year it's converted into a haunted house for Halloween. Dark rooms, creepy music, and actors dressed as monsters leaping out from corners—did they scare her? Far from it. *She scared them.* Not only did she not jump, she approached the costumed employees to talk to them and one of them leapt back in fright when she tried to touch his mask.

What's wrong with her? SM-046 has an extremely rare genetic disorder known as Urbach-Wiethe disease. Only about four hundred cases of it have ever been reported. Someone who has it looks and acts normal for the most part. You might notice SM-046 has a hoarse voice or that her skin looks a tad weathered but nothing out of the ordinary. Her grey matter is very different, though. The disease causes parts of the brain to calcify; they actually harden and die. Often it's the amygdala, the area most associated with fear. SM-046 has a normal IQ and can feel joy, sadness, and other emotions just fine. But no fear.

She can remember being terrified by a Doberman when she was a child, long before the damage to her brain occurred. But in her adult life she has never been scared.

The disorder actually makes her much more open and nice. Research has shown subjects with complete bilateral amygdala damage judge strangers to be much more approachable and trustworthy than normal people do.

Just as with Ashlyn's lack of pain, a total lack of fear is as much a blessing as a curse. SM-046 doesn't instinctively take the precautions you and I naturally do. Without fear, she has trouble detecting danger.

She's been the victim of numerous crimes. She's had a knife to her throat and been held at gunpoint—twice. She was nearly beaten to death by her first husband. Even during these horrible events she was never afraid. Police reports corroborated her lack of fear. She returned to the park where she was held at knifepoint the next day.

Researchers think she might not even be capable of PTSD—no fear, no stress.

In 2013, researchers were able to make her feel fear by having her inhale a carbon dioxide gas mixture through an oxygen mask. But this was under lab conditions. She's still never experienced real fear in that place called life. This is why we only know her as SM-046. Researchers feel her identity needs to be guarded to protect her because she's simply not capable of protecting herself.

So there's a reason to not be fearless. And a reason to not be wildly overconfident. Very bad things can happen. Often in life, it's better to be a little unsure.

We learned the downsides of confidence: denial and jerk-itude. As Tomas Chamorro-Premuzic explained in a piece for the *Harvard Business Review,* reversing just these two problems can have big positive effects:

> Lower self-confidence reduces not only the chances of coming across as arrogant but also of being deluded. Indeed, people with low self-confidence are more likely to admit their mistakes—instead of blaming others—and rarely take credit for others' accomplishments. This is arguably the most important benefit of low self-confidence because it points to the fact that low self-confidence can bring success, not just to individuals but also to organizations and society.

This leads us to the strengths of being less than confident. Confidence makes it very hard for us to learn and improve. When we think we know all the answers, we stop looking for them. Marshall Goldsmith says, "Although our self-confident delusions can help us achieve, they can make it difficult for us to change."

When we're less sure, we're more open to new ideas and we're actively and passively scanning the world for new ones. When we have that confident feeling of power, we don't pay as much attention, because we feel we don't need to. A study aptly titled "Power,

Competitiveness, and Advice Taking: Why the Powerful Don't Listen" showed that just making someone feel powerful was enough to make them ignore advice from not only novices but also experts in a field.

Listening to other people's ideas increases brainpower. One study showed that social interactions can actually make us smarter. But there's a catch: to get the cognitive boost, you need to take the other person's perspective. And you can't do that if you're not paying attention.

Hubris has the double whammy of making you so sure you're right that you don't listen, and over the long term you act like such a tool that nobody wants to talk to you, let alone disagree with you. When you do fall on your face, they'll be gleefully clapping. Even Machiavelli, who was not known for recommending sensitivity, warned that leaders need people who will be honest with them in private lest they end up surrounded by fearful sycophants. James Baldwin once wrote, "Not everything that is faced can be changed, but nothing can be changed until it is faced."

Tomas Chamorro-Premuzic says there are two benefits to humility: it's a reality check and it keeps us from being arrogant. He argues that humility actually drives self-improvement because we can see the gap between where we are and where we want to be. Also, being more competent than people assume we are is much better than not living up to our swagger.

Even *forcing* people to be humble has incredible results. Doctors are known for being on the arrogant side. When a hospital decided it wanted to reduce infections among patients, they insisted that all physicians follow a checklist before procedures. This was a little demeaning, but the administration was serious—so serious that they gave authority to nurses to intervene (with political cover from the top brass) if doctors didn't follow every step. The results? "The ten-day line-infection rate went from 11 percent to zero." Cocky doctors had been skipping steps, but when they were made to play by the rules the effects were dramatic. In one hospital the fifteen-month experiment saved eight lives and two million dollars.

So knocking yourself down a peg might be a good thing, as long as it doesn't take you off the course you were on. Tomas Chamorro-Premuzic said:

Low self-confidence may turn you into a pessimist, but when pessimism teams-up with ambition it often produces outstanding performance. To be the very best at anything, you will need to be your harshest critic, and that is almost impossible when your starting point is high self-confidence.

Ahhh. Negativity has a purpose. It's not some objectively bad thing, like having a flat tire. Approaching issues with a critical eye can discourage you because you're finding faults, but it's also the first step toward improvement. Psychological research shows that negative emotions produce a motivation to learn. If you get an A on a test, you just smile and move on. If you get an F, you want to learn *how* you screwed up. Another study, titled "Tell Me What I Did Wrong," showed that a shift takes place when people are on the path to expertise. Novices seek and need positive feedback because it keeps them working at something they're not very good at. But there's a tipping point. As someone becomes an expert they deliberately seek out negative feedback so they know how to keep improving now that their mistakes are fewer and subtler.

This ties in with what we learned about optimism and grit. Positive beliefs keep you going but they are, to a degree, illusions. It was depressed people who saw the world more accurately. Research shows that pessimistic entrepreneurs are more successful, optimistic gamblers lose more money, and the best lawyers are pessimists. We need optimism and confidence to keep going and convince others to join our cause, but negativity and pessimism help us see problems so we can make them better. Yes, the former feel much better, but both are necessary.

Abraham Lincoln is a great example. He embodied many of the upsides of lower confidence that we've looked at. He was open to different ideas and spent an enormous amount of time at the War

Department's telegraph office so he could be plugged in to what strategies were being proposed. (In fact, Lincoln was so drawn to new ideas, he's the only U.S. president to hold a patent.)

Lincoln also had an open-door policy. Donald T. Phillips, author of *Lincoln on Leadership*, says he was probably the most accessible president in the history of the country. He spent more than 75 percent of his time meeting with people. It's believed he met every single Union soldier who enlisted early during the Civil War.

Was he a bully? Hardly. Lincoln would have liked the "friend" idea of networking. He didn't coerce or threaten to get his way. In his own words, "So with men, if you would win a man to your cause, first convince him that you are his sincere friend." And how did he deal with people who were outright hostile? "I destroy my enemies when I make them my friends."

Was he humble? Yup. He had no problem admitting fault. In a letter to Ulysses S. Grant he was more than blunt about it: "I now wish to make the personal acknowledgement that you were right, and I was wrong."

The research shows this kind of humility pays off. Bosses who show vulnerability and underrate themselves are the most popular. Frank Flynn of Stanford found that people who feel guilt are seen as better leaders by their peers. Research from the U.S. Navy shows that esteemed leaders are democratic and have solid listening skills. The only time crews wanted a leader to make decisions without consulting people was during times of crisis (just like pirates).

We think of leaders as tending toward narcissism, and as we established, narcissists do tend to become leaders, but they don't thrive there. The performance of narcissists is relative to how much of a chance there is for them to look cool. This produces a really negative effect: when things are at their worst and leaders are needed the most, narcissists are the least likely to be engaged.

The truth is, if you wanted to pick a "bad" personality type who performs well as a CEO, don't go with a narcissist—pick a junkie. David J. Linden, professor of neuroscience at Johns Hopkins University School of Medicine, explains that their addictive nature can lead them to work obsessively when it counts:

> The risk-taking, novelty-seeking, and obsessive personality traits often found in addicts can be harnessed to make them very effective in the workplace. For many leaders, it's not the case that they succeed in spite of their addiction; rather, the same brain wiring and chemistry that make them addicts also confer on them behavioral traits that serve them well.

You've heard both sides: Overconfidence makes you feel good, gives you grit, and impresses others—but can also make you an arrogant jerk who alienates people, doesn't improve, and possibly loses everything because of denial. Being less confident gives you the drive and tools to become an expert and makes other people like you . . . but it doesn't feel so good and can send a lousy signal to others about your competence.

Kinda sucks, doesn't it? Seems like there's no easy answer. You can impress people and make them angry or have them like you but not respect you. It feels like a contradiction. So how about this: *What if you throw the whole confidence paradigm in the trash?*

Don't scream heresy just yet. Plenty of research shows that looking through the lens of self-esteem might be the real reason the debate over confidence is so fraught with grief. But what's the alternative to self-confidence? University of Texas professor Kristin Neff says it's "self-compassion." Compassion for yourself when you fail means you don't need to be a delusional jerk to succeed and you don't have to feel incompetent to improve. You get off the yo-yo experience of absurd expectations and beating yourself up when you don't meet them. You stop lying to yourself that you're so awesome. Instead, you focus on forgiving yourself when you're not.

Research shows increasing self-compassion has all the benefits of self-esteem—but without the downsides. You can feel good and perform well while not turning into a jerk or being unable to improve. Unlike self-confidence, self-compassion doesn't lead to delusion. In fact, one study, "Self-Compassion and Reactions to Unpleasant Self-Relevant Events: The Implications of Treating Oneself Kindly," showed that people high in the trait had increased clarity. They saw themselves and the world *more* accurately but didn't judge themselves as harshly when they failed. Meanwhile, people focused on self-esteem often feel the need to delude themselves or to dismiss negative—but useful—feedback in order to still feel good about themselves. They cling to their self-validating theories instead of seeing the real world. This leads to hubris and narcissism. When you check the numbers, there is a solid correlation between self-esteem and narcissism, while the connection between self-compassion and narcissism is pretty much zero.

What happens when you feel good about yourself and your abilities without inflating your ego? People like you. Neuroscience research shows that developing self-compassion leads to feeling compassion for others, instead of the loss of empathy that comes with overconfidence. Under an fMRI, people who were forgiving of themselves had the same areas light up that are activated when we care for other people. With romantic couples, self-compassion was evaluated as a better predictor of being a good partner than self-esteem.

As we discussed earlier in the chapter, one of the things self-confidence definitely does is make you happier. Guess what? Self-compassion does too, but without all the negatives: "Research suggests that self-compassion is strongly related to psychological wellbeing, including increased happiness, optimism, personal initiative, and connectedness, as well as decreased anxiety, depression, neurotic perfectionism, and rumination."

Pretty impressive, right? So why does compassion succeed where self-esteem fails? Because self-esteem is always either delusional or contingent, neither of which lead to good things. To always feel like you're awesome you need to either divorce yourself from reality or be on a treadmill of constantly proving your value. At some point you won't measure up, which then craters your self-esteem. Not to mention relentlessly proving yourself is exhausting and unsettling. Self-compassion lets you see the facts and accept that you're not perfect. As famed psychologist Albert Ellis once said, "Self-esteem is the greatest sickness known to man or woman because it's conditional." People with self-compassion don't feel the need to constantly prove themselves, and research shows they are less likely to feel like a "loser."

I know what some of you are thinking: *Is always forgiving myself going to make me passive? Am I going to lose my motivation and edge if I'm not worried about maintaining self-esteem?*

It's actually *lack* of self-compassion that makes you passive. When you're self-confident you ignore feedback that doesn't match your internal reality, right? So no need to change. When you lack confidence you can see problems but may feel not up to the challenge of overcoming them. Being self-compassionate lets you see issues and do something about them. Research suggests that having this forgiving approach allows you to take more responsibility for problems while being less saddened by them. Studies show that because people with self-compassion don't beat themselves up, they have less fear of failure, which translates into less procrastination as well as more grit.

Forgiving yourself is also *easier* than maintaining self-confidence. You don't need to constantly revise the inflated stories you tell yourself and you don't need to slay a dragon every day to prove you're worth something. Research shows what's probably obvious: we like to hear good things about ourselves, but we also like to hear things that are true. The reason it's so difficult to increase self-esteem is that, sadly, we can't always do both. Self-compassion says that's okay.

So how do you develop self-compassion? It starts with something you saw with Navy SEAL James Waters: talking to yourself. But instead of building yourself up with motivational stuff you may not believe and compliments that may not be true, just talk to yourself nicely, gently, like Grandmom would. Don't beat yourself up or be critical when things don't go your way. As researcher Kristin Neff explains, "Who is the only person in your life who is available 24/7 to provide you with care and kindness? You."

You also want to accept your humanity. You *are* fallible. You don't have to be perfect all the time like Batman. You can't be. Nobody can. Trying to be is irrational, and that's what leads to all the frustrating emotions.

Finally, recognize your failures and frustrations without either denying them or seeing them as the end of the world. No rationalizing or melodrama. Then do something about them. Studies show that taking the time to jot down nice thoughts to yourself, how you're a fallible human and how you can see problems without turning them into emotional disasters, made people feel better and increased self-compassion. Meditation and mindfulness paid off too. Throw them into the mix for better results.

Is this gonna improve your life overnight? Heck, no. But with time, improvement is possible as opposed to the confidence/non-confidence spectrum, which always seems to come with side effects.

All right, time to round up everything we've learned about the confidence dilemma, get some tips we can use, and find out one more thing about self-compassion that's pretty darn amazing.

*

He'd lost everything. An entire family fortune. And with it, he lost his mind.

But Joshua Norton did not lose his confidence. Oh no. Some people lose their marbles and become barely functional and unemployed. Not Norton. In fact, he got a much, much, much better job.

On September 17, 1859, Norton became Emperor Norton I. If you weren't aware the United States had an emperor, well, you're all that much more prepared for tonight's episode of *Jeopardy*. (Don't worry. President James Buchanan didn't know either.) Of course, that's *self-proclaimed* emperor of the United States, but whatever.

For twenty-one years Norton proudly roamed the streets of San Francisco wearing a military uniform complete with epaulets, a saber, and a beaver hat that had peacock feathers emerging from it. Two stray dogs, Bummer and Lazarus, often trailed behind him like an entourage. In William Drury's biography of Norton he wrote,

"He carried a dignified and regal air about him, but was seen as a kind, affable man, inclined to be jocular in conversation. He spoke rationally and intelligently about any subject, except about himself or his empire." He was ambitious too. He later added "Protector of Mexico" to his title. These days San Francisco has a reputation for accepting crazies the way the Statue of Liberty welcomes immigrants. It wasn't much different back then. The city didn't merely tolerate him; they played along graciously and made him San Francisco's unofficial mascot.

Restaurants gave him free meals, theater owners always saved an opening-night seat for him, and the city created a budget to cover their ruler's lodging and to get him a new military uniform when the old one started to fall apart. (To say thanks, Norton bequeathed the city's supervisors with a "patent of nobility in perpetuity.") Citizens happily paid "taxes" to His Majesty to make sure the royal coffers didn't run dry. A print shop kindly created Norton's official government bonds, which local vendors accepted as currency from the emperor with a wink and a nod. Shops even sold Emperor Norton dolls.

When a police officer mistook His Royal Highness for the crazy person he was and arrested him, the citizens of San Francisco were furious. Norton was immediately freed and the chief of police apologized personally. Always gracious, the emperor issued an "imperial pardon." From that day on, members of the police department saluted Norton when they saw him about town.

But don't think that all this deference led to Norton shirking his duties. No, no. He confidently executed the responsibilities of his office, regularly issuing royal decrees that the local newspapers were all too happy to publish. His famous proclamations ranged from ordering the governor of Virginia fired, to telling Congress they could no longer convene in Washington, DC, to abolishing both the Republican and Democratic parties when their feuding caused too much grief. The emperor proudly defended the city's honor. He announced that anyone calling his homeland "Frisco" would be fined $25, which is equivalent to about $430 today. (And, yes, he ordered the city's Board of Supervisors arrested after they failed to follow his decrees.)

On the sad day when his rule came to an end, the *San Francisco Chronicle* headline read "*Le Roi Est Mort*": "The King Is Dead." Another newspaper covered his passing in great detail—while the inauguration of California's new governor received just thirty-eight words. Norton's funeral procession stretched two miles with over ten thousand citizens in attendance. (Wealthy donors covered the funeral costs.) Flags were put at half-mast. His gravestone reads EMPEROR OF THE UNITED STATES AND PROTECTOR OF MEXICO. (Nope, there are no quotation marks around that title.) His legacy is secure. Both Mark Twain and Robert Louis Stevenson immortalized him in their work. Norton's bonds are now valuable collector's items. And in 1980 the city commemorated the centennial of his death.

You could argue that he was a successful emperor. A few of those decrees ended up becoming reality, even if it wasn't the least bit due to him. His support of women and minorities would end up becoming widely adopted. He advocated for a league of nations that predated the UN. Norton's demand that a bridge be built stretching from Oakland to San Francisco came to pass, and recently there have been a number of efforts to have the Bay Bridge renamed in his honor.

Mark Twain would write that Norton "filled an emptiness in his life with the delusion of royalty." Had Norton not executed his office with such confidence people would not still remember him fondly more than a century later. But if you're not careful, confidence can make you an emperor nowhere but in your own head.

So what can we confidently say we've learned about confidence?

BELIEVING IN YOURSELF IS NICE.
FORGIVING YOURSELF IS BETTER.

Self-compassion beats self-esteem. I'd like to think that I'm the Jason Bourne of social science writing, but I'm probably a lot closer to its court jester. And that's okay. We don't need to see ourselves as larger than life and it's often better if we don't. You don't want to fall into denial or be a jerk. You want to keep learning but not feel bad about yourself. You need to avoid self-worth that is contingent on fantasy-based illusions or constantly proving yourself. So be self-compassionate. It's got all the upsides of confidence without the downsides.

ADJUST FOR YOUR NATURAL LEVEL OF SELF-ESTEEM

Are you normally pretty confident? Then enjoy the benefits but keep an eye out for delusion and stay empathetic. Seek situations that challenge you to keep yourself humble. Strive to keep an open mind instead of assuming you already know the answer. Be nice. Don't end up as an emperor in your own mind.

Do you lack confidence? No problem. You'll naturally learn faster than those know-it-alls and you'll make more friends. Focus your efforts in quantifiable areas where competence can be accurately measured so you don't have to sweat issues of perception. (Nobody cares if I'm confident in person as long as the words come out okay on the page.) Become great at what you do and confidence will increase. Which leads us to our next point . . .

ABSOLUTELY HAVE TO HAVE MORE CONFIDENCE? EARN IT.

Confidence is a result of success, not a cause. So in spite of my fevered recommendation of self-compassion, if you still want to focus on confidence, the surest path is to become really good at what you do. When Daniel Chambliss studied top swimmers, he found that by them focusing on "small wins" every day their skills progressed and their confidence in their abilities did too. When you have a competitive mind-set you always risk underperforming and feeling like a loser. When challenged, focus on improving your skills—not doing well or looking good. Studies show "get-better goals" increase motivation, make tasks more interesting, and replenish energy. This effect carries over to subsequent tasks. As always, pick the right pond. G. Richard Shell of Wharton said that surrounding yourself with those who believe in you can lead to "transferred expectations" and a self-fulfilling prophecy, which increases confidence. You can become more confident over time with hard work. As Alfred Binet, inventor of the IQ test, said about intelligence, "It is not always the people who start out the smartest who end up the smartest."

DON'T BE A FAKER

Faking it is too hard and the price of failure is too high. The short-term benefits of impressing others aren't worth being labeled untrustworthy and moving to Moldova. Even if you're successful in tricking others, this all too often leads to tricking yourself, which is the most dangerous scenario of all. As Richard Feynman famously said, "The first principle is that you must not fool yourself and you are the easiest person to fool."

I know. There are critical times when you need to make a good impression and faking seems like the best option. Instead of pretending to be what you're not, the best answer is to focus on presenting *the best version of yourself.* In the study "Your Best Self Helps Reveal Your True Self: Positive Self-Presentation Leads to More Accurate Personality Impressions," the researchers found exactly that. You don't have to be a method actor. Be you on your best day and people will see the real you.

What's that extra thing that self-compassion brings us that's so darn special? It's a little thing called "wisdom." I'm not being sappy or poetic here either. In a study titled "Self-Kindness When Facing Stress," they found that being compassionate with yourself was actually correlated with being wise. Not just IQ points or knowledge, wisdom. (How many things that you do every day can you really say are making you wiser?)

Harshly judging yourself as good or bad, as immediately successful or unsuccessful, is very black and white and narrow-minded. To achieve wisdom, you need a little more flexibility, acceptance, and the learning that comes with growth. Think about the wisest people you've known. Were they full of bluster and hubris? Or utterly without confidence? They were probably calm and understanding, forgiving and less judgmental. We'd all like to achieve that level of wisdom one day. And self-compassion is a great first step.

All right, hopefully I've resolved the confidence debate for you. (If not, I compassionately forgive myself.)

Confidence operates at the level of feelings and appearances. But what about the real brass tacks work that needs to get done? How many hours do you need to put in? Many successful people are unapologetic workaholics, but your vision of success might involve work–life balance and occasionally getting some sleep. How hard do you really need to work to be successful?

CHAPTER 6

Work, Work, Work . . .

or Work–Life Balance?

How to Find Harmony Between Home and the Office,
Courtesy of Spider-Man, Buddhist Monks, Albert
Einstein, Professional Wrestlers, and Genghis Khan

Anyone who knows baseball knows Ted Williams. He played professionally from 1939 to 1960 and is one of the undisputed greatest hitters of all time, right up there with Babe Ruth. But whether you're familiar with him or not, I have news for you: Ted Williams never played baseball. Nope, he never did.

The problem there is the verb: Williams wasn't *playing*. To him, hitting a baseball wasn't a game. He always took it very, very seriously. In a 1988 interview he said as a child he literally wished on a falling star that he would become the greatest hitter to ever live. But he didn't sit around and wait for the dream to come true. His obsessive, perfectionist work ethic would bring him more success than any descending celestial body would. Williams said, "I . . . insist that regardless of physical assets, I would never have gained a headline for hitting if I [had not] kept everlastingly at it and thought of nothing else the year round . . . I only lived for my next time at bat."

Ten thousand hours to achieve expertise? Williams probably did that a few times over. He was obsessed. After school, he'd go to a local field and practice hitting until nine P.M., only stopping because that's when they turned the lights out. Then he'd go home and practice in the backyard until his parents made him go to bed. He'd get to school early so he could fit in more swings before classes started. He'd bring his bat to class. He picked courses that had less homework, not because he was lazy but so he'd have more time for hitting.

That still wasn't enough practice time for Ted. In a move that would make chapter 3's Spencer Glendon and Peter Drucker proud, he ignored fielding almost altogether. Occasionally he could be seen on the field with his *back* facing home plate. And even then he'd be swinging his glove like a bat, practicing, much to the frustration of his fellow players. As for girls? No time. He was a virgin until his second year in the major leagues. When he joined the majors he lied about his birthday, saying it was October instead of August. Why? A birthday during the baseball season might be a distraction. Williams told *Time* magazine, "Hundreds of kids have the natural ability to become great ballplayers but nothing except practice, practice, practice will bring out that ability."

It wasn't mere hours that made Williams so great. It was how he spent those hours. He was a perfectionist, constantly trying to improve. He turned the game of baseball into pure science, long before sabermetrics or *Moneyball*. Williams even visited MIT to learn more about the physics of baseball. He studied the best batters and would eventually write a book, *The Science of Hitting*, that to this day is still considered the best book on the subject.

His secret sauce was the intensity with which he studied pitchers. Williams believed in "knowing your enemy." And he certainly saw pitchers as the enemy, often joking, "What do you think is dumber than a pitcher? Two pitchers." He would say, "You're not playing the Cincinnati Reds or the Cleveland Indians, you're playing that pitcher . . . and he's the guy you concentrate on."

He kissed up to the umpires to get their insights on various pitchers' styles and kept notes on them in a little black book. He interrogated older players for more info on the opposition. "I don't guess what they throw. I figure out what they're going to throw," he said. People would marvel at how he could recount the habits and preferences of different pitchers decades after his career came to a close. But this perfectionist sensitivity that made him perform so well led to much strife with sportswriters who covered him. Their criticism enraged a man who already put so much pressure on himself to be the best.

His bats were rubbed with alcohol on a nightly basis to keep them clean, and he weighed them to make sure they weren't being affected by condensation. They had their own locker next to his in the clubhouse. Williams handled them lovingly, like a baby—and then he would practice his hitting with them until his hands bled.

It paid off. In a *New Yorker* profile of Ted Williams, John Updike wrote, "No other player so constantly brought to the plate that intensity of competence that crowds the throat with joy." But, excuse the pun, life can throw you a curve ball . . .

When World War II began, Williams was called to serve. His response to having to derail his career? Well, if he had to be a Marine combat pilot, he'd be great at that too. John Glenn, a friend of Williams's, wrote in his autobiography, "He gave flying the same perfectionist's attention he gave to his hitting." Despite not having more than a high school education, Ted was ruled by a rage to master any task in front of him, and he quickly became competent at whatever was needed.

Due to the war, he missed three full seasons of baseball. When he returned to the game, did he miss a step? Nope. He doubled his already insane batting regimen and joined the lineup three weeks later.

While most professional sports are undeniably a young man's game, Williams competed in the major leagues until the age of forty-two. During his final year in the pros his home-run percentage was the best of his career, a stellar 9.4. He even hit a home run during his final at bat before retirement in 1960.

He then became a manager for the Washington Senators. While his perfectionism rendered him temperamentally ill-suited for the job, it still produced amazing results. His attitude seemed to be *I got my ten thousand hours and I'm going to be sure you do too.* He was convinced that playing golf messed up hitting technique and fined players a thousand dollars for being on the greens during the baseball season. He launched marathon batting practices, set up a curfew, limited alcohol consumption, tried to get them to take naps before night games, and even did his best to keep the team celibate. Batters who couldn't remember the pitching styles of opponents were treated to Williams's famous temper.

But this also paid off. Hits went up, strikeouts went down, and attendance at games soared. The team emerged with their best record in twenty-four years. The same sportswriters he loathed (and who loathed him back) had no choice but to name him American League Manager of the Year.

Perfectionism aside, one cannot work 24/7. We all need rest. A hobby. Something approximating work–life balance. Ted Williams loved to go fishing, a famously placid, relaxing sport . . . Um, no, not in this case. He was a driven achiever even when supposedly taking it easy. A friend said, "When he was pulling on a fish he would use more expletives in one sentence then I'd ever heard in my life. It was almost poetic. It was lyrical, like him singing a song. He didn't do it vindictively or in anger, he was just being himself, always trying to top himself." And, yes, he earned his way into the National Fresh Water Fishing Hall of Fame as well as the International Game Fish Association Hall of Fame.

In 1999, *The Sporting News* put him as eighth on their list of best 100 Greatest Baseball Players. He was awarded the Presidential Medal of Freedom by George H. W. Bush in 1991.

Ted Williams was great because he never stopped working.

Does all this hard work really produce extreme success? The answer is an unequivocal yes. Our expert on great achievers, Dean Keith Simonton, provides a daunting formula for eminence: "People who wish to do so must organize their whole lives around a single enterprise. They must be monomaniacs, even megalomaniacs, about their pursuits. They must start early, labor continuously, and never give up the cause. Success is not for the lazy, procrastinating, or mercurial." (Does that mean it's a good thing that I'm writing these lines at 3:25 A.M.?)

If you wanted to hear you can make millions and be renowned by only working when you feel like it and not making sacrifices, well, just close the book now and go watch some "no money down real estate" infomercials. You've come to the wrong place.

Still here? Good. Frank Barron, a renowned professor at UC Santa Cruz, said, "Voluminous productivity is the rule and not the exception among the individuals who have made some noteworthy contributions." Even hair-styling mogul Vidal Sassoon once quipped, "The only place where success comes before work is a dictionary." Yes, to be the very best you must be a little nuts in the effort department.

Dean Keith Simonton sums it up: "Those individuals with the highest total output will, on average, produce the most acclaimed contributions as well." The Price Law is a great illustration of just how important feverish work is. Take the number of top people in a field. To make the math easy, we'll just say it's one hundred. Then take the square root of that number, which in our example is ten. The Price Law says those ten people will be responsible for 50 percent of the notable achievements in that field. Ten people out of one hundred will produce half the stuff worth paying attention to. And Simonton notes that the Price Law "holds for every major domain in the arts and sciences."

But you're not a botanist or a painter, you say? Doesn't matter. In all professional jobs you see a similar effect: "The top 10 percent of workers produce 80 percent more than the average, and 700 percent more than the bottom 10 percent." And that requires hours. When Harvard professor John Kotter looked at top managers across various industries he found that sixty-plus-hour weeks were not uncommon. And what did Stanford professor Jeffrey Pfeffer (whom we met in chapter 2) mention first in his list of keys to corporate success? "Energy and stamina." Because you're going to need it.

Can you be productive at something without spending a ton of time at it? To a degree, of course, but assuming equal talent and efficiency, the person who spends more time wins. And the issue of hours seems to be the real distinguishing factor between the pretty good and the truly great. Yeah, being smart helps, but the "threshold hypothesis" shows that smarts ain't everything, especially when it comes to big breakthroughs. When you look at eminent people, the majority are smarter than average. Without an IQ of 120, very few people end up producing anything that will be groundbreaking and remembered in the history books. But the twist is that as long as you're past the 120 mark, many studies show more IQ points have little effect. What makes the difference? Not luck. It's all those hours. A Manhattan Project physicist IQ of 180 might be nice, but those 60 points don't make the difference that more hours will.

Some people do insane amounts of work and see nothing from it. By the time of his death, Robert Shields had produced a diary that was 37.5 million words long. He spent four hours a day recording everything from his blood pressure to the junk mail he received. He even woke up every two hours so he could detail his dreams. This didn't make him rich and didn't even garner him a *Guinness Book of World Records* listing. It just made him a crazy man with one of the most morbidly fascinating obituaries ever.

Hours alone also aren't enough. Those hours need to be *hard*. You need to be pushing yourself to be better, like Ted Williams. You've spent a lot of hours in your life driving, right? Are you ready to compete in NASCAR or Formula 1? Probably not. Trying to improve isn't something we are doing in the vast majority of activities we engage in every day—including work. With results that may make you scared to go to the hospital, studies have shown that doctors and nurses don't get much better at their jobs over time. Without a "rage to master," like you behind the wheel, they just do their thing, hour after hour, rather than push to become experts. As Michelangelo once said, "If people knew how hard I worked to achieve my mastery, it wouldn't seem so wonderful after all." In Benjamin Bloom's classic study of top athletes, scientists, and artists, he found that one of the critical elements of a great mentor wasn't just secret knowledge and emotional support; it was pushing you harder. A great mentor's "expectations and demands were constantly raised until they were at a point where the student was expected to do virtually all that was humanly possible."

Research shows ambition alone is predictive of success, and motivation predicts career success better than intelligence, ability, or salary. Combine them with tons of hours and one thing's for certain: I sure don't want to be standing between you and your goals because I'll end up looking like a flattened Wile E. Coyote with tire tracks across my face.

Ted Williams thought of nothing but hitting, he put in an astronomical number of hours always trying to improve, and he became so successful that most boys of that generation dreamed of being him one day. And now you're wondering if success means a misery-inducing schedule along with a massive coronary by age fifty, I've got a surprise for you: it *can* mean the exact opposite.

In general, overwork is bad for you. It's correlated with reduced exercise, fewer visits to the doctor, and more smoking. Worse than that, a study entitled "To Your Happiness? Extra Hours of Labor Supply and Worker Well-Being" showed the success benefits often are outweighed by the negatives in terms of happiness and stress. To put a cherry on top, one of the top five regrets of people on their deathbed is "I wish I didn't work so hard."

But things change when you find your job meaningful. I've mentioned the Terman Study before, which followed people from youth all the way to the ends of their lives. Since this study allowed the researchers to see the big picture, what did they find in relation to hard work in a meaningful career? As the *WSJ* reports, "Those who stayed very involved in meaningful careers and worked the hardest, lived the longest." Meaningful work means doing something that's (a) important to you and (b) something you're good at. Plenty of research shows that if you do those things you're uniquely good at (psychologists call them "signature strengths"), they're some of the biggest happiness-boosting activities of all. A Gallup study reported, "The more hours per day Americans get to use their strengths to do what they do best, the less likely they are to report experiencing worry, stress, anger, sadness, or physical pain." Imagine what life would be like if your job entailed using your signature strengths all day, every day. Of course you'd work long hours. Who'd want to go home?

The problem here is the word "work." We often use it to mean something bad. "I hate having to do all this work." But we also use the word to mean "job." When your job is fulfilling, it's not a bad thing. As Mark Twain wrote in *The Adventures of Tom Sawyer*, "Work consists of whatever a body is obliged to do. Play consists of whatever a body is not obliged to do." When you enjoy your work, you may still experience stress but it's worth it in the end. Nobody is happy during mile twenty of a marathon. When you're halfway up Mount Everest, you wonder why you ever thought this was a good idea. Getting a Ph.D. can take years of grueling, lonely effort. And yet these are the things people are the most proud of. The best example is having kids. Parenthood is certainly stressful. It can be difficult. For some people it's a full-time job. But nobody seriously says "All that parenting is going to kill you. You should stop doing it." Sometimes it *feels* like it's going to kill you, sure, but it's the most meaningful thing in most people's lives, and the challenge just makes the rewards that much sweeter. A career you love is no different.

If a meaningful career boosts longevity, what kills you sooner? Unemployment. Eran Shor, a professor at McGill University, found that being jobless increases premature mortality by a whopping 63 percent. And preexisting health issues made no difference, implying that it's not a correlation, it's very likely causation. This was no small study. It covered forty years, twenty million people, and fifteen countries. That 63 percent figure held no matter where the person lived.

The unhappiness effects of unemployment might be even *worse*. Most of the research shows that your happiness level is fairly consistent throughout life. Getting married makes you happier, but in a few years most people return to their prior level of satisfaction. If your spouse passes away you'll be sadder for an average of seven years, but after that, boom—back to baseline. However, there are a few things that can put a permanent dent in how often you smile, like suffering a serious illness or getting divorced. Or losing your job. In fact, happiness levels do not fully recover even after you get a new job. Being out of work can leave a mark that lasts a lifetime.

What about retirement? That's the "good" unemployment, right? Wrong. Retiring is associated with cognitive decline, heart disease, and cancer. Those effects weren't due to aging but because people stop being active and engaged.

It's not really fair to compare long hours against no job at all. However, having a job you dislike can be even worse than unemployment. According to a 2010 survey by Gallup, people who felt "emotionally disconnected" from their jobs enjoyed their lives less than people who had no jobs at all. And a study of Swedish workers showed monotonous work was associated with a higher rate of myocardial infarction. Yes, a boring job can kill you.

Remember how I said that working too hard was one of the biggest regrets people had on their deathbed? Definitely true. But what was the number-one regret? "I wish I'd had the courage to live a life true to myself, not the life others expected of me." Career was a solid number two, right behind education and ahead of relationships. We spend so much of our time at work. I'm guessing the people who regretted working so much didn't like their jobs—and that many of those who didn't live a life true to who they were picked the wrong careers. Challenging, meaningful work makes us happy and fulfilled. But then again, when it's meaningful, it's not really work, is it?

Okay, the successful workaholics have presented their case. Let's hear what the less obsessed folks have to say about whether there's a downside to all this frantic labor.

(Note to lazy people: it's safe to start reading again.)

*

Albert Einstein and Charlie Chaplin attended the premiere of *City Lights* together. The crowd went wild for the two superstars, and Chaplin said to the great scientist, "They cheer me because they all understand me, and they cheer you because no one understands you."

How true. Ask people what Einstein did and they'll say "Relativity." (Ask them what relativity is and you'll get an awkward silence. All most people understand about it is that you're supposed to know it's important.) As Walter Isaacson said in his wonderful biography, Einstein "devised a revolutionary quantum theory of light, helped prove the existence of atoms, explained Brownian motion, upended the concept of space and time, and produced what would become science's best known equation." His work was so impactful that everyone knew he would one day win a Nobel Prize—but he had achieved so much that people weren't sure for *which* breathtaking accomplishment he would get it. When he finally did win the prize in 1921, ironically, he didn't get it for relativity theory. And the bulk of the work he was celebrated for he accomplished in one year, 1905, when he was twenty-six years old. (Not bad for a guy who was rejected for military service because he had sweaty feet.)

Unlike Newton, Einstein was charming, committed to social justice, and had a family and children. But similar to his reclusive predecessor, he lived in a world of ideas, in his own head. Obviously, he was a genius, but his real superpower was the incredible time and focus he put into his work. Though surrounded by fame, friends, and family, he still lived a life that was often cerebrally detached, the better to explore his ideas. This obviously paid off in terms of career success.

It was a Faustian bargain, though Einstein did not pay the price. His family did. Isaacson said, "One of his strengths as a thinker, if not as a parent, was that he had the ability, and the inclination, to tune out all distractions, a category that to him sometimes included his children and family." When they demanded his attention, he doubled down on his work.

This strained his family to the breaking point. Einstein said, "I treat my wife as an employee whom I cannot fire." And this was not merely a barb thrown out in the heat of anger. When his marriage began to break down he presented his wife with a *contract* that detailed what he expected of her if the relationship was to continue:

CONDITIONS:

A. You will make sure
1. that my clothes and laundry are kept in good order;
2. that I will receive my three meals regularly in my room;
3. that my bedroom and study are kept neat, and especially that my desk is left for my use only.

B. You will renounce all personal relations with me insofar as they are not completely necessary for social reasons. Specifically, you will forego
1. my sitting at home with you;
2. my going out or traveling with you.

C. You will obey the following points in your relations with me:
1. you will not expect any intimacy from me, nor will you reproach me in any way;
2. you will stop talking to me if I request it;
3. you will leave my bedroom or study immediately without protest if I request it.

D. You will undertake not to belittle me in front of our children, either through words or behavior.

She reluctantly agreed, but unsurprisingly the marriage still fell apart due to his distance and the affairs he carried on with younger women, who did not make emotional demands of him.

While he was an attentive father when his boys were young, as the years passed Einstein would spend more and more time in his head. After his divorce, he saw his children rarely, focusing more on his work. His son Eduard struggled with mental illness and attempted suicide, eventually dying in a psychiatric hospital. Einstein had not visited him for more than three decades. His other son, Hans Albert, is quoted as saying, "Probably the only project he ever gave up on was me."

Hard work creates talent. And talent plus time creates success . . . but how much is too much?

Did I mention what Ted Williams's obsessive work ethic and perfectionism did to his relationships? No? (I'm sneaky like that.) Well, sadly, it's a similar story to Einstein.

Ted Williams's incredible ability came from the fact that he spent all his time focused on baseball, but his weakness was also *that he spent all his time focused on baseball.* Rob Kaufman, the son of Williams's late-life partner Louise Kaufman, said, "He was totally lacking in social skills. He spent too much time in the locker room. He was intelligent, but he didn't learn any of the skills that his peers learned."

Williams divorced three times. One woman he dated, Evelyn Turner, repeatedly refused his marriage proposals. She said she would be his wife only if he assured her she would come first in his life. Ted responded, "It's baseball first, fishing second, and you third." When he fought with wife number three, Dolores Wettach, she threatened to write a sequel to Williams's biography titled *My Turn at Bat Was No Ball.* Shelby Whitfield, a friend of Ted's, said, "Williams was probably one of the worst people to be married to that you could imagine."

He was no better as a father. Williams even admitted it: "As a father, I struck out . . . I was never there. I was always gone. I had my commitments. I just didn't do the job." The hours on the field that brought him glory destroyed his relationship with his three children. When his daughter Bobby-Jo would ask him about his childhood, he told her to read his autobiography.

Though Williams had success as a team manager, the same pattern was visible in his relationships with the players he oversaw. Red Sox infielder Ted Lepcio said, "He had a hard time understanding why guys like me couldn't hit better. I think he had a hard time relating to nonperfectionists."

And as a perfectionist of the highest order, he wanted to control everything. When he couldn't he would explode. Stories of his temper are legion and legendary. Williams had a rage to master everything in his life, but when things presented themselves that he couldn't control—like wives, children, and family—mastering wasn't an option. And that left him with only rage.

His temper was an *intensifier* (which you'll recall from chapter 1). Wife number three, Dolores, spoke of his anger: "It was his best friend, because it gave him power to do things which saved him, which was important. If he had to swing the bat, and he was angry, that ball would fly. If he was fishing, and he was angry, that fly would just fly, and the fish didn't stand a chance." But in relationships it was crippling. If Williams lost a chess match in a friendly family game, he'd throw the board across the room. As biographer Ben Bradlee wrote, "Ultimately, Dolores felt the source of Ted's rage was his inability to satisfy the perfectionist ambitions that he set for himself. When he failed to meet his own expectations, no matter how innocuous the activity, he could snap." Satisfaction forever eluded him because of these constant towering expectations of himself and others. Teammate Jimmy Piersall once asked him why he was so mad all the time. Williams responded, "You know why? Because I've got to be good every day. You don't have to be."

One time Williams returned to the dugout furious and critical of himself. He felt he should not have swung at that final pitch. He could not get over it. We've all been in a situation like this: you feel like you've made a mistake and you can't stop beating yourself up about it. But Williams had just hit a home run. A home run that had won the game. It didn't matter. As his teammates went crazy over the win, Williams stewed. He felt he could have done better.

That attitude may bring incredible results (if not happiness) in a talent-driven contest like baseball. But it doesn't work with relationships. Sadly, his innate drive and long hours of practice only reinforced this perspective and Williams could not turn it off. The intensifier that made him one of the greatest baseball players to ever live meant he would forever be at odds with the people who loved him most.

As George Bernard Shaw said, "The true artist will let his wife starve, his children go barefoot, his mother drudge for his living at seventy, sooner than work at anything but his art." And where was Mozart when his wife was giving birth to their first child? In the other room composing, of course.

The same is seen in doctors who are passionate about their jobs. A study of over one thousand Dutch medical specialists showed the top reasons for burnout were interference of family life and perfectionism. Psychologist Richard Ryan says, "One of the reasons for anxiety and depression in the high attainers is that they're not having good relationships. They're busy making money and attending to themselves and that means there's less room in their lives for love and attention and caring and empathy and the things that truly count." This phenomenon of neglecting family for one's passion isn't the least bit new. The ancient Romans had an expression, "*libri aut liberi*," which translates to "books or children." If you're very serious about creating things, you sacrifice family.

The issue of energy is critical as well. Creative workers not only spend less time with their spouses but a study from the *Academy of Management Journal* found that the time they do spend is of lower quality. When they get home their brains are pooped. There's no gas left in the tank to be an attentive partner. One study found people high in perfectionism were 33 percent less likely to have satisfying relationships.

Some push the intensity of those hours to unnatural levels. The esteemed science journal *Nature* did an informal survey of 1,400 of its readers. Twenty percent had used drugs to increase focus and concentration, the most common being the stimulant Ritalin. In Mason Currey's analysis of the habits of geniuses he also found a significant number used amphetamines, just like Paul Erdös. Sean Esteban McCabe of the University of Michigan analyzed American undergrads and reported 4.1 percent were doing the same. (Excuse me while I refill my coffee.)

So having a calling one is obsessively passionate about can bring success and fulfillment, but it can also crowd out relationships, which are key to happiness. Harvard researcher Shawn Achor echoed this, "The people who survive stress the best are the ones who actually increase their social investments in the middle of stress, which is the opposite of what most of us do. Turns out that social connection is the greatest predictor of happiness we have when I run them in my studies." What was number four in that list of biggest regrets of the dying? "I wish I had stayed in touch with my friends."

Unchecked, getting those ten thousand hours of deliberate practice can lead to a dark place. Howard Gardner, professor at the Harvard School of Graduate Education, studied a number of eminent creators like Picasso and Freud:

> My study reveals that, in one way or another, each of the creators became embedded in some kind of a bargain, deal, or Faustian arrangement, executed as a means of ensuring the preservation of his or her unusual gifts. In general, the creators were so caught up in the pursuit of their work mission that they sacrificed all, especially the possibility of a rounded personal existence.

In an interview, chess legend Bobby Fischer said almost exactly that. When a reporter asked what his life would have been like had he not been so obsessed with chess, Fischer replied, "Well, it would have been better, you know. A little more balanced . . . a little more rounded." Franz Kafka went even further: "What will be my fate as a writer is very simple. My talent for portraying my dreamlike inner life has thrust all other matters into the background; my life has dwindled dreadfully, nor will it cease to dwindle. Nothing else will ever satisfy me."

The same issue of opportunity/cost that we looked at in chapter 2 with Spencer Glendon and Peter Drucker applies here. Every hour at work is an hour you're not with friends and family. Is this really necessary to be successful at a global scale? Sadly, it may be. The paper "Why Productivity Fades with Age: The Crime–Genius Connection" shows that, at least with men, marriage has a noticeably negative effect on output among scientists, authors, jazz musicians, painters, and even criminals. The author of the study, Satoshi Kanazawa writes, "Scientists rather quickly desist after their marriage, while unmarried scientists continue to make great scientific contributions later in their lives."

All of this is if you have your ultimate dream job. What if you don't (which is true for most of us)? I'm sure this comes as no surprise, but working like crazy when you're not obsessively passionate has some serious negative effects. In Japan, this has gotten completely out of hand. It is not unheard of for people to literally die from overwork. The problem has become so prevalent the Japanese have a name for it: *karōshi*. Far from a rare curiosity, the term was added to the dictionary in 2002. It has become such a problem that it is legally recognized and the government began tracking it in 1987. The number of people dying from *karōshi* in Japan is comparable to the number of traffic fatalities.

The deaths are usually directly attributable to heart attack or stroke, but suicide is not unheard of and that even garnered its own name, *karōjisatsu*. Insurance companies have repeatedly paid out on lawsuits regarding the problem, with families receiving the equivalent of more than a million dollars in damages. When surveyed, 90 percent of Japanese workers weren't even familiar with the concept of work–life balance. To stem the problem, some offices now play a recorded message at the end of the workday, basically telling employees "GO HOME."

Most of us will never take overwork to the level of heart attack or suicide. Nah, we'll just settle for making ourselves utterly miserable. We commonly refer to the problem as "burnout," but what's fascinating is that psychologists have realized that burnout isn't just an acute overdose of stress; it's pretty much plain ol' clinical depression.

The paper, "Comparative Symptomatology of Burnout and Depression," said, "Our findings do not support the view hypothesizing that burnout and depression are separate entities."

We all experience stress and most of us bounce back from it fine after a break. Christina Maslach, one of the leading researchers in the field, says true burnout occurs when we're not right for the job we're in. That's also why passionate people may destroy their relationships or physically pass out from exhaustion but not burn out the frazzled way the average worker might. Researchers Cary Cherniss and David Kranz found that burnout was "virtually absent in monasteries, Montessori schools, and religious care centers where people consider their work as a calling rather than merely a job." But when you're not clicking with your role, you're overloaded, and your duties aren't aligned with your expectations or values, it's not merely the stress that gets to you; you actually experience a perspective shift. You feel you can't make progress, you disengage, and you eventually become cynical and pessimistic.

So burnout is *the flip side of grit*. When we talked about Navy SEAL James Waters and the research of Martin Seligman, we saw that resilience often comes from optimism. Burnout is the result of a pessimistic attitude toward your job. *This isn't getting me anywhere. I can't handle this. It's never going to get any better.*

Some may think you just need to tough it out, but when you're pessimistic and miserable it's very hard to achieve success. As Julia Boehm and Sonja Lyubomirsky published in the *Journal of Career Assessment,* success does not lead to happiness as often as happiness leads to success. Just as optimism keeps you going, burnout creates a pessimistic downward spiral where it's hard to fulfill your duties because it all seems futile. In the end, you might find yourself hoping for *karōshi.*

What's the fix for all this? Many think getting that big raise is going to make it all worth it, but they're wrong. The study "How Do Objective and Subjective Career Success Interrelate over Time?" showed that pay doesn't increase job satisfaction. More money doesn't make a job a better fit; therefore, it's unlikely to reduce burnout. If you're overworked in a job that isn't right for you, it may be time to make a change.

If you're obsessively pursuing a career you're passionate about, the solution there won't surprise you too much either. You need time for relationships. When the American Medical Association surveyed top doctors to find out how they avoided burnout, one of the key things mentioned was "sharing issues with family and friends."

We all have limits, and for a well-rounded life, we need both a career that suits us as well as supportive loved ones. As writer Sam Harris said in an interview with *The Atlantic:*

> It's probably true that certain human accomplishments depend upon people's neurotic needs for achievement or their lust for money or power. A lot of art comes from a place of being captivated by selfish illusions. And if a person were to permanently dispel the illusion of the self, he might not write great novels or start the next Apple. Buddhahood might be incompatible with being the next Nabokov or Steve Jobs. Luckily, no one has ever had to choose between becoming a great artist or entrepreneur, or the next Buddha. The relevant question for me is how neurotic and unhappy and self-deceived do we have to be while living productive lives. I think the general answer is, far less than most of us are.

So while obsessive work may be necessary for the heights of success, it doesn't lead to a fulfilling, balanced life.

That raises other questions: If we do want to achieve success and don't want to be cut off from friends and family or suffer the depression of burnout, can less really be more? Can we have fun and be successful or is that just a pipe dream?

*

There was nothing more the Japanese fighters could do. They were being roundly beaten at their own game. And it was embarrassing.

The Gracie family of Brazil had taken the grappling style of jiujitsu to an all-new level, and in the exploding sport of mixed martial arts, their name had become synonymous with victory. Jiujitsu is a Japanese art—a Japanese word, even—but it had been elevated to seeming perfection by another nation on the other side of the world. The Gracies learned Japanese jiujitsu early in the twentieth century and evolved it in the back alleys of Rio de Janeiro through street fights and later in no-rules competitions. They took the art and made it a science.

Ever since the first Ultimate Fighting Championship, in which Royce Gracie devastated three opponents in a single night, Gracie jiujitsu had caused a paradigm shift in martial arts. There was no debate: anyone wanting to compete in MMA had to know Gracie jiujitsu or they would be defeated by it. That included fighters from the very nation that had invented jiujitsu.

Japan has always loved fighting sports. K-1 kickboxing events filled football-size stadiums. When Pride FC launched in 1997 as the nation's premier mixed martial arts organization, it too garnered huge audiences. But many of the Japanese fighters who competed in it were seen as sacrificial offerings to foreign fighters like the Gracies. They were derided as "tomato cans" because at the end of the match, battered, they would be leaking red the way a damaged container of sauce might.

In this new world of mixed martial arts, Japan desperately wanted to regain its storied fighting history, but there seemed to be no way to outdo the Gracies. Members of that family had literally been rolling on grappling mats since before they could walk. Just working more or working harder would not be enough. Gracie jiujitsu was a drug-resistant virus infecting all of martial arts.

Was there an antidote that could restore the fighting honor of Japan?

Yes, but it would come from the most unlikely of places . . .

No one questioned the talent of Kazushi Sakuraba. They did, however, question his sanity. Often called "Saku" for short, he wasn't a classically trained martial artist. He was a professional wrestler. His style of "catch wrestling" is a hybrid grappling form created in the 1800s that gained attention in carnivals and fairs. In something that resembles a *Rudolph, the Red-Nosed Reindeer* story set in the world of fighting, a pro wrestler whose style was something out of a circus would become Japan's MMA "white knight."

One of the most difficult challenges in Gracie jiujitsu is called "passing the guard." It involves getting past your opponent's attempts to control you with their legs so you can move to a more dominant position on the mat. This is often a grueling back-and-forth chess match as fighters struggle for advantage. How did Saku pass the guard? By doing a *cartwheel*. Flying over the defenses of his opponent, he looked more like Spider-Man than an MMA fighter. And it worked.

This guy wasn't from the Shaolin Temple—more like Ringling Bros. Clown College. Before his fights, fans would be on edge; they knew they'd get a great fight, but the anticipation was more about *What's this awesome crazy guy going to do next?!?*

Not only was Saku's innovative fighting style electrifying, but from start to finish he was a consummate showman. The Japanese media had often referred to one of his opponents, fighter Kevin Randleman, as "Donkey Kong." So Saku entered the ring for their fight dressed as Mario.

Saku also did something else few fighters ever did during a fight: he smiled. There was no doubt to anyone watching that his guy was having fun. Though he clearly took his training very seriously, he never took *himself* all that seriously.

He was also doing something else: winning. Though frequently competing against fighters who outweighed him by as much as fifty pounds, Saku, after his first appearance in the UFC, went undefeated for eleven fights. Only one question remained: *Could he possibly beat a Gracie?* Other than by decision, no member of the Gracie family had lost a professional fight in *decades*.

On November 21, 1999, Saku caught Royler Gracie in a *kimura* armlock, and the proud member of the Gracie family refused to tap out in submission. But when Royler's arm was clearly dislocated, the referee intervened to stop the bout. Saku had won.

This sent a shockwave through the MMA community. A Gracie

had been defeated. And it was the crazy clown from pro wrestling who had done it.

In just over a year Kazushi Sakuraba brought down four top fighters from the first family of martial arts, which garnered him another nickname: "The Gracie Hunter." After defeating Royce, Hélio Gracie, the patriarch of the family extended a hand to Sakuraba, who happily shook it and bowed. The proud Brazilian family recognized a more than worthy opponent. Japanese fighters had regained their honor.

Kazushi Sakuraba's record includes victories over seven UFC champions. The former pro wrestler is regarded as "Japan's greatest mixed martial artist." And I doubt any fighter has had as much fun in the ring.

This new apex predator of mixed martial arts wasn't someone who did Gracie jiujitsu better than the Gracies; he was a lunatic who dyed his hair orange and did cartwheels in the ring. Sakuraba didn't win solely by doing more or working harder. Sometimes more is not the answer. Sometimes more isn't even possible. Sometimes we need to relax and have fun—and maybe act a little bit crazy—to be at our best.

Scientists surveyed 254 adult students on playfulness and then looked at their transcripts. Guess what? A playful attitude was associated with better grades. It actually went further than that: playful students more often read class material that wasn't even required. They were curious and motivated. Other research has found a connection between amount of recess time for kids and academic performance. More playing equals more learning.

Fun helps us bond with others not only in our personal lives but also at the office. After all, how well do you know someone if you've never shared a laugh with them? When William Hampes did a study of ninety-eight students, he found a significant relationship between humor and trust. We're more likely to have faith in the people we joke around with.

But you can't be focused on fun if you're the boss, right? Wrong.

You'd better think about everyone having a good time if you're trying to recruit top talent. A study from the *Journal of Leadership and Organizational Studies* found that "workplace fun was a stronger predictor of applicant attraction than compensation and opportunities for advancement." Yeah, that means exactly what you think: money and promotions weren't nearly as important to people as working somewhere fun.

You still need to work long hours, right? More hours means more results. Or does it? Let's examine the best of the best . . . or the worst of the worst. (Depends on how you look at it, really.)

Management consulting is legendary for its long hours and demanding workloads. Eighty-hour weeks are not uncommon, there's tons of travel and constant email checking, and many suffer from "death by PowerPoint." Leslie Perlow and Jessica Porter wanted to see what would happen if a top consulting firm did the absolutely unthinkable: they gave their employees a consistent day off from work. What a concept. For the manic pace of employees at the Boston Consulting Group this was unthinkable. Sure, you get time off, but if an emergency comes up—and there's *always* an emergency—we need you. So what Perlow calls "predictable time off" wasn't really an option. When she first raised the topic with BCG, the first partner she talked to said no. It took six months to find another partner at the firm who was willing to give this insane idea a shot.

I'm sure you're not shocked that the employees liked this. Compared to workers under the old system, consultants who got the predictable time off were 23 percent more likely to say they were satisfied with their jobs and 24 percent more likely to say they were excited to go to work in the morning. Across a range of metrics they felt better about their jobs and lives, and were more likely to stay at the company. Of course. Time off feels good. But that wasn't the only result. The consultants were also 11 percent more likely to say they were providing better service to their clients. The clients confirmed this: ratings of the teams with predictable time off were, at worst, the same as the non-PTO teams and, at best, far better than they had been.

BCG got the message. Four years later, 86 percent of the teams in the firm's Northeast divisions were giving predictable time off a shot. Employees were working *less* and the company was getting better results. So there's clearly a limit for the average employee. When quantity of work gets too high, quality suffers. And quality of life suffers for workers.

Thirty-nine percent of Americans work fifty or more hours a week and eighteen percent work sixty or more, according to a 2014 Gallup poll. What's the added benefit of all those extra hours? Research from Stanford says close to nothing. Productivity declines so steeply after fifty-five hours that "someone who puts in seventy hours produces nothing more with those extra fifteen hours." All they are creating is stress.

A paper from the *Journal of Socio-Economics* found that the happiness decrease that overtime stress produces is bigger than the happiness boost that extra overtime pay produces. The math doesn't work.

How else is fun and relaxation related to success? Well, these days it seems every company is screaming about innovation. They say they need creativity, but do all these hours at the office lead to new ideas? Nope. Study after study shows that creativity comes from being relaxed, not stressed and overworked.

In fact, you're engaging in your prime creative time long before you get to the office. Most people come up with their best ideas in the shower. Scott Barry Kaufman of the University of Pennsylvania found that 72 percent of people have new ideas in the shower, which is far more often than when they're at work. Why are showers so powerful? They're relaxing. Remember, Archimedes didn't have his "Eureka" moment at the office. He was enjoying a nice warm bath at the time.

The go, go, go environment of many modern workplaces is downright antithetical to creative thinking. Harvard's Teresa Amabile found that under high levels of time pressure you're 45 percent less likely to come up with that creative solution. All the stress instead creates what she calls a "pressure hangover." Your muse exits the building and may not come back for days.

To really be creative, you need to step out of that hyperfocused state of tension and let your mind wander. Researchers speculate that daydreaming is actually akin to problem solving. It uses the same areas of the brain engaged when you're working on a puzzle. People whose minds wander more have been shown to be better problem solvers.

Speaking of downtime, you and I need to have a heart-to-heart about that daily block of big downtime: sleep. I'm sure I'm not the first to mention that it's important for a whole bevy of reasons (but I do promise to be the most annoying).

Research shows that not getting enough shut-eye makes you out-and-out dumber. John Medina, professor at the University of Washington School of Medicine, explains:

> Take an A student used to scoring in the top 10 percent of virtually anything she does. One study showed that if she gets just under seven hours of sleep on weekdays, and about forty minutes more on weekends, she will begin to score in the bottom 9 percent of non-sleep-deprived individuals.

And you don't fully recover that brainpower as fast as you might think. A 2008 study in Stockholm showed that even after a week of normal sleep people still weren't 100 percent after just a few five-hour nights.

Sleep has been shown to affect decision-making, ethics, your health, and how much you time you pointlessly screw around on the Internet. Research also shows beauty sleep is real. When scientists had subjects look at photos of people before and after sleep deprivation, the shots in which they were tired were consistently rated as less attractive.

I know, I know: you think you're fine. No, you're not. You're like a drunk shouting they're okay to drive. That's the really sneaky thing about sleep deprivation: you're not necessarily aware of it. Just because you don't feel tired doesn't mean you're well rested and performing optimally. Your sleepy gauge just isn't that well calibrated, my friend. The *New York Times* reported on the work of University of Pennsylvania sleep researcher David Dinges: After 2 weeks of 4 hours of sleep a night, test subjects said they were tired but okay. Then the researchers gave them a battery of tests and it turned out their brains were Jell-O. Dinges also found that after 2 weeks of 6 hours a night they were effectively drunk. How much sleep does the average American get per night? Gallup says it's 6.8 hours. (So you're probably pretty wasted as you read this.)

Now, there are people who don't need more than a few hours of sleep a night, but you are almost certainly not one of them. "Short sleepers" make up only 1 to 3 percent of the population. (They're actually hard to study because this is one of the few disorders nobody ever goes to a hospital complaining about.) You know the morning people who are almost pathologically chipper and upbeat? Short sleepers are like that *all* the time. Researchers call it "behaviorally activated." It's believed they may have subclinical hypomania, the same kind of disorder we talked about in chapter 1. Again, that's like mania but with the volume turned way down. They're not crazy, just optimistic, full of pep, and very emotionally resilient. The "disorder" runs in families and is believed to be caused by a mutation of the *hDEC2* gene. So if you don't have that genetic issue, no, you're not a short sleeper; you're just too tired to realize how tired you are.

What happens when you and I try to emulate these people? Let's look at the most extreme of cases, because frankly that's more fun.

Randy Gardner set the record for staying awake by remaining conscious for over eleven days. Researchers documented the whole thing and found that he experienced no long-lasting health issues and was back to normal after finally getting some sleep. That said, during the event his brain completely went haywire. After a while his speech slurred, he hallucinated, he had trouble focusing his eyes, and for a short time he came to believe he was an African American football player, despite being a Caucasian teenager. The *Guinness*

Book doesn't even have a category for sleep deprivation anymore because of how much it screws you up. Don't try this at home, kids.

Sleep doesn't just affect how tired you are or how clearly you think. It also affects your emotions. You and I have had days when we're tired and cranky, but it goes deeper than that, down to the neuroscience level. When we're exhausted, our brains can't help but focus on the negative. Remember the amygdala? That part of the brain wasn't working in the woman who couldn't feel fear. Research by Matthew Walker at the University of California at Berkeley shows that sleep deprivation puts us in a state that's almost the opposite of that woman: the world gets more negative. When students were kept awake for thirty-five hours, fMRI analysis showed their amygdala response to bad things shot up to 60 percent higher than people who had slept normally. When we get our eight hours, our brains "reset" and we are on a more even keel. Without shut-eye, our brains overreact to bad stuff. Plain and simple: when you're tired it's harder to stay happy.

Your mood in the morning also affects how you perform the entire day. How you sleep, as well as a stressful commute, can influence your productivity from the moment you hit the office until the second you leave for the evening. A study from Wharton showed that your mood in the morning influences how you react to events. Is your coworker's error a minor annoyance or an utter disaster? (By the same token, if the boss comes into the office looking angry, you may want to wait until tomorrow to ask for that raise.)

Those early hours are important for another reason: they're usually when you're most productive. When I spoke to Duke professor Dan Ariely, he said, "It turns out that most people are productive in the first two hours of the morning. Not immediately after waking, but if you get up at 7 you'll be most productive from around from 8 to 10:30." Don't waste them being exhausted and cranky.

To think about this another way, do you accomplish more in three hours when you're sleep deprived or in one hour when you feel energetic, optimistic, and engaged? Ten hours of work when you're exhausted, cranky, and distracted might be far less productive than three hours when you're "in the zone." So why not focus less on hours and more on doing what it takes to make sure you're at your best?

Okay, time for *Scared Straight: Sleep Edition*. British researchers looked at white-collar workers who normally slept six to eight hours a night but subsequently slept less, then the researchers followed up with them more than a decade later. What was the result? A lot more dead people. The study reported, "There is good evidence that participants whose sleep decreased from six, seven, or eight hours per night were at higher risk of all-cause and cardiovascular mortality than those who retained the same sleep duration across the phases."

So why aren't we getting enough sack time? We all like sleep. Of course, the answer is work. (If you didn't know I was going to say that, please take a nap right now.) University of Pennsylvania medical school researcher Mathias Basner said, "The evidence that time spent working was the most prominent sleep thief was overwhelming. It was evident across all sociodemographic strata and no matter how we approached the question." And nothing beats video game programmer Evan Robinson's insight on what's happening here. To paraphrase: Why is it that companies that wouldn't think twice about firing you for being drunk on the job don't mind creating conditions that effectively make you drunk on the job?

You're not a computer that can run 24/7 without a hitch. You need rest. But you'll be punished for sleeping on the job. Meanwhile, sleeping on the job turns out to be a *really good idea*. The evidence for naps improving performance is pretty overwhelming.

Now, if we're gonna talk about naps we have to talk about astronauts.

To sleep properly, you're dependent on cues from your environment. When it's bright out your brain thinks it should be awake; when it's dark out, beddy-bye. This creates a whole heck of a lot of grief for astronauts, because when you're not on planet Earth, these cues can get all out of whack. You and I experience the sun coming up once a day. In the same twenty-four hours, astronauts can see that happen a dozen times. So NASA has had to do a lot of research on sleep, because when astronauts are too tired to do their jobs correctly, the results can be deadly. They developed the Fatigue Countermeasures Program, which is what a multibillion-dollar government agency has to call a "nap." A study by the space agency showed naps made the pilots sharper: "The results clearly demonstrated that a 40-minute planned inflight rest period significantly improved performance and physiological alertness in long-haul flight operations."

We talked about how being sleep deprived made it harder to be happy. Guess what? Taking a ninety-minute nap reversed the effect. Not only did a siesta reduce the brain's overactive response to negative stuff, it also increased the response to good things.

How else does resting and having some fun help? Naps are short so let's go big: vacations. A German study of teachers showed that taking a two-week vacation increased work engagement and decreased burnout for up to a month. Vacations refill your gas tank. (Feel free to tear this page out and put it on your boss's desk.) Now, this doesn't mean you can justify overwork and depriving yourself of sleep just because you have a trip on the calendar. The researchers found that too much stress after coming back to work made the effects last less than a month. You're emptying the gas tank again. Meanwhile, having more fun after you return home increased how long the vacation helped.

We need fun. We need rest. They increase our chances of success and they benefit your employer as well. Hard work doesn't necessarily mean good work. If a lot of surfing on the Internet has taught us anything it's that quantity often doesn't mean quality. Don't do more work if you can do better work. You want to keep in mind that 80/20 perspective Peter Drucker talked about and do things that move the needle instead of spending all your time shuffling emails.

Author Tony Schwartz says, "Energy, not time, is the fundamental currency of high performance." It's a qualitative lens instead of a quantitative one. All hours are not created equal. We're not machines, and the time model is a machine model. Our job isn't to be a machine—it's to give the machines something brilliant to do.

We've heard from both sides. Yes, passionate obsessives like Ted Williams work like crazy and see great results but they often pay the price in terms of relationships. Those of us who aren't in our dream jobs have far more to lose and less to gain from long hours. Nobody wants to be the next *karōshi* statistic. Having fun, getting sleep, and taking vacations may take time away from work but can more than make up for it in terms of quality and engagement.

So why is the work–life balance question such a dilemma? It didn't seem to be such an issue in the past . . . Or was it? What's the real problem here and how do we fix it? It turns out the world *has* changed. There has been a real shift. But there is something you can do about it.

To better illustrate this, we really should talk about Spider-Man . . .

*

Peter Parker was exhausted again.

He was tired pretty much all the time lately. While fighting crime can certainly be draining, his superpowers had always defended him against this type of exhaustion. But something was different now.

In his adventures as Spider-Man, Parker had found a new costume. Instead of his classic blue and red duds, this outfit was black and white. Not only did it look really cool, but it augmented his powers. The costume could perfectly mimic any type of clothing so he never had to cover it up. Nice feature when you have a secret identity. It also provided him with a near-inexhaustible supply of stronger webbing. Again, good to have when you're a web-slinging crime fighter.

But since he'd gotten it, he was tired. All the time. Of course, it couldn't be the costume. It was just fabric, after all. Until one night Peter Parker took the outfit off and collapsed into bed, quickly falling asleep . . .

And then the costume *moved*. It crept back onto his body, covering him once again. It stood him up. And out the window they went, swinging from web to web, Parker still asleep inside its confines the whole time.

The next day Peter woke up, exhausted again but still not understanding why. He knew he had to do something.

Peter sought the help of Reed Richards, leader of the Fantastic Four and a great scientist. Richards ran some tests and had very disturbing news. The new costume was not a costume. And it certainly was not made of fabric. It was *alive*. Biologically, it was a symbiote, like a parasite. It was quite intelligent. And it had motives of its own. It was feeding off Spider-Man's superpowers and attempting to fuse with Peter—permanently. He would become part of it. It would not live to serve him; he would live to serve it.

But there was a bigger problem: not only did Peter now know the truth, *it* knew that he knew. And he couldn't get the symbiote off him . . .

We'll stop there for a second. I know what some of you are thinking: *Why is this guy rambling on about superhero costumes?* Sorry. I'll get concrete for the non-comic fans:

When you first got your job, did it feel like a great opportunity? Did it offer you salary and benefits that seemed impressive and beneficial? But on your path to success, did you find it was draining you? That you were tired all the time? Did it have you working at night, feeding it, when you should be sleeping? Did it seem far more like you were becoming part of it than it was becoming part of you? Did you fight to maintain your independence but realize you couldn't get it off you no matter how hard you tried?

Yeah. Exactly.

I'll be your Reed Richards here: You may not have a job. You may have a symbiote.

And now, Spider-Man or Spider-Woman, we need to find a way to fight back.

Who understands better than anyone the pressures the world puts on us? How strapped for time you and I have become? How impatient we've been forced to be? Elevator designers.

Author James Gleick notes that every nine days or so the products of the Otis Elevator company lift the population of the Earth. And riders want everything faster. They want the elevator to come faster, they want it to go faster, they want the doors to open faster. Elevator designers have tried all sorts of solutions to deal with our endless frustration with any delay. Algorithms allow the lifts to anticipate demand and minimize wait time. Mitsubishi created one that rises as fast as a plane—over forty feet a second. But we're still tapping our feet and rolling our eyes. Not fast enough.

They've realized we can wait about fifteen seconds on average. At forty seconds, we start clenching our fists. When surveyed, people who had to wait two minutes report it as ten minutes. So they've tried tricking us. Those mirrored elevator lobbies? That's not elegant design. Those mirrors are there because when we can stare at ourselves we pay less attention to how long the wait time is and complaints drop.

But it's no better once we get inside. The designers call it "door dwell"—how long before the doors close. It's usually under four seconds. Doesn't matter. Not fast enough. What's consistently the button that gets hit so much that the paint is wearing off? Gleick confirms it's DOOR CLOSE.

Which brings our conversation to work–life balance. Have we always been this strapped for time? Did our parents and grandparents have this same stretched-too-thin feeling? In the ten years from 1986 to 1996 work–life balance was mentioned in the media thirty-two times. In 2007 alone it was mentioned 1,674 times. The times they are a changin'.

For one thing, people are working more hours. When *Harvard Business Review* surveyed over fifteen hundred people earning salaries in the top 6 percent of Americans, they found 35 percent worked over sixty hours a week and 10 percent put in a colossal eighty-plus hours at the office. Of college-educated men with a full-time job in the United States, 22.2 percent worked fifty-hour weeks in 1980. By 2001 it was 30.5 percent. This explains why so many of us may feel "money rich, time poor." Then again, a lot of us feel "money poor, time poor" too.

Of course, all those hours need to come from somewhere. When *HBR* talked to those top 6 percent of earners working sixty or more hours a week, they found "more than 69 percent believe they would be healthier if they worked less extremely; 58 percent think their work gets in the way of strong relationships with their children; 46 percent think it gets in the way of good relationships with their spouses; and 50 percent say their jobs make it impossible to have a satisfying sex life."

As you might imagine, that has big effects on happiness. Most studies in the past have shown adults to be happier than younger people. Not anymore. Since 2010, people under thirty are happier than previous generations of young people. But people over thirty aren't as happy as people in their age group used to be. Why might this be? Researcher Jean Twenge explained:

American culture has increasingly emphasized high expectations and following your dreams—things that feel good when
you're young. However, the average mature adult has realized
that their dreams might not be fulfilled, and less happiness is
the inevitable result. Mature adults in previous eras might not
have expected so much, but expectations are now so high they
can't be met.

Another study showed that between 1976 and 2000 high school seniors' ambitions and expectations rose to absurd levels—and were continuing to grow with time. A little bit of math and . . . yup, they're the disappointed adults now. In the words of the great philosopher Tyler Durden, "We've all been raised on television to believe that one day we'd all be millionaires, and movie gods, and rock stars, but we won't. And we're slowly learning that fact. And we're very, very pissed off."

What's going on? In the modern era, the standards of success have gotten absurd. They're not difficult to reach; they're impossible. TV shows you twenty-something Silicon Valley billionaires. Think you're good at something? There's someone on the Internet who is better, works less, and is happier. They have nice teeth too. For most of human existence when we looked around us there were one or two hundred people in our tribe and we could be the best at something. We could stand out and be special and valuable. Now our context is a global tribe of seven-plus billion. There's always someone better to compare yourself to, and the media is always reporting on these people, which raises the standards just when you think you may be close to reaching them.

If these mental expectations weren't bad enough, the modern world has actually made things *more* competitive. The talent market is global—which means if you can't hack it, companies don't sweat it. Someone on the other side of the planet certainly can. Computers make things more efficient, requiring fewer people, and the global talent market offers ten times as many applicants for every spot.

The world says "More, more, more." And so do we. J. Walker Smith of Yankelovich Partners told *The Wall Street Journal,* "Right now, there's no aspiration to be middle class. Everyone wants to be at the top." We probably have far more now than we ever had in the past, but we're probably not much happier. And instinctively we think the problem can still be fixed by more. More money. More food. More things. Just more. We're not even sure what we need more of, but whatever we have now sure as hell isn't doing it, so turn it up to eleven, Bertha. This isn't an anticapitalist rant or your grandfather saying "You kids don't appreciate anything." It's another example of our instincts gone awry. The problem is that in the quest for "What makes me feel good" there's no finish line. It's a pie-eating contest and first prize is more pie.

These expectations make it harder to achieve the goals we naturally inherit from our surroundings, but that's not the worst part. In today's world, *it's all our fault.* Or at least it feels like it.

We love choices and the twenty-first century has given us nearly infinite choices. With technology, we now always have the choice to be working. The office doors don't close at five P.M. anymore. Every minute we spend with friends or playing with our kids is a minute we could be working. So every moment is a decision. That decision didn't exist in the past. But having it in the back of our heads all the time is enormously stressful.

When I spoke to Swarthmore College professor Barry Schwartz, who has studied the problems inherent in choice and happiness, he said:

These days, when you come home, your work comes with you. In fact, no matter where you go, your work comes with you. You're at a ballgame, your work is in your pocket, right? What that means is not necessarily you want to work all the time but you have to make a decision not to work. There's no constraint. "Should I play with my kid or should I answer these emails?" That was not an issue thirty years ago. You're home; of course you play with your kid. No decision. Now there's a decision to be made.

Technology has increased choices dramatically in good and bad ways. Remember that study of the top six percent of earners? "Seventy-two percent said that technology helps them do their jobs well, fifty-nine percent said that it lengthens their working day, and sixty-four percent noted its encroachment on family time." During Leslie Perlow's research, one executive looked at his smartphone and said, "I love the thing and I hate it at the same time. The reason I love it is that it gives me so much power. And the reason I hate it is that it has so much power over me."

Barry Schwartz explains that when the world doesn't give you much choice and things don't work out the way you want, it's the world's fault. What else could you have done? But when you have one hundred options and you don't choose well, the burden shifts because you could have picked better.

Here's the problem: We love *having* choices. We hate *making* choices. Having choices means having possibilities. Making choices means losing possibilities. And having so many choices increases the chance of regret. When work is always a choice, everything is a trade-off. More time working means less time with your friends, spouse, or kids. And if you choose wrong, it's your fault, making choices even more stressful. We work harder but feel worse because everything is being judged, constantly.

In his book *OverSuccess,* Jim Rubens describes a study showing the effects this is having on us:

> [A] survey of 2,300 consumers earning $50,000 and up found the group "highly aspirational and stressed, disconnected, and anxious." Fewer than four in ten respondents reported that they "feel like a part of my community," "have the right balance in my life," or "have a lot of close friends." Only three in ten were happy with their personal appearance and only 18 percent were happy in their romantic relationships.

In 2008, 52 percent of people said they'd lain awake at night due to stress; 40 percent said their stress levels made them want to cry. One in three women said that, on a ten-point scale, they'd peg their stress level at eight, nine or ten.

It hits family time just as hard. Between the years 1980 and 1997, the number of household conversations dropped by 100 percent. Yes, 100 percent. The author of the study said that means that "in 1997 the average American family spent no time per week when talking as a family was the primary activity." He continued: "In a 2000 national YMCA poll of a representative sample of American teens, 21 percent of teens rated 'not having enough time together with parents' as their top concern." (Okay, when the average surly American teenager's top concern is that they're not seeing their parents enough, there's *definitely* a problem.)

But when we feel such intense pressure to succeed both at work and at home, when there are always choices and it feels like it's our fault, we become desperate for a solution. Some of us set aside a facet of our lives so that other categories can thrive. Laura Nash and Howard Stevenson, the authors of *Just Enough,* and HBS professor Clay Christensen call this strategy "sequencing." The attitude being *First I'll work a job I hate and make a lot of money and* then *I'll have a family and* then *I'll do what I want and be happy.*

This doesn't work with relationships, though. Christensen rightly points out that "by the time serious problems arise in those relationships, it often is too late to repair them. This means, almost paradoxically, that the time when it is most important to invest in building strong families and close friendships is when it appears, at the surface, as if it's not necessary."

The authors of *Just Enough* confirmed this was true in their research with top executives. Yes, the group was quite accomplished career-wise, but behind the veil things sounded a lot more like Ted Williams and Albert Einstein: "When we probed further, we found that many were not necessarily doing very well with their other targets: family, long-term business health, building a place to work that people actually value, developing a personal character that holds up when they got out of the public spotlight." We can't sequence relationships. They need regular, consistent attention. As Ralph Waldo Emerson said, "We are always getting ready to live, but never living."

All right, enough doom and gloom: What can you do about this?

You need a *personal* definition of success. Looking around you to see if you're succeeding is no longer a realistic option. Trying to be a relative success compared to others is dangerous. This means your level of effort and investment is determined by theirs, which keeps you running full speed all the time to keep up. Vaguely saying you want to "be number one" isn't remotely practical in a global competition where others are willing to go 24/7. We wanted options and flexibility. We got them. Now there are no boundaries. You can no longer look outside yourself to determine when to stop. The world will always tell you to just keep going.

Brace yourself. I'm going to say something unpleasant: You have to make a decision. The world will not draw a line. You must. You need to ask *What do* I *want?* Otherwise you're only going to get what *they* want. Sorry to have to break this to you but in today's world "having it all" isn't possible when others determine the limits in each category. We used to rely on the world to tell us when we were done, but now the balance must come from you. Otherwise you risk ending up with that number-one regret of the dying: not having had the courage to live the life you wanted and instead lived the life others prescribed.

Entrepreneur Ken Hakuta said, "Success is something you will confront constantly in business. You will always be interpreting it against something, and that something should be your own goals and purpose."

Barry Schwartz says we have to become "choosers" instead of "pickers." A picker selects from the options available, leading us into false dichotomies created by the options we see in front of us. But a chooser "is thoughtful enough to conclude that perhaps none of the available alternatives are satisfactory, and that if he or she wants the right alternative, he or she may have to create it."

What combination of things makes you feel you have enough? What kills the need for more? What, in this world of infinite, perpetually screaming options, makes you lean back from the table and calmly say "I'm good, thanks"? The authors of *Just Enough* did more than sixty interviews with very high-achieving professionals and surveyed ninety high-level executives. It turns out that most of these people didn't know the answer to these questions either. What was interesting was that they made consistent mistakes, and by looking at these mistakes the researchers were able to get a handle on what we need in life and the best way to go about getting it.

We all know the good life means more than money . . . but none of us is exactly sure what those other things are or how to get them. Let's face it: money's pretty easy to count and it consistently brings some happiness for at least a short period of time. We all know love and friends and other stuff are important too . . . but they're a heck of a lot more complicated and we can't just have them delivered to our house by Amazon Prime.

Evaluating life by one metric turns out to be a key problem. We can't use just one yardstick to measure a successful life.

In *Just Enough* the authors refer to it as a "collapsing strategy"—collapsing everything into one barometer of whether or not our life is on track. Most of us find it easy to focus just on money and say "Make the number go up." Convenient, simple . . . and dead wrong. As we saw, the insanely successful people the authors spoke to often felt they were missing out in another area of life, like their relationships. When we try to collapse everything into one metric we inevitably get frustrated.

The researchers realized multiple yardsticks for life were necessary. For instance, to have a good relationship with your family you need to spend time with them. So hours spent together is one way to measure. But if that time is spent screaming at each other, that's not good either. So you need to measure quantity and quality.

The study came up with four metrics that matter most:

1. HAPPINESS: having feelings of pleasure or contentment in and about your life
2. ACHIEVEMENT: achieving accomplishments that compare favorably against similar goals others have strived for
3. SIGNIFICANCE: having a positive impact on people you care about
4. LEGACY: establishing your values or accomplishments in ways that help others find future success

They also came up with a simple way to interpret the feelings these four need to provide in your life:

1. HAPPINESS = ENJOYING
2. ACHIEVEMENT = WINNING
3. SIGNIFICANCE = COUNTING (TO OTHERS)
4. LEGACY = EXTENDING

How much of each metric do you need to feel like a success? It can be intimidating to have to determine, right now, what balance of these four will provide what you need for the rest of your life. You don't need to go that far. What made you feel fulfilled at age ten isn't true at twenty and won't be true at eighty. Things will change and that's okay. Specifics will shift, but your values probably won't move nearly as much.

You want to be contributing to the four needs on a regular basis. If you ignore any of them, you're headed for a collapsing strategy. Measuring life by one yardstick won't work. Delay any for too long and you're sequencing. A favorite quote of mine by Warren Buffett sums that up: "I always worry about people who say, 'I'm going to do this for ten years; I really don't like it very well. And then I'll do this . . .' That's a lot like saving sex up for your old age. Not a very good idea."

All this makes sense, but we have to get to the crux of the work–life balance issue: Where do you draw the line? How do you know when you're doing enough "winning" and need to put more into the "counting" or "extending" categories?

A good starting point is asking yourself *What's "good enough"?*

This attitude does not go over well with many people—and that's why we have the work–life balance problem in the first place. Saying "only the best" does not work in a world where options and competition are limitless. There used to be twenty-six different types of Head and Shoulders shampoo. Procter & Gamble said "Enough" and cut it down to a slightly more reasonable fifteen, which produced a 10 percent bump in profits.

Barry Schwartz says that what we often fail to realize is those constraints are welcome. They make decisions easier. They make life simpler. They make it "not your fault." So they make us happier. We believe these constraints are ultimately worth the trade-off. Limitless freedom is alternately paralyzing and overwhelming. Plus, the only place we get good limits these days is when we determine them ourselves, based on our values.

People handle having lots of choices in two ways: by "maximizing" or "satisficing." Maximizing is exploring all the options, weighing them, and trying to get the best. Satisficing is thinking about what you need and picking the first thing that fulfills those needs. Satisficing is living by "good enough."

In the modern world, maximizing is impossible and unfulfilling. Imagine exploring Amazon.com for the "best book for you." Good luck evaluating every single one. You'd need years. But there's a deeper, less obvious problem. You might think that evaluating more possibilities would lead to objectively better results—and you'd be right. But it also leads to less subjective happiness with what you end up with.

That's exactly what was found in a study done by Barry Schwartz and Sheila Iyengar. Students who were maximizers in trying to get the best job after graduation ended up better off—they got salaries that were 20 percent higher. But they ended up more unhappy with their jobs than satisficers did. Maximizers are on that treadmill of expectations and experience more regret because they always feel they could do better. Certainly if we're comparing brain surgeons, maximizing might be a good idea, but in most areas of life it just makes us unhappy. Nobel Prize–winner Herbert Simon, who created the idea of maximizing and satisficing, said that in the end, when you calculate all factors of stress, results, and effort, satisficing is actually the method that maximizes.

As Nash and Stevenson point out, "You cannot maximize two things if they are trade-offs." It's the Spencer rule again. You have only twenty-four hours in a day and only so much energy. With multiple categories you must draw a line. You cannot go all in on one and have a successful life all around.

It all comes down to the question *What do I want?* If you don't decide, the world will decide for you. As you saw, that's a treadmill of always chasing, never arriving. Ellen Galinsky did a study asking kids, "If you were granted one wish and you only have one wish that could change the way your mothers or your fathers work affects your life, what would that wish be?" Most popular answer? They wished their parents were "less stressed and less tired."

Want work–life balance? Then remember what Barry Schwartz told me: "Good enough is almost always good enough."

Okay, so you need to think about the big four and reach "good enough" in each. You want to be a chooser, not a picker. You want to "conquer the world." But you also want to get home by six P.M. and not work weekends. It feels impossible. Well, you know who successfully did the impossible? You know who *actually* conquered the world?

Genghis Khan. How did he do it? He had a *plan* . . .

*

Temujin was born in a terrible place at a terrible time. The steppes of Asia in the twelfth century were like the Wild West—but worse. Survival alone was hard, and the fight for resources meant the nomadic tribes of the area just couldn't get along.

Simple things like getting a wife was difficult because many men were so poor they could not afford to pay a dowry. So they kidnapped one. Seriously. Though kidnapping your future spouse was quite common, nobody was thrilled with having a daughter forcibly taken away. So this, along with theft and violence, produced a non-stop feuding between tribes.

Hard times meant hard measures, and everyone was always reacting to the last injustice they suffered. Maybe you'd win a battle and shout "Hurray" (yes, that word comes from the Mongol language), but sure enough, next week someone would attack you in revenge. And you'd attack back. And this would go on forever and nobody got anywhere. Historically we think of the Mongols as barbarians. And they pretty much were . . .

Until Temujin.

We are not sure when he was born (1162 is a good guess), and we don't know where he was born. His youth was marked by the troubles of the times: his father was poisoned by an enemy tribe, and for a time he himself was enslaved. He never learned to read or write. He did not have the education or resources handed to him that Alexander the Great did. But he was the Mozart of military strategy. So good, in fact, that his enemies even accused him of using magic and hanging out with devils to achieve his victories.

How did an illiterate young man in a horrible place during a horrible time conquer more territory in twenty-five years than the Romans did in four hundred? How did he build an empire that spanned over twelve million contiguous miles? And do it with an army that never grew larger than a hundred thousand men, which, as author Jack Weatherford explains, is "a group that could comfortably fit into the larger sports stadiums of the modern era"?

Everyone else on the steppe was always reacting to whatever awful thing had recently been perpetrated on them. Temujin stepped outside of this vicious cycle. He did not merely react. He thought about what he wanted. And he made *plans*.

First, he set out to unite the tribes of the steppe. He smashed the kinship structure that had kept the nomadic tribes caught in a cycle of feuding. He established a meritocracy where skill and loyalty were rewarded and bloodlines and politics were ignored. He abolished wife-napping and harshly punished lawbreakers to prevent the spiral of vendettas that had plagued the area. He discarded the names of the various tribes. They would now all be united as People of the Felt Walls. By 1206, the Mongol nomads of the steppe were one. Temujin then took the title by which he is known to this day: Genghis Khan.

This alone was a huge success. But how did he defeat more advanced civilizations, like China and Europe? How did he vanquish vast armies that were better trained and better equipped and with only a hundred thousand nomads? Oh, he had a plan for this, too.

His strategy was not to beat his enemies at their own game but to use the advantages that came naturally to his people. Mongols rode horses from the age of three. A simple people without modern technology, they overcame bigger, better-equipped armies by using greater speed and mobility. Jack Weatherford writes, "Genghis Khan's innovative fighting techniques made the heavily armored knights of medieval Europe obsolete, replacing them with disciplined cavalry moving in coordinated units." Used to living off the land, they had no need to drag slow supply chains behind their army. Each fighter brought three to five extra horses with him so they would never have a tired mount. This allowed Mongol horsemen to travel six hundred miles in only nine days, centuries before the combustion engine.

They fought the way modern armies do. They descended upon foes like a "swarm of bees, with separate groups all attacking independently from multiple angles." When you look at how the Mongol army waged war, you'd think they had the advantage of seeing into the future, yet modern generals learned it from *him*. They all studied his style, replacing horses with tanks and planes. He was blitzkrieg-ing centuries before the Germans.

Khan's army looked like peasants, so they were often underestimated, which Khan used to his advantage. He also did not reactively lash out with bravado. If his enemies thought he was weak, great. His favorite plan in battle became faking a retreat. When the enemy was sure they had won, they would give chase, breaking their formation . . . and charging right into a waiting ambush, where Mongol archers would rain arrows down upon their cornered prey.

Of course, there were constantly new challenges. Khan always had a plan, but he was also *adaptable*. He learned from each and every skirmish. Most would have expected him to be stymied when his army encountered the walled fortresses of China. The Mongols didn't even have two-story structures in the steppes let alone the knowledge of how to assault such fortifications. They had no experience with siege warfare, catapults, or trebuchets. But they didn't have to.

Khan knew there were things he didn't know, or things he didn't have time to learn, so he was always recruiting. Among conquered peoples, anyone who was useful was allowed to join them. One enemy archer had managed to shoot the Khan's own horse out from under him. When the man was caught, Khan did not execute him; *he made him a general.* Along the same lines, the Mongols absorbed a number of Chinese engineers familiar with siege warfare. Eventually Khan's army became so successful at it that it "ended the era of walled cities."

Khan's plans were so solid that the empire did not crumble after his death. It kept expanding for another hundred fifty years. (Next time you mail a letter, think of Genghis Khan. His reign brought us the first international postal system.)

He was a fatherless, illiterate nobody from a terrible place at a terrible time but became one of the most powerful men to ever live. Genghis Khan did not blindly react to problems. He thought about what he wanted. He made plans. And then he imposed his will on the world.

That's what you need: a plan. Most of us don't take the time. We're reactive, like the tribes of the steppes. And the problem with work–life balance is that the old limits are no longer in place for us. We can't rely on the world to tell us when to power down or shift gears. It's on you now. That means you need a plan, or you're always going to feel like you're not doing enough. You won't be facing Chinese armies or Eastern European enemies. Your war is first and last with yourself. But that's a battle you can definitely win with the right plan. What works for you will be a little different from what works for everyone else, but there are some tools to help . . .

As Barry Schwartz made clear, we have so many options these days that we end up being pickers, not choosers, and that's a big part of the problem here. We don't decide what we want and then go get it. Things are shoved in our faces and then we shrug and say, "Okay, I guess." Basically, we let other people tell us what to do. Aristotle said God was the "unmoved mover." He moved other things, but nobody told him how to move. We can definitely benefit from emulating this strategy.

Being reactive doesn't just hurt your chances of getting what you want; it also reduces your chances of real happiness. Research shows we often don't choose to do what really makes us happy; we choose what's easy. Mihály Csikszentmihályi found that watching TV made teenagers truly happy 13 percent of the time. Hobbies scored

34 percent and sports or games got 44 percent. But what did teens choose to do most often? They spent four times as many hours watching television. Without a plan, we do what's passive and easy—not what is really fulfilling.

Robert Epstein surveyed thirty thousand people in thirty countries and found that the most effective method for reducing stress was having a plan. When we think about obstacles ahead of time and consider how to overcome them, we feel in control. That's the secret to really getting things done. As fMRI studies show, a feeling of control motivates us to act. When we think we can make a difference, we're more likely to engage. Things aren't as scary when we have our hands on the wheel. And the most interesting part—and the most helpful to us—is that it's not actually being in control that causes all these changes. It's just the *feeling* of control. Joe Simpson couldn't control his situation when he was stranded on that mountain with a broken leg, but making it a game made him feel like he could.

The importance of control goes all the way down to the neuroscience level. Quick summary: when you're stressed out, you literally can't think straight. Under stress, your center of rational thought— the prefrontal cortex—just throws up its arms and quits. Your limbic system, that ol' lizard brain of emotions, takes the reins. A study by Amy Arnsten of the Yale School of Medicine said, "Even quite mild acute uncontrollable stress can cause a rapid and dramatic loss of prefrontal cognitive abilities." In an interview, Arnsten also said, "The loss of prefrontal function only occurs when we feel out of control. It's the prefrontal cortex itself that is determining if we are in control or not. Even if we have the illusion that we are in control, our cognitive functions are preserved." Your heart doesn't like lack of control either. A study from the journal *Health Psychology* found that when you feel like you don't have control over things, there's a big increase in heart attacks. Guess which people saw the biggest jump? Those normally at low risk for heart problems.

To get a better idea of the day-to-day importance of control, let's look at entrepreneurs. A survey of nearly two thousand small business owners showed that more than 50 percent work more than forty hours a week. The job isn't less demanding. While 41 percent said working for themselves reduced stress, 32 percent said it increased it. But guess what? A whopping 79 percent expressed satisfaction with running a small business and 70 percent were happy with their lifestyle. That crushes the job satisfaction numbers among non-self-employed people we saw earlier. So comparable hours, comparable stress, but they're far happier. Why? When asked the reason they started their own business, the number-one answers were "To be my own boss," "To make my own decisions," "To do it my way." They wanted control. And despite few changes in overall hours and stress, they were happier.

What about productivity and success? The London School of Economics and Political Science looked at how 357 CEOs in India used their time and the effect it had on profits. When the big cheese worked more hours, the company made more money. But it was *how* they used those hours that made all the difference. The extra profits were all attributable to scheduled activities with employees. Hours when the CEOs deviated from their plan didn't make the company an extra nickel.

So a plan is vital if you want to be successful and happy. What you'll find next is a framework of steps for you to implement, starting *now*. But before we get into the specifics, it's important to remember one point: this is *your* plan. And the thing most likely to get in the way of it working is, well, you. Knee-jerk responses of "I can't do that" and "My boss will never let me" are what got you into this position in the first place. Not everyone can implement the following ideas exactly as written, but just dismissing the things that seem like a stretch is a mistake. Obey the spirit of the law even if you can't follow the letter. Simply put: try.

Another big mistake people make is looking at a list, seeing the things they already do, and saying, "I do that! I'm smart! I can close the book now." Reassuring yourself feels nice. But you're here to improve your life. Focus on the stuff in the plan that you *don't* do. Remember, emphasizing the negative can feel crummy, but it's the path to improvement. That's what the experts do.

You cannot balance your time if you don't know where it's going. Former Intel CEO Andy Grove once said, "To understand a company's strategy, look at what they actually do rather than what they say they will do." Write down where each hour goes as it happens. Don't rely on your fallible memory. Do this for a week. Where are your activities taking you? Is it where you want to go? Note: this will be depressing. I assure you, you're wasting more time than you think. Beyond that, note which hours are contributing to which of the big four:

1. HAPPINESS = ENJOYING
2. ACHIEVEMENT = WINNING
3. SIGNIFICANCE = COUNTING (TO OTHERS)
4. LEGACY = EXTENDING

Or is that hour going in the "None of the above" bucket?

To improve how you use your time, take a lesson from criminology. To reduce crime in a city, tracking people isn't nearly as effective as looking at geography. Researchers discovered that half of crimes happen in just 5 percent of the city. This is called "hot spot" policing. Giving those few areas twice the number of police patrols cut crime in half in the hot spots and reduced citywide emergency calls by 6 to 13 percent.

So look for hot spots in your schedule. When do you waste the most time? When do you overdo one of the big four at the expense of another? You'll get more bang for your buck changing your routines around these hot spots than by a vague notion of "working less" or "trying to spend more time with the family." By the same token, look for trends that are working. When do you get disproportionate results? Early morning or late evening? At home or at the office? Try to make those moments more consistent.

Remember, you cannot maximize two things that are both dependent on the same resource: time. You also don't want to eliminate any categories with a sequencing or collapsing strategy. You want the balance of the big four that works for you. Make a decision on how much time you want to allot to each per week. You can revise it later, but you need an answer now. Seriously, write it down. I'll wait. *(Author hums softly to himself.)* Once you hit the number of hours in one category, address the hot spots in another.

As we talked about in the grit chapter, turning things into a game can make tricky problems more fun and engaging. Renowned venture capitalist Vinod Khosla certainly stays on top of how well his investments are doing, but he also has had his assistant record how many times a month he has dinner with his family. Coming up with a clever metric that works for you can make all the difference. Kevin Bolen, managing director of Strategic Investments and Growth Initiatives at KPMG, wanted more time with his wife and two sons. His main hot spot was traveling for work. So he focused on *losing* his platinum status on all his frequent-flier accounts. That became his goal. He got fewer free flights and perks, but it became a great barometer for how successful his work–life balance efforts were.

TALK TO YOUR BOSS

Some will say they just don't have the latitude to make big changes. Their boss won't let them. If you really want a better work–life balance, don't make assumptions. Sit down with your boss and actually discuss it. No, you don't say "Hey, I want to work less." Ask your boss for a clear idea of your role and their expectations, and whether this or that change would really be an issue. You'll probably be surprised by the answer, especially if you think about their needs and try to make it a win-win. Ask for an estimate of how much time they want you doing "shallow work," like responding to emails and sitting in meetings, and how much they want you cranking on "deep work" that really produces results. Just having this conversation can drop your stress levels. A study in the *Journal of Occupational Health Psychology* showed that getting more clarity about what you're expected to do reduces strain when work demands are high. It's easier to make the right decisions and not worry.

This chat will be good for the boss too, whether they realize it or not. The *Harvard Business Review* detailed a strategy called "active partnering" in which employees and managers disclosed what they wanted to achieve personally and professionally. A study of 473 executives showed that after a year of active partnering, 62 who wanted to leave the firm decided to stick around. A number of them even got promoted.

You'll want to have more of these conversations over time as you tweak your plan, but in all likelihood your boss will appreciate it. Proactive employees who have plans, ask about priorities, and try to head off problems are valuable. The people the boss has to come to after the fact to correct errors are the real difficult ones. And when you produce results, you'll get more latitude. More latitude means more freedom and control to execute your plan. Handle it right and it's an upward spiral for everyone.

You know your troublesome hot spots and what gets you dispro-portionate results. You're allotting hours to all of the big four, and you've gotten direction and approval from your boss. Now you can really make a difference . . .

TO-DO LISTS ARE EVIL. SCHEDULE EVERYTHING.

Georgetown University professor Cal Newport is the Genghis Khan of productivity. And Cal thinks to-do lists are the devil's work. Because the lists don't give any consideration to time. Ever wonder why you never seem to get to the bottom of that list? You can easily list twenty-eight hours worth of activities for a twenty-four-hour day. You need to be realistic about what you can get done in the time you have. The only way to do that is to schedule things on a calendar instead of making an endless list.

Decide when you want to leave work and you'll know how many hours you have. Slot in what you need to get done by priority. Cal calls this "fixed schedule productivity." You need boundaries if you want work–life balance. This forces you to be efficient. By setting a deadline of six P.M. and then scheduling tasks, you can get control over that hurricane of duties, and you can be realistic instead of shocked by what is never going to happen.

Most of us use our calendars all wrong: we don't schedule work; we schedule interruptions. Meetings get scheduled. Phone calls get scheduled. Doctor appointments get scheduled. You know what often doesn't get scheduled? *Real work.* All those other things are distractions. Often, they're other people's work. But they get dedicated blocks of time and your real work becomes an orphan. If real work is the stuff that affects the bottom line, the stuff that gets you noticed, the thing that earns you raises and gets you singled out for promotion, well, let me utter blasphemy and suggest that maybe it deserves a little dedicated time too.

Also, at least an hour a day, preferably in the morning, needs to be "protected time." This is an hour every day when you get real work done without interruption. Approach this concept as if it were a religious ritual. This hour is inviolate. Emails, meetings, and phone calls are often just "shallow work." You want to use this hour for what Cal calls "deep work." One hour when you will actually move things forward instead of just treading water. Shallow work stops you from getting fired—but deep work is what gets you promoted. And you don't want this at the end of the day when it may get bumped. You want to be able to bring your full brainpower to the tasks that matter. Research shows that two and a half to four hours after waking is when your brain is sharpest. Do you want to waste that on a conference call or a staff meeting?

What if you're totally overwhelmed at the office? If you never get a break from interruptions, then do your protected time at home for an hour before work. Peter Drucker cites a Swedish study of twelve executives that showed they literally could not work twenty minutes without being interrupted. The only one who was able to make thoughtful decisions was the one who spent ninety minutes working from home before entering the maelstrom of the office.

Planning out every day so rigorously is a pain at first but it works. For extra credit, you may want to start planning out your free time too. Before you recoil in horror at the thought, I've got some data for you. A study of 403 people in the *Journal of Happiness Studies* showed that managing your free time is associated with higher quality of life. What was fascinating was that increasing people's free time had no effect on their happiness, but scheduling that time in advance made all the difference. As we discussed earlier, we often don't use our time off wisely—we do what is easy instead of what makes us happy. By taking some time to plan, you can make it much more likely you'll really have fun instead of being a couch potato.

So scheduling everything and using protected time can make sure the important stuff gets done. But I know what you're thinking: all that shallow work isn't going away. A good way to deal with the busy work is in "batches." Rather than reactively living in your inbox, schedule a few intervals when you process emails, return phone calls, and shuffle the papers that need shuffling. After that session is over, turn off notifications, silence the phone, and get back to important stuff. Three batches a day works for me, but a job that requires frequent interaction may need more. The point is to be able to control and schedule these periods as much as possible so they don't creep into the time you're doing deep work. We got to the moon and built the pyramids without email and Facebook. You can go a couple of hours without checking them. What if your boss demands quick replies? Set up an email filter so you only get notifications from the head honcho or whoever else really matters. The rest can wait.

There's one more scheduling item you need to keep in mind to make sure you don't undo all the good you've accomplished so far: learn to say no. If you get rid of unnecessary activities, schedule everything, use protected time, and batch busy work but you can't stop people from piling unimportant tasks on your desk, you'll forever be mired in the shallows. You have your priorities from your boss and you'll align your tasks with how many hours you actually have in the day. If something doesn't have priority and there's just not time for it, you need to say no. To quote Warren Buffett, "The difference between successful people and very successful people is that very successful people say no to almost everything."

CONTROL YOUR CONTEXT

It matters. More than you think. It influences your decisions even when you don't realize it. When I spoke to Duke professor Dan Ariely he said:

One of the big lessons from social science in the last forty years is that environment matters. If you go to a buffet and the buffet is organized in one way, you will eat one thing. If it's organized in a different way, you'll eat different things. We think that we make decisions on our own, but the environment influences us to a great degree. Because of that we need to think about how to change our environment.

We can't control our environment everywhere we go, of course, but we have more control than we usually choose to exercise. Distractions literally make you stupid. Students whose classroom was situated near a noisy railroad line ended up academically a full year behind students with a quiet classroom. When the noise was dampened, the performance difference vanished. Offices aren't much different. Research shows that the most productive computer programmers have one thing in common. It's not experience, salary, or hours spent on a project. They had employers who gave them an environment free from distraction.

This is where you can actually use being reactive to your advantage. Shawn Achor recommends the "twenty second rule." Make the things you should do twenty seconds easier to start and make the things you shouldn't be doing twenty seconds harder. Sounds tiny but it makes a big difference. By rearranging your workspace so temptations aren't visible, you can trick yourself into making better choices. Ariely told me of a simple study done at Google's New York office. Instead of putting M&M's out in the open, they put them in containers. No big deal. What was the result? People ate three million fewer of them in a single month. So close that web browser. Charge your phone on the other side of the room.

I know controlling your environment can be hard. Shared workspaces, open-plan offices, chatty colleagues, and bosses that look over your shoulder. This is why I recommend a simple solution for at least part of the day: hide. Book a conference room and work from there. Not only will you be distraction-free, but you'll probably be more creative. Stanford professors Jeffrey Pfeffer and Bob Sutton note that "a large body of research shows that the more that authority figures hang around, the more questions they ask, and especially the more feedback they give their people, the less creative the work will be. Why? Because doing creative work entails constant setbacks and failure, and people want to succeed when the boss is watching—which means doing proven, less creative things that are sure to work."

END THE DAY RIGHT—AND ON TIME

You used "fixed schedule productivity," right? You decided when you wanted to leave work and arranged your schedule around that. Good, because Leslie Perlow said the key to getting those work–life balance results is to impose a "strict time-off mechanism." You want to know when you're leaving the office so you can make sure you're adding to the buckets of enjoying, winning, counting, and extending—not just working, working, and working.

Unless you want to hate your job, how you end the day matters a lot more than you might think. To explain, I need to talk to you about getting things shoved in your butt. Yes, literally getting things shoved in your butt. Nobel Laureate Daniel Kahneman and Daniel Redelmeier looked at how much pain people remembered after colonoscopies. It turns out that how long the procedures lasted and the average amount of pain didn't influence people's recollections. What really seemed to matter was the peak amount of discomfort and how it ended. A longer colonoscopy with a higher average amount of pain but a low peak and a gentle ending was remembered as less uncomfortable. Meanwhile, a quick one with a low average but a sharp peak and an unpleasant conclusion was remembered as being far worse. Whether it's arguments with your spouse or the last lines of a Hollywood movie, endings matter. So take the time to end the day well. Those last moments at the office every day loom large in terms of how you feel about your job.

Cal Newport recommends a "shutdown ritual" in which you take the time to close out the day's business and prepare for tomorrow. Research shows that writing down the things you need to take care of tomorrow can settle your brain and help you relax. As neuroscientist Daniel J. Levitin explains, when you're concerned about something and your grey matter is afraid you may forget, it engages a cluster of brain regions referred to as the "rehearsal loop." And you keep worrying and worrying. Writing your thoughts down and making a plan for tomorrow switches this off.

Then get yourself some downtime. What are the best ways to destress? It's far better to engage in a hobby or spend time with friends. Research shows that weekends are great because it's the extra time with the people you care about. You get an average of 1.7 extra hours of friend time on the weekend, and this creates a happiness boost. And don't neglect sleep. You don't want to start hallucinating that you're a football star.

Now that you have your rough plan, write it down. (Genghis Khan couldn't do that, but you can.) Research by Roy Baumeister shows not only can this help you achieve your goals but it also stops your brain from continuing to obsess about stuff when it's time to relax.

Your plan won't be perfect right out of the gate. You'll screw up. It's okay. Don't forget the self-compassion. Forgiving yourself both makes you feel better and prevents procrastination. A study of 119 students showed that those who forgave themselves for procrastinating on studying for one test subsequently procrastinated less on a second test. They felt better, and rather than beating themselves up, they were able to move on and perform better.

As you see what works and what doesn't, tweak your plan. Which of the big four isn't getting enough hours? Adjust until you're closer to the balance you want. This method of tracking, reviewing, and improving is how Peter Drucker says you can get where you want to go. A plan will move you a lot closer to all-around life success.

Currently on this planet, 0.5 percent of all men are one of Genghis Khan's descendants. That's one in two hundred. So by, um, *many* standards he was successful. He had a plan. You don't need to conquer the world, literally or metaphorically. "Good enough" is good enough if you keep the big four in mind.

Steven Jay Ross, who helped build the TimeWarner corporation, put it best:

> There are three categories of people—the person who goes into the office, puts his feet up on his desk, and dreams for twelve hours; the person who arrives at five A.M. and works sixteen hours, never once stopping to dream; and the person who puts his feet up, dreams for one hour, then does something about those dreams.

We've covered a lot in these six chapters. To put it all in perspective, let's see just how bad things can possibly get—and the heights of how great we can make them if we try.

What Makes a Successful Life?

Brace yourself. These next words are going to sting a bit.

"I hope you die."

That's a hard thing to hear. Especially when a mother says them to a son. But her Martin was gone. He lay in bed, motionless. Brain dead. She just couldn't bear to see him this way anymore.

Martin's parents took care of him every day, his father waking up every two hours at night to move him so he did not get bedsores. Caring for him had placed a tremendous strain on the family. They continued to tend to the body that had been their son because they loved him, even though the doctors said he would never recover. He had been like this for years.

But Martin wasn't brain-dead. In fact, he was completely aware. Martin was "locked in"— cognizant of the world around him but unable to move. He had heard what his mother said. He just had no way to signal it to her.

Sure, the words hurt, but not as much as you might think. After all, he wished he was dead too. She didn't hate him. She had watched her energetic son vanish into this living corpse, and she wanted the horrible state he was in to finally end. Martin wasn't angry with her for saying it. He felt compassion.

Ever since a mysterious illness struck him at age twelve he had been bedridden and assumed brain dead. But a few years later he had woken up inside a body he was no longer able to control, and for eleven unfathomably long years this was his life.

Having your mother wish you would die is awful, but it was still attention. Which was unique because long ago the entire world had started seeing him as an inanimate object. He was something to be dealt with, moved, arranged, and cleaned but not interacted with. He wasn't a person. At best he was a persistent burden.

People act differently when they don't think you're human anymore. They would pick their nose and eat it in front of him. They check their image in a mirror over and over again without fear of being called a narcissist. They let out that big fart they've been holding in while with "real" people.

What was constant and nearly overwhelming was Martin's feeling of powerlessness. Everything in his life was decided for him. Whether he ate or not. Whether he lay on his left side or his right side. Caretakers at the hospital were callous with him. And on numerous occasions he was outright abused. But he could do nothing and say nothing.

Ever been alone at night in bed with frightening thoughts? This was his life all the time. The thoughts were all he had. *You are powerless.* It was like a song you can't get out of your head. *You are alone.* There was no hope.

Out of sheer survival, to not go insane, Martin inadvertently became a Zen master. He detached from his thoughts. Without any training, he discovered mindfulness. Hours or days or even weeks could go by in an instant because he had removed himself from life, from his thoughts. But the void was not nirvana. It was blackness. There was no bad, but there was no hope either. He did allow one thought to occasionally creep in. The same one his mother had expressed: *I hope I die.*

Occasionally the world would intrude. It would grab him and yank him back into reality. What did this most often? What would become his nemesis?

Barney.

That insufferable purple dinosaur and his relentlessly cheery singing on the television was always so happy it only served to remind Martin how miserable he was. Powerless to change the channel or smash the TV, he listened to it over and over.

Martin couldn't escape the world, so he chose a different path. He began to escape into his imagination. He dreamed about all the wonderful things that could happen, not bound by the laws of physics or reality and certainly not by the stubborn body that ignored his every command. He fantasized about all the things he wanted from life. And it passed the time.

Then two things changed. In his midtwenties he slowly regained some control of his body; he could grasp things with his hands. And a nurse, tracking his eye movements, started to believe he might still be in there. She encouraged the doctors to test him again. And they realized he *was* in there.

Things then changed very quickly. With a joystick and a computer he could communicate. With a wheelchair he could move. Martin felt extraordinary relief. But, as the podcast *Invisibilia* notes, he was not complacent. Not after all that dreaming. He started chasing those dreams.

Two years later he had a job at an office. But that wasn't enough. Having always had a knack for things mechanical, he became a freelance web designer. Then he started his own company.

He went to college.

He wrote a memoir of his experiences, *Ghost Boy*, which was roundly praised.

He learned to drive a car.

And in 2009 he was no longer alone. At thirty-three, he got married to Joanna, a friend of his sister's whom he'd met over Skype. For over a decade he couldn't move his face. Now his face hurt from smiling too much.

Interviewed by the BBC, he said:

> Success is strange in that it cultivates more success. Once I had achieved something it encouraged me to try even harder. It expanded my perception of what was possible. If I could do this, then what else could I do?

Martin is still in a wheelchair and cannot speak without computer assistance. But he's educated, successful, and happily married. He has a good life. To think how much further he had to go to get there than any of us boggles the mind.

Few people ever face the challenges Martin Pistorius did, but all of us often feel trapped in a tough situation. Almost "locked in." We try to mentally escape or to just let the world go by, but just as Steven Jay Ross said, it's by dreaming and then doing something about those dreams that we can achieve success. In fact, it's the only way we can.

Success comes in many forms. Some success is incredibly impressive, some simple and quaint, others almost absurd. We get hung up on the heights of success we see in the media and forget that it's our personal definition of success that matters. And you can achieve that.

Don't worry about innate talent. Benjamin Bloom's research on successful people—from sculptors to Olympians to mathematicians—revealed that talent usually doesn't control what you can achieve in life. Bloom said, "After forty years of intensive research on school learning in the United States as well as abroad, my major conclusion is: What any person in the world can learn, almost all persons can learn, if provided with the appropriate prior and current conditions of learning."

What's holding you back from your personal definition of success? In most cases, there is nothing you cannot overcome with time and effort. When I think about the limits of success, my mind usually turns to Scrabble. Nigel Richards is the greatest Scrabble player to ever live. He's the French Scrabble champion. The website FiveThirtyEight.com reports, "The difference between his official rating and the second-place player's is about the same as the difference between second place and 20th." He didn't even start playing the game until he was twenty-eight. The first time he competed in a national tournament, he won. Nobody plays French Scrabble better than he does. Oh, one more thing I should mention . . .

Nigel Richards doesn't speak French.

To give his acceptance speech, he needed a translator. After dominating the English Scrabble world for years, he turned his attention to the Gallic language and just started memorizing words. He doesn't know what they mean. And French Scrabble is harder than North American Scrabble because it has almost two hundred thousand more words. He wanted to be the French champion and he didn't let not speaking French hold him back.

We've talked about a lot of things related to success in this book, from how the perils of mountain climbing illustrate the power of grit to Nobel Prize winners doing research on the happiness implications of getting stuff shoved in your butt. Let's end things simply (and with less discomfort than a colonoscopy).

What's the most important thing to remember when it comes to success?

One word: alignment.

Success is not the result of any single quality; it's about alignment between who you are and where you choose to be. The right skill in the right role. A good person surrounded by other good people. A story that connects you with the world in a way that keeps you going. A network that helps you, and a job that leverages your natural introversion or extroversion. A level of confidence that keeps you going while learning and forgiving yourself for the inevitable failures. A balance between the big four that creates a well-rounded life with no regrets.

As Howard Stevenson and Laura Nash write about their study of successful people who struggled for balance:

> When you align your values with the employment of your signature skills in a context that reinforces these same strengths, you create a powerful and emotionally engaging force for achievement, significance, happiness, and legacy. When your internal choice of success goals aligns with the group in which you operate, the rewards are even higher.

How do you find alignment? As the Oracle at Delphi said so long ago, "Know thyself." What are your intensifiers? Are you a Giver, a Taker or a Matcher? Are you more introverted or more extroverted? Underconfident or overconfident? Which of the big four do you naturally fulfill and which do you consistently neglect?

Then align those qualities with the world around you. Pick the right pond. Find a job that leverages your intensifiers. Create a story that keeps you going. Make little bets that expand your horizons. Use WOOP to turn your dreams into realities.

What's the most important type of alignment? Being connected to a group of friends and loved ones who help you become the person you want to be. Financial success is great, but to have a successful life we need happiness. Career success doesn't always make us happy, but the research shows that happiness does bring success.

Your relationships are what bring you happiness. Researcher and bestselling author Shawn Achor reports, "In a study I performed on 1,600 Harvard students in 2007, I found that there was a 0.7 correlation between perceived social support and happiness. This is higher than the connection between smoking and cancer." How much money would it take to increase your happiness as much as a good social life does? Data from the *Journal of Socio-Economics* says you'd have to earn an extra $121,000 a year.

What happens when you look at the big picture? When you are on your deathbed, what will success mean? One researcher found out. George Valliant led the Grant Study, which followed a group of men for their entire lives, from college until their death. What did he say to sum up their findings from this decades-long research? "The only thing that really matters in life are your relationships to other people."

Is all this relationship and love stuff too warm and fuzzy for your success aspirations? It shouldn't be. Valliant and his team scored the subjects in terms of their relationships at age forty-seven (how long had they been married, did they have kids, were they close to them, how many friends did they have). The results nearly matched how successful the men had been in their careers. The relationship score was like a crystal ball for how much money they made and how impressive their careers were. The men who scored highest made more than twice as much money as those who scored lowest. Was this effect and not cause? That's unlikely. The guys who were the most empathic earned two and half times what the most narcissistic did.

Those relationships not only improve success; they can save your life. Remember Spencer Glendon and his health issues? I mentioned he received a liver transplant. When he first fell seriously ill, the doctors knew he might eventually need a new liver and his friends were all tested to see if any were a match. (The liver is unique in that it regenerates; so both donor and recipient will eventually grow a full organ with time.) His friend Carl was a good match. Years went by and Spencer's health continued to decline. The doctors said they had run out of options. Spencer would require a transplant.

Carl didn't merely volunteer. He revealed that ever since the positive donor match he had quietly been on a dedicated regimen of diet and exercise. He'd spent the past few years getting himself into peak shape so that when the time came, he could give Spencer the healthiest liver possible. Because of Carl's sneaky plan, both friends are healthy and happy today. I hope you and I are lucky enough to have friends like Carl.

If you align your knowledge of yourself with your career and the people around you, it can form an upward spiral that leads to not only career success but also happiness and fulfillment.

So our journey has come to a close. You've seen crazy cyclists, people who don't feel pain and fear, oddball pianists, serial killers, pirates, prison gangs, Navy SEALs, Toronto raccoons, Shaolin monks, how long you can be Batman, Erdös numbers, Newton and Einstein, Ted Williams and Spider-Man, radar wars between Harvard and MIT, ghost armies and hostage negotiators, the emperor of the United States (may he rest in peace), confident chess computers, Japanese wrestlers with orange hair, Genghis Khan, and a guy who flew around the world just to say "Thanks." I appreciate you taking the time to read all this insanity and going on this trip with me.

In this book, I wanted to get to the truth about what research and great stories show really brings success in life. Did I succeed? Well, that's up to you. I don't have all the answers. I'm just an introverted orchid, hopeful monster, unfiltered leader, and Matcher who would like to be a Giver who is often overconfident and needs to work on his self-compassion. But I think I've picked the right pond and aligned myself with some wonderful friends. That's good enough for me. Take the time to figure out what you are and find the right body of water for you.

If you want to learn more, visit my website: Bakadesuyo.com. I have additional materials for you there. Just like that problematic word "networking," your lizard brain doesn't really understand the concept of author or writer guy, so let's stick to what it does know: I'm your friend. Feel free to email me if you want to say hi. I'm at ebarker@ucla.edu.

I wish you great success.

Acknowledgments

Robert DeNiro told me to never name drop.

—BOB WAGNER

Walter Green flew around the world to say thanks. The least I can do is express my gratitude to a few folks who helped get this book in your hands—many by keeping the author sane during its creation.

Everyone will tell you how hard it is to write a book but most don't mention how lonely it is. I could not have done it without these fine people:

Uber-agent Jim Levine and my editors Hilary Lawson and Genoveva Llosa.

All the people featured in the book for sharing their stories, research, and ideas.

Once again, to my parents, without whom I would not be possible.

All the wonderful people who read my blog. (Yeah, there will be an email on Sunday.)

Jason Hallock, who is the best Wilson that House could ever hope for.

Don Elmore. Without Lucius Fox, there is no Batman.

Tyler Cowen, who told the interwebz about this nobody blogger they should check out.

Andrew Kevin Walker, Julie Durk, and Drew Holmes for getting me out of the house and inducting me into "The Rally Pals."

Friends and unindicted co-conspirators: Debbie "Couchfire" Rosa, Nick Krasney, Mike Goode, Raghu Manavalan, and Chris Voss.

My cousin Ryan, who is the closest thing to a brother I will ever have. My aunt Clare, whose birthday cards to a starving writer always included a check. And my aunt Barbara who sent me care packages in college.

For advice and counsel on the process of writing a book: Dan Pink, Adam Grant, David Epstein, Shane Snow, John Richardson, and Sheila Heen.

The Sedona Illuminati: James Clear, Ryan Holiday, Josh Kaufman, Steve Kamb, Shane Parrish, Nir Eyal, and Tim Urban.

The lovely people who supported my semi-insane endeavors: Bob Radin, Paulo Coelho, Chris Yeh, Jennifer Aaker, and Detective Jeff Thompson (who asked me if I'd like to come train with the NYPD Hostage Negotiation Team—like I'm gonna say no to that.)

And to my girlfriend junior year in college who laughed in my face when I said I wanted to be a writer. Thanks for the motivation.

References

A man will turn over half a library to make one book.

—SAMUEL JOHNSON

INTRODUCTION: WHAT REALLY PRODUCES SUCCESS?

Auerbach, Stephen. *Bicycle Dreams.* Auerfilms, 2009. Film.

Coyle, Daniel. "That Which Does Not Kill Me Makes Me Stranger." *New York Times,* February 5, 2006. www.nytimes.com/2006/02/05/sports/playmagazine/05robicpm.html?pagewanted=all&_r=0.

"Limits of the Body." *Radiolab.* Season 7, episode 3. Radio broadcast, 32:07. Aired April 16, 2010. www.radiolab.org/story/91710-limits-of-the-body/.

Snyder, Amy. *Hell on Two Wheels.* Chicago: Triumph Books, 2011.

CHAPTER 1: SHOULD WE PLAY IT SAFE AND DO WHAT WE'RE TOLD IF WE WANT TO SUCCEED?

Alexander, Susan. "How Neil Young Became the First Artist to Get Sued for Not Being Himself." Lateral Action. http://lateralaction.com/articles/neil-young/.

Altman, Sam. "Lecture 9: How to Raise Money (Marc Andreessen, Ron Conway, and Parker Conrad)." How to Start a Startup. Stanford University class lecture. http://startupclass.samaltman.com/courses/lec09/.

Arnold, Karen D. *Lives of Promise.* San Francisco: Jossey-Bass, 1995.

Barnett, J. H., C. H. Salmond, P. B. Jones, and B. J. Sahakian. "Cognitive Reserve in Neuropsychiatry." *Psychological Medicine* 36, no. 08 (2006): 1053–64. http://dx.doi.org/10.1017/S0033291706007501.

Bazzana, Kevin. *Wondrous Strange.* Toronto: McClelland and Stewart, 2010.

Belsky, Jay, Charles R. Jonassaint, Michael Pluess, Michael Vicente Stanton, B. H. Brummett, and R. B. Williams. "Vulnerability Genes or Plasticity Genes?" *Molecular Psychiatry* 14, no. 8 (2009): 746–54. doi:10.1038/mp.2009.44.

Chambliss, Daniel F. "The Mundanity of Excellence: An Ethnographic Report on

Stratification and Olympic Swimmers." *Sociological Theory* 7, no. 1 (Spring 1989): 70–86. doi:10.2307/202063.

Christian, Brian. *The Most Human Human*. New York: Anchor, 2011.

"Congenital Insensitivity to Pain." NIH, U.S. National Library of Medicine. Last modified November 2012. https://ghr.nlm.nih.gov/condition/congenital-insensitivity-to-pain.

Coryell, W., J. Endicott, Monika Keller, N. Andreasen, W. Grove, R. M. A. Hirschfeld, and W. Scheftner. "Bipolar Affective Disorder and High Achievement: A Familial Association." *American Journal of Psychiatry* 146, no. 8 (1989): 983–88. doi:10.1176/ajp.146.8.983.

Dobbs, David. "Can Genes Send You High or Low? The Orchid Hypothesis A-bloom." DavidDobbs.net. June 8, 2013. http://daviddobbs.net/smoothpebbles/orchids-dandelions-abloom-best-of-wired-nc-10/.

Dobbs, David. "The Science of Success." *The Atlantic,* December 2009. www.theatlantic.com/magazine/archive/2009/12/the-science-of-success/307761/.

Ellis, Bruce J., and W. Thomas Boyce. "Biological Sensitivity to Context." *Current Directions in Psychological Science* 17, no. 3 (2008): 183–87. doi:10.1111/j.1467-8721.2008.00571.x.

El-Naggar, Mona. "In Lieu of Money, Toyota Donates Efficiency to New York Charity." *New York Times,* July 26, 2013. www.nytimes.com/2013/07/27/nyregion/in-lieu-of-money-toyota-donates-efficiency-to-new-york-charity.html.

Gaskin, Darrell J., and Patrick Richard. "Appendix C: The Economic Costs of Pain in the United States," from *Relieving Pain in America*. Institute of Medicine (U.S.) Committee on Advancing Pain Research, Care, and Education. Washington, DC: National Academies Press, 2011. www.ncbi.nlm.nih.gov/books/NBK92521/.

Gino, Francesca, and Dan Ariely. "The Dark Side of Creativity: Original Thinkers Can Be More Dishonest." *Journal of Personality and Social Psychology* 102, no. 3 (2012): 445–59. doi:10.1037/a0026406.

Götz, Karl Otto, and Karin Götz. "Personality Characteristics of Successful Artists." *Perceptual and Motor Skills* 49, no. 3 (December 1979): 919–24. doi:10.2466/pms.1979.49.3.919.

Gould, Stephen Jay. "Return of the Hopeful Monster." The Unofficial Stephen Jay Gould Archive. www.stephenjaygould.org/library/gould_hopeful-monsters.html.

Haynes, V. Dion. "Being at Head of Class Isn't Same as Having Inside Track on Life." *Chicago Tribune,* June 11, 1995. http://articles.chicagotribune.com/1995-06-11/news/9506110252_1_valedictorians-boston-college-achievers.

Heckert, Justin. "The Hazards of Growing Up Painlessly." *New York Times Magazine,* November 15, 2012. www.nytimes.com/2012/11/18/magazine/ashlyn-blocker-feels-no-pain.html?pagewanted=all.

Herbert, Wray. "On the Trail of the Orchid Child." *Scientific American,* November 1, 2011. www.scientificamerican.com/article/on-the-trail-of-the-orchid-child/.

Howe, Sandra. "Valedictorians Don't Stay at the Head of the Class, Says Education

Researcher." *Boston College Chronicle* 4, no. 5 (1995). www.bc.edu/bc_org/rvp/pubaf/chronicle/v4/N2/ARNOLD.html.

Inouye, Dane. "Congenital Insensitivity to Pain with Anhidrosis." *Hohonu* 6 (2008). http://hilo.hawaii.edu/academics/hohonu/documents/Vol06x04CongenitalInsensitivitytoPainwithAnhidrosis.pdf.

Interview with Gautam Mukunda by author. "Gautam Mukunda of Harvard Explains Secret to Being a Better Leader." *Barking Up the Wrong Tree* (blog). March 18, 2013. www.bakadesuyo.com/2013/03/interview-harvard-business-school-professor-gautam-mukunda-teaches-secrets-leader/.

Interview with Shawn Achor by author. "Be More Successful: New Harvard Research Reveals a Fun Way to Do It." *Barking Up the Wrong Tree* (blog). September 28, 2014. www.bakadesuyo.com/2014/09/be-more-successful/.

Johnson, Steven. *Where Good Ideas Come From.* New York: Riverhead Books, 2011.

Judson, Olivia. "The Monster Is Back, and It's Hopeful." Opinionator. *New York Times,* January 22, 2008. http://opinionator.blogs.nytimes.com/2008/01/22/the-monster-is-back-and-its-hopeful/.

Lacy, Susan. "Inventing David Geffen." *American Masters.* TV documentary, 1:55:00. Aired November 20, 2012.

Levine, Mark. "The Age of Michael Phelps." *New York Times,* August 5, 2008. www.nytimes.com/2008/08/05/sports/05iht-05phelps.15022548.html?_r=0.

Lewis, Randy. "Listen to What Got Him Sued." *Los Angeles Times,* June 15, 2011. http://articles.latimes.com/2011/jun/15/entertainment/la-et-neil-young-treasure-20110615.

McMenamin, Brigid. "Tyranny of the Diploma." *Forbes,* December 28, 1998. www.forbes.com/free_forbes/1998/1228/6214104a.html.

Mueller, Jennifer S., Jack Goncalo, and Dishan Kamdar. "Recognizing Creative Leadership: Can Creative Idea Expression Negatively Relate to Perceptions of Leadership Potential?" Cornell University, School of Industrial and Labor Relations. 2010. http://digitalcommons.ilr.cornell.edu/articles/340/.

Mukunda, Gautam. *Indispensable.* Boston: Harvard Business Review Press, 2012. Kindle Edition.

Nagasako, Elna M., Anne Louise Oaklander, and Robert H. Dworkin. "Congenital Insensitivity to Pain: An Update." *Pain* 101, no. 3 (2003): 213–19. doi:10.1016/S0304-3959(02)00482-7.

Papageorge, Nicholas W., Victor Ronda, and Yu Zheng. "The Economic Value of Breaking Bad Misbehavior, Schooling, and the Labor Market." Social Science Research Network. June 1, 2016. http://dx.doi.org/10.2139/ssrn.2503293.

Pete, Steven. "Congenital Analgesia: The Agony of Feeling No Pain." BBC News Magazine. July 17, 2012. www.bbc.com/news/magazine-18713585.

Pressfield, Steven. "Suing Neil Young." StevenPressfield.com. July 31, 2013. www.stevenpressfield.com/2013/07/suing-neil-young/.

Rao, Hayagreeva, Robert Sutton, and Allen P. Webb. "Innovation Lessons from Pixar: An Interview with Oscar-Winning Director Brad Bird." *McKinsey Quarterly,* April 2008. www.mckinsey.com/business-functions/strategy-and-corporate-finance/our-insights/innovation-lessons-from-pixar-an-interview-with-oscar-winning-director-brad-bird.

Rubin, Shira. "The Israeli Army Unit That Recruits Teens with Autism." *The Atlantic,* January 6, 2016. www.theatlantic.com/health/archive/2016/01/israeli-army-autism/422850/.

Silvia, Paul J., James C. Kaufman, Roni Reiter-Palmon, and Benjamin Wigert. "Cantankerous Creativity: Honesty–Humility, Agreeableness, and the HEXACO Structure of Creative Achievement." *Personality and Individual Differences* 51, no. 5 (2011): 687–89. doi:10.1016/j.paid.2011.06.011.

Simonton, Dean Keith. *Greatness.* New York: Guilford Press, 1994.

Simonton, Dean Keith. "The Mad-Genius Paradox: Can Creative People Be More Mentally Healthy but Highly Creative People More Mentally Ill?" *Perspectives on Psychological Science* 9, no. 5 (2014): 470–80. doi:10.1177/1745691614543973.

Simonton, Dean Keith. *The Wiley Handbook of Genius.* Hoboken, NJ: Wiley-Blackwell, 2014.

Sokolove, Michael. "Built to Swim." *New York Times Magazine,* August 8, 2004. www.nytimes.com/2004/08/08/magazine/built-to-swim.html.

Stanley, Thomas J. *The Millionaire Mind.* Kansas City, MO: Andrews McMeel, 2001.

Stein, Joel. "Thirteen Months of Working, Eating, and Sleeping at the Googleplex." *Bloomberg Businessweek,* July 22, 2015. www.bloomberg.com/news/features/2015-07-22/thirteen-months-of-working-eating-and-sleeping-at-the-googleplex.

Tough, Paul. *How Children Succeed.* Boston: Houghton Mifflin Harcourt, 2012.

Weeks, David, and Jamie James. *Eccentrics, A Study of Sanity and Strangeness.* New York: Villard, 1995.

Westby, Erik L., and V. L. Dawson. "Creativity: Asset or Burden in the Classroom?" *Creativity Research Journal* 8, no. 1 (1995): 1–10. doi:10.1207/s15326934crj0801_1.

CHAPTER 2: DO NICE GUYS FINISH LAST?

Axelrod, Robert. *The Evolution of Cooperation.* New York: Basic Books, 2006.

Bachman, W. "Nice Guys Finish First: A SYMLOG Analysis of U.S. Naval Commands." In *The SYMLOG Practitioner: Applications of Small Group Research.* Edited by R. B. Polley, A. P. Hare, and P. J. Stone. New York: Praeger, 1988, 60.

Baumeister, Roy F., Ellen Bratslavsky, Catrin Finkenauer, and Kathleen D. Vohs. "Bad Is Stronger than Good," *Review of General Psychology* 5, no. 4 (2001): 323–70. https://carlsonschool.umn.edu/file/49901/download?token=GoY7afXa.

Bernerth, Jeremy B., Shannon G. Taylor, Jack H. Walker, and Daniel S. Whitman. "An Empirical Investigation of Dispositional Antecedents and Performance-Related Outcomes of Credit Scores." *Journal of Applied Psychology* 97, no. 2 (2012): 469–78. http://dx.doi.org/10.1037/a0026055.

Blackburn, Keith, and Gonzalo F. Forgues-Puccio. "Why Is Corruption Less Harmful in Some Countries than in Others?" *Journal of Economic Behavior and Organization* 72, no. 3 (2009): 797–810. doi:10.1016/j.jebo.2009.08.009.

Bowden, Mark. "The Man Who Broke Atlantic City." *The Atlantic,* April 2012. www.theatlantic.com/magazine/archive/2012/04/the-man-who-broke-atlantic-city/308900/.

Butler, Jeffrey, Paola Giuliano, and Luigi Guiso. "The Right Amount of Trust." NBER Working Paper No. 15344, National Bureau of Economic Research, Cambridge, MA, September 2009. Revised June 2014. doi:10.3386/w15344.

Chan, Elaine, and Jaideep Sengupta. "Insincere Flattery Actually Works: A Dual Attitudes Perspective." *Journal of Marketing Research* 47, no. 1 (2010): 122–33. doi:http://dx.doi.org/10.1509/jmkr.47.1.122.

Cottrell, Catherine A., Steven L. Neuberg, and Norman P. Li. "What Do People Desire in Others? A Sociofunctional Perspective on the Importance of Different Valued Characteristics." *Journal of Personality and Social Psychology* 92, no. 2 (2007): 208–31. http://dx.doi.org/10.1037/0022-3514.92.2.208.

DeSteno, David. *The Truth About Trust.* New York: Penguin, 2014.

Dutton, Kevin. *The Wisdom of Psychopaths.* New York: Macmillan, 2010.

Falk, Armin, Ingo Menrath, Pablo Emilio Verde, and Johannes Siegrist. "Cardiovascular Consequences of Unfair Pay." IZA Discussion Paper No. 5720, Institute for the Study of Labor, Bonn, Germany, May 2011. http://repec.iza.org/dp5720.pdf.

Friedman, Howard S., and Leslie R. Martin. *The Longevity Project.* New York: Plume, 2012.

Gambetta, Diego. *Codes of the Underworld.* Princeton, NJ: Princeton Univ. Press, 2011.

Gino, Francesca, Shahar Ayal, and Dan Ariely. "Contagion and Differentiation in Unethical Behavior: The Effect of One Bad Apple on the Barrel." *Psychological Science* 20, no. 3 (2009): 393–98. doi:10.1111/j.1467-9280.2009.02306.x.

"The Good Show." *Radiolab.* Season 9, episode 1. Radio broadcast, 1:05:07. Aired December 14, 2010. www.radiolab.org/story/103951-the-good-show/.

Grant, Adam. *Give and Take.* New York: Penguin, 2013.

Helliwell, John F., and Haifang Huang. "Well-Being and Trust in the Workplace." *Journal of Happiness Studies* 12, no. 5 (2011): 747–67. doi:10.3386/w14589.

Ilan, Shahar. "Thou Shalt Not Be a Freier." *Haaretz,* January 28, 2007. www.haaretz.com/print-edition/opinion/thou-shalt-not-be-a-freier-1.211247.

Interview with Adam Grant by author. "Adam Grant Teaches You the Right Way to Give and Take." *Barking Up the Wrong Tree* (blog). April 9, 2013. www.bakadesuyo.com/2013/04/interview-wharton-business-school-professor-teaches-approach-give/.

Interview with Robert Cialdini by author. "Robert Cialdini Explains the Six Ways to Influence People—Interview." *Barking Up the Wrong Tree* (blog). June 3, 2013. www.bakadesuyo.com/2013/06/robert-cialdini-influence/.

Interview with Robert Sutton by author. "The Leadership Secret Steve Jobs and Mark

Zuckerberg Have in Common." *Barking Up the Wrong Tree* (blog). November 19, 2013. www.bakadesuyo.com/2013/11/scaling-up-excellence/.

James Jr., Harvey S. "Is the Just Man a Happy Man? An Empirical Study of the Relationship Between Ethics and Subjective Well-Being." *Kyklos* 64, no. 2 (2011): 193–212. doi:10.1111/j.1467-6435.2011.00502.x.

Kivimäki, Mika, Jane E. Ferrie, Eric Brunner, Jenny Head, Martin J. Shipley, Jussi Vahtera, and Michael G. Marmot. "Justice at Work and Reduced Risk of Coronary Heart Disease Among Employees." *Archives of Internal Medicine* 165, no. 19 (2005): 2245–51. doi:10.1001/archinte.165.19.2245.

Kordova, Shoshana. "Word of the Day Freier פראייר." *Haaretz,* January 14, 2013. www.haaretz.com/news/features/word-of-the-day/word-of-the-day-freier-1508-1512-1488-1497-1497-1512.premium-1.493882.

Lambert, Craig. "The Psyche on Automatic." *Harvard Magazine,* November–December 2010. http://harvardmagazine.com/2010/11/the-psyche-on-automatic?page=all.

Leeson , Peter T. "An arrgh chy: The Law and Economics of Pirate Organization." *Journal of Political Economy* 115, no. 6 (2007): 1049–94. doi:10.1086/526403.

Leeson, Peter T. *The Invisible Hook.* Princeton, NJ: Princeton Univ. Press, 2009.

Leeson, Peter T. "Pirational Choice: The Economics of Infamous Pirate Practices." *Journal of Economic Behavior and Organization* 76, no. 3 (2010): 497–510. doi:10.1016/j.jebo.2010.08.015.

Malhotra, Deepak. "How to Negotiate Your Job Offer—Prof. Deepak Malhotra (Harvard Business School)." YouTube video, 1:04:23. Posted November 20, 2012. www.youtube.com/watch?v=km2Hd_xgo9Q.

Markman, Art. "Are Successful People Nice?" *Harvard Business Review,* February 9, 2012. https://hbr.org/2012/02/are-successful-people-nice.

Marks, Michelle, and Crystal Harold. "Who Asks and Who Receives in Salary Negotiation." *Journal of Organizational Behavior* 32, no. 3 (2011): 371–94. doi:10.1002/job.671.

Miller, Marjorie. "It's a Sin to Be a Sucker in Israel." *Los Angeles Times,* July 25, 1997. http://articles.latimes.com/1997/jul/25/news/mn-16208.

Mogilner, Cassie, Zoë Chance, and Michael I. Norton. "Giving Time Gives You Time." *Psychological Science* 23, no. 10 (2012): 1233–38. doi:10.1177/0956797612442551.

Morrow, Lance. "Dr. Death." Books, *New York Times,* August 29, 1999. www.nytimes.com/books/99/08/29/reviews/990829.29morrowt.html.

Niven, David. *The 100 Simple Secrets of Successful People.* New York: HarperCollins, 2009.

Nowak, Martin, and Karl Sigmund. "A Strategy of Win-Stay, Lose-Shift That Outperforms Tit-for-Tat in the Prisoner's Dilemma Game." *Nature* 364 (1993): 56–58. doi:10.1038/364056a0.

Nowak, Martin, and Roger Highfield. *SuperCooperators.* New York: Free Press, 2012.

Nyberg, A., L. Alfredsson, T. Theorell, H. Westerlund, J. Vahtera, and M. Kivimäki. "Managerial Leadership and Ischaemic Heart Disease Among Employees: The

Swedish WOLF Study." *Occupational and Environmental Medicine* 66 (2009): 51–55. doi:10.1136/oem.2008.039362.

Pfeffer, Jeffrey. *Power*. New York: HarperBusiness, 2010.

Reuben, Ernesto, Paola Sapienza, and Luigi Zingales. "Is Mistrust Self-Fulfilling?" *Economics Letters* 104, no. 2 (2009): 89–91. http://ssrn.com/abstract=1951649.

Schnall, Simone, Jean Roper, and Daniel M. T. Fessler. "Elevation Leads to Altruistic Behavior." *Psychological Science* 21, no. 3 (2010): 315–20. doi:10.1177/0956797609359882.

Schwitzgebel, Eric. "Do Ethicists Steal More Books? More Data." *The Splintered Mind* (blog). December 08, 2006. http://schwitzsplinters.blogspot. com/2006/12/do-ethicists-steal-more-books-more-data.html.

Skarbek, David. *The Social Order of the Underworld*. Oxford: Oxford Univ. Press, 2014.

Smith, Pamela K., Nils B. Jostmann, Adam D. Galinsky, and Wilco W. van Dijk. "Lacking Power Impairs Executive Functions." *Psychological Science* 19 no. 5 (2008): 441–47. doi:10.1111/j.1467–9280.2008.02107.x.

Stewart, James B. *Blind Eye*. New York: Simon and Schuster, 2012.

Sutton, Robert I. *Good Boss, Bad Boss*. New York: Piatkus, 2010.

University of California, Berkeley. "Gossip Can Have Social and Psychological Benefits." Public release. January 17, 2012. www.eurekalert.org/pub_ releases/2012-01/uoc--gch011712.php.

University of Nebraska, Lincoln. "To Be Good, Sometimes Leaders Need to Be a Little Bad." Public release. October 19, 2010. www.eurekalert.org/pub_ releases/2010-10/uon-tbg101910.php.

Van Kleef, Gerben A., Astrid C. Homan, Catrin Finkenauer, Seval Gündemir, and Eftychia Stamkou. "Breaking the Rules to Rise to Power: How Norm Violators Gain Power in the Eyes of Others." *Social Psychological and Personality Science* 2, no. 5 (2011): 500–7. doi:10.1177/1948550611398416.

Veenhoven, R. "Healthy Happiness: Effects of Happiness on Physical Health and the Consequences for Preventive Health Care." *Journal of Happiness Studies* 9, no. 3 (2008): 449–69. doi:10.1007/s10902-006-9042-1.

Weiner, Eric. *Geography of Bliss*. New York: Twelve Books, 2008.

Wu, Long-Zeng, Frederick Hong-kit Yim, Ho Kwong Kwan, and Xiaomeng Zhang. "Coping with Workplace Ostracism: The Roles of Ingratiation and Political Skill in Employee Psychological Distress." *Journal of Management Studies* 49, no. 1 (2012): 178–99. doi:10.1111/j.1467-6486.2011.01017.x.

CHAPTER 3: DO QUITTERS NEVER WIN AND WINNERS NEVER QUIT?

Abramson, Leigh McMullan. "The Only Job with an Industry Devoted to Helping People Quit." *The Atlantic,* July 29, 2014. www.theatlantic.com/business/ archive/2014/07/the-only-job-with-an-industry-devoted-to-helping-people-quit/375199/.

"The Acceptance Prophecy: How You Control Who Likes You." *Psyblog,* August 27, 2009. www.spring.org.uk/2009/08/the-acceptance-prophesy-how-you-control-who-likes-you.php.

Akil II, Bakari. "How the Navy SEALs Increased Passing Rates." *Psychology Today,* November 09, 2009. www.psychologytoday.com/blog/communication-central/200911/how-the-navy-seals-increased-passing-rates.

Albert Einstein College of Medicine. "'Personality Genes' May Help Account for Longevity." News release. May 24, 2012. http://www.einstein.yu.edu/news/releases/798/personality-genes-may-help-account-for-longevity/.

Alloy, Lauren B., and Lyn Y. Abramson. "Judgment of Contingency in Depressed and Nondepressed Students: Sadder but Wiser?" *Journal of Experimental Psychology* 108, no. 4 (1979): 441–85. http://dx.doi.org/10.1037/0096-3445.108.4.441.

Amabile, Teresa, and Steven J. Kramer. "The Power of Small Wins." *Harvard Business Review,* May 2011. https://hbr.org/2011/05/the-power-of-small-wins.

Amabile, Teresa, and Steven J. Kramer. *The Progress Principle.* Boston: Harvard Business Review Press, 2011.

American Heart Association. "Optimism Associated with Lower Risk of Having Stroke." ScienceDaily. July 22, 2011. www.sciencedaily.com/releases/2011/07/110721163025.htm.

Anonymous. "The Effects of Too Much Porn: 'He's Just Not That Into Anyone.'" *The Last Psychiatrist* (blog). February 15, 2011. http://thelastpsychiatrist.com/2011/02/hes_just_not_that_into_anyone.html.

Ariely, Dan. *The Upside of Irrationality.* New York: HarperCollins, 2010.

Ariely, Dan. "What Makes Us Feel Good About Our Work?" Filmed October 2012. TEDxRiodelaPlata video, 20:26. www.ted.com/talks/dan_ariely_what_makes_us_feel_good_about_our_work.

Association for Psychological Science. "In Hiring, Resume Info Could Help Employers Predict Who Will Quit." August 19, 2014. www.psychologicalscience.org/index.php/news/minds-business/in-hiring-resume-info-could-help-employers-predict-who-will-quit.html.

Association for Psychological Science. "Keep Your Fingers Crossed! How Superstition Improves Performance." News release. July 13, 2010. www.psychologicalscience.org/index.php/news/releases/keep-your-fingers-crossed-how-superstition-improves-performance.html.

Association for Psychological Science. "Why Are Older People Happier?" ScienceDaily. January 12, 2012. www.sciencedaily.com/releases/2012/01/120106135950.htm.

Babcock, Philip S., and Mindy Marks. "The Falling Time Cost of College: Evidence from Half a Century of Time Use Data." NBER Working Paper No. 15954, National Bureau of Economic Research, Cambridge, MA, April 2010. www.nber.org/papers/w15954.

Bakalar, Nicholas. "Future Shock Concept Gets a Personal Twist," *New York Times,* February 22, 2005. www.nytimes.com/2005/02/22/health/psychology/future-shock-concept-gets-a-personal-twist.html.

Baumeister, Roy F. "Suicide as Escape from Self." *Psychological Review* 97, no. 1 (1990): 90–113. doi:10.1037//0033-295X.97.1.90.

Baumeister, Roy F., and John Tierney. *Willpower.* New York: Penguin, 2011.

Ben-Shahar, Tal. *Choose the Life You Want.* New York: The Experiment, 2014.

Boudarbat, Brahim, and Victor Chernoff. "The Determinants of Education-Job Match among Canadian University Graduates." IZA Discussion Paper No. 4513, Institute for the Study of Labor, Bonn, Germany, October 2009. http://ftp.iza.org/dp4513.pdf.

Brad. "BUD/S Pool Comp Tips." SEAL Grinder PT, December 18, 2013. http://sealgrinderpt.com/navy-seal-workout/buds-pool-comp-tips.html/.

Brooks, David. *The Road to Character.* New York: Random House, 2015.

Carrére, Sybil, Kim T. Buehlman, John M. Gottman, James A. Coan, and Lionel Ruckstuhl. "Predicting Marital Stability and Divorce in Newlywed Couples." *Journal of Family Psychology* 14, no. 1 (2000): 42–58. http://dx.doi.org/10.1037/0893-3200.14.1.42.

Collins, Jim. "Best New Year's Resolution? A 'Stop Doing' List." JimCollins.com. December 30, 2003. www.jimcollins.com/article_topics/articles/best-new-years.html.

Cooper, Douglas P., Jamie L. Goldenberg, and Jamie Arndt. "Empowering the Self: Using the Terror Management Health Model to Promote Breast Self-Examination." *Self and Identity* 10, no. 3 (2011): 315–25. doi:10.1080/15298868.2010.527495.

Courtiol, A., S. Picq, B. Godelle, M. Raymond, and J.-B. Ferdy. "From Preferred to Actual Mate Characteristics: The Case of Human Body Shape." *PLoS ONE* 5, no. 9 (2010): e13010. doi:10.1371/journal.pone.0013010.

Cowen, Tyler. "Be Suspicious of Stories." Filmed November 2009. TEDxMidAtlantic video, 15:57. http://www.ted.com/talks/tyler_cowen_be_suspicious_of_stories.

Coyle, Daniel. "How to Prepare for a Big Moment." The Talent Code. January 21, 2014. http://thetalentcode.com/2014/01/21/how-to-prepare-for-a-big-moment/.

Csikszentmihályi, Mihály. *Creativity.* New York: HarperCollins, 2009.

Csikszentmihályi, Mihály. *Finding Flow.* New York: Basic Books, 2007.

Currey, Mason. *Daily Rituals.* New York: Knopf, 2013.

Diener, Ed, and Micaela Y. Chan. "Happy People Live Longer: Subjective Well-Being Contributes to Health and Longevity." *Applied Psychology: Health and Well-Being* 3, no. 1 (2011): 1–43. doi:10.1111/j.1758-0854.2010.01045.x.

Dignan, Aaron. *Game Frame.* New York: Free Press, 2011.

"The Dilbert Index? A New Marketplace Podcast." Freakonomics podcast, 5:13. February 23, 2012. http://freakonomics.com/2012/02/23/the-dilbert-index-a-new-marketplace-podcast/.

Dreifus, Claudia. "A Surgeon's Path from Migrant Fields to Operating Room." *New York Times,* May 13, 2008. www.nytimes.com/2008/05/13/science/13conv.html?_r=0.

Drucker, Peter. *The Effective Executive.* New York: HarperBusiness, 2006.

Duckworth, Angela. *Grit*. New York: Scribner, 2016.

Duckworth, Angela L., Christopher Peterson, Michael D. Matthews, and Dennis R. Kelly. "Grit: Perseverance and Passion for Long-Term Goals." *Journal of Personality and Social Psychology* 92, no. 6 (2007): 1087–101. http://dx.doi.org/10.1037/0022-3514.92.6.1087.

Feiler, Bruce. *The Secrets of Happy Families*. New York: William Morrow, 2013.

"Fighting Germs with Fun." YouTube video, 2:40. Posted by dw3348p, December 15, 2009. www.youtube.com/watch?v=p9nCRJo73oI.

Frankl, Viktor E. *Man's Search for Meaning*. Boston: Beacon Press, 2006.

Fry, Prem S., and Dominique L. Debats. "Perfectionism and the Five-Factor Personality Traits as Predictors of Mortality in Older Adults." *Journal of Health Psychology* 14, no. 4 (2009): 513–24. doi:10.1177/1359105309103571.

Gardner, Howard E. *Creating Minds*. New York: Basic Books, 2011.

Gerster, Jane. "Toronto Vows to Outsmart Its Raccoons." *Wall Street Journal*, August 23, 2015. www.wsj.com/articles/toronto-vows-to-outsmart-its-raccoons-1440373645.

Ghofrani, Hossein A., Ian H. Osterloh, and Friedrich Grimminger. "Sildenafil: From Angina to Erectile Dysfunction to Pulmonary Hypertension and Beyond." *Nature Reviews Drug Discovery* 5 (2006): 689–702. doi:10.1038/nrd2030.

Gilbert, Daniel. *Stumbling on Happiness*. New York: Vintage, 2007.

Gilovich, Thomas, and Victoria Husted Medvec. "The Experience of Regret: What, When, and Why." *Psychological Review* 102, no. 2 (1995): 379–95. doi:10.1037/0033-295X.102.2.379.

Gino, Francesca. *Sidetracked*. Boston: Harvard Business Review Press, 2013.

Glass, Ira. "Tough Room Act One: Make 'em Laff." *This American Life*. Episode 348. Radio broadcast, 59:00. Aired February 8, 2008. www.thisamericanlife.org/radio-archives/episode/348/tough-room?act=1#play.

Gonzales, Laurence. *Deep Survival*. New York: W. W. Norton, 2004.

Gottschall, Jonathan. *The Storytelling Animal*. Boston: Mariner, 2013.

Gottschall, Jonathan. "Why Fiction Is Good for You." *Boston Globe,* April 29, 2012. www.bostonglobe.com/ideas/2012/04/28/why-fiction-good-for-you-how-fiction-changes-your-world/nubDy1P3viDj2PuwGwb3KO/story.html.

Grant, Adam. *Give and Take*. New York: Penguin, 2013.

Gurari, Inbal, Michael J. Strube, and John J. Hetts. "Death? Be Proud! The Ironic Effects of Terror Salience on Implicit Self-Esteem." *Journal of Applied Social Psychology* 39, no. 2 (2009): 494–507. doi:10.1111/j.1559-1816.2008.00448.x.

Holiday, Ryan. *The Obstacle Is the Way*. New York: Portfolio, 2014.

"How Many Doctors Does It Take to Start a Healthcare Revolution?" Freakonomics podcast, 53:56. April 9, 2015. http://freakonomics.com/2015/04/09/how-many-doctors-does-it-take-to-start-a-healthcare-revolution-a-new-freakonomics-radio-podcast/.

Interview with Dan Ariely by author. "How to Motivate People—4 Steps Backed by Science." *Barking Up the Wrong Tree* (blog). April 6, 2014. www.bakadesuyo.com/2014/04/how-to-motivate-people/.

Interview with James Pennebaker by author. "How to Deal with Anxiety, Tragedy, or Heartache—4 Steps from Research." *Barking Up the Wrong Tree* (blog). November 15, 2014. www.bakadesuyo.com/2014/11/how-to-deal-with-anxiety/.

Interview with James Waters by author. "A Navy SEAL Explains 8 Secrets to Grit and Resilience." *Barking Up the Wrong Tree* (blog). January 13, 2015. www.bakadesuyo.com/2015/01/grit/.

Interview with Peter Sims by author. "The System That All Creative Geniuses Use to Develop Their Ideas." *Barking Up the Wrong Tree* (blog). September 24, 2013. www.bakadesuyo.com/2013/09/peter-sims/.

Interview with Richard Wiseman by author. "How to Attract Good Luck: 4 Secrets Backed by Research." *Barking Up the Wrong Tree* (blog). July 19, 2015. www.bakadesuyo.com/2015/07/how-to-attract-good-luck/.

Interview with Shawn Achor by author. "Be More Successful: New Harvard Research Reveals a Fun Way to Do It." *Barking Up the Wrong Tree* (blog). September 28, 2014. www.bakadesuyo.com/2014/09/be-more-successful/.

Interview with Spencer Glendon by author. Unpublished.

Isabella, Jude. "The Intelligent Life of the City Raccoon." *Nautilus,* October 9, 2014. http://nautil.us/issue/18/genius/the-intelligent-life-of-the-city-raccoon.

Iyengar, Sheena. *The Art of Choosing.* New York: Twelve, 2011.

Johnson, Steven. *Everything Bad Is Good for You.* New York: Riverhead Books, 2006.

Johnson, Steven. *Where Good Ideas Come From.* New York: Riverhead Books, 2011.

Jonas, Eva, Jeff Schimel, Jeff Greenberg, and Tom Pyszczynski. "The Scrooge Effect: Evidence That Mortality Salience Increases Prosocial Attitudes and Behavior." *Personality and Social Psychology Bulletin* 28, no. 10 (2002): 1342–53. http://dx.doi.org/10.1177/014616702236834.

Kivetz, Ran, Oleg Urminsky, and Yuhuang Zheng. "The Goal-Gradient Hypothesis Resurrected: Purchase Acceleration, Illusionary Goal Progress, and Customer Retention." *Journal of Marketing Research* 43, no. 1 (2006): 39–58. doi:http://dx.doi.org/10.1509/jmkr.43.1.39.

Lee, Louise. "Don't Be Too Specialized If You Want a Top Level Management Job." Insights by Stanford Business. August 1, 2010. www.gsb.stanford.edu/insights/dont-be-too-specialized-if-you-want-top-level-management-job.

Lee, Spike W. S., and Norbert Schwarz. "Framing Love: When It Hurts to Think We Were Made for Each Other." *Journal of Experimental Social Psychology* 54 (2014): 61–67. doi:10.1016/j.jesp.2014.04.007.

Lench, Heather C. "Personality and Health Outcomes: Making Positive Expectations a Reality." *Journal of Happiness Studies* 12, no. 3 (2011): 493–507. doi:10.1007/s10902-010-9212-z.

Levitt, Steven D., and Stephen J. Dubner. *Think Like a Freak.* New York: William Morrow, 2014.

Liberman, Varda, Nicholas R. Anderson, and Lee Ross. "Achieving Difficult Agreements: Effects of Positive Expectations on Negotiation Processes and Outcomes." *Journal of Experimental Social Psychology* 46, no. 3 (2010): 494–504. http://dx.doi.org/10.1016/j.jesp.2009.12.010.

Linden, David J. *The Compass of Pleasure*. New York: Penguin, 2012.

Lockhart, Andrea. "Perceived Influence of a Disney Fairy Tale on Beliefs on Romantic Love and Marriage." Ph.D. diss., California School of Professional Psychology, 2000.

Lyubomirsky, Sonja, Rene Dickerhoof, Julia K. Boehm, and Kennon M. Sheldon. "Becoming Happier Takes Both a Will and a Proper Way: An Experimental Longitudinal Intervention to Boost Well-Being." *Emotion* 11, no. 2 (2011): 391–402. doi:10.1037/a0022575.

MacDonald, Kevin. *Touching the Void*. Final Four Productions, 2003. Film.

Martin, Michael. "Illegal Farm Worker Becomes Brain Surgeon." *Tell Me More*. Radio broadcast, 13:51. Aired December 5, 2011. www.npr.org/2011/12/05/143141876/illegal-farm-worker-becomes-brain-surgeon.

McGonigal, Jane. *Reality Is Broken*. New York: Penguin, 2011.

McRaney, David. "Confabulation." You Are Not So Smart podcast, 28:00. May 30, 2012. http://youarenotsosmart.com/2012/05/30/yanss-podcast-episode-three/.

Meredith, Lisa S., Cathy D. Sherbourne, Sarah J. Gaillot, Lydia Hansell, Hans V. Ritschard, Andrew M. Parker, and Glenda Wrenn. *Promoting Psychological Resilience in the U.S. Military*. Santa Monica: RAND Corporation, 2011. Ebook. www.rand.org/pubs/monographs/MG996.html.

Miller, Gregory E., and Carsten Wrosch. "You've Gotta Know When to Fold 'Em: Goal Disengagement and Systemic Inflammation in Adolescence." *Psychological Science* 18, no. 9 (2007): 773–77. doi:10.1111/j.1467-9280.2007.01977.x.

Minkel, J. R. "Dark Knight Shift: Why Batman Could Exist—But Not for Long." *Scientific American,* July 14, 2008. www.scientificamerican.com/article/dark-knight-shift-why-bat/.

Mischel, Walter. *The Marshmallow Test*. Boston: Back Bay Books, 2015.

Munroe, Randall. *What If?* Boston: Houghton Mifflin Harcourt, 2014.

The NALP Foundation. "Keeping the Keepers II: Mobility and Management of Associates." Associate Attrition Reports. www.nalpfoundation.org/keepingthekeepersii.

Newheiser, Anna-Kaisa, Miguel Farias, and Nicole Tausch. "The Functional Nature of Conspiracy Beliefs: Examining the Underpinnings of Belief in the Da Vinci Code Conspiracy." *Personality and Individual Differences* 51, no. 8 (2011): 1007–11. doi:10.1016/j.paid.2011.08.011.

Niven, David. *100 Simple Secrets of Successful People*. New York: HarperCollins, 2009.

Oettingen, Gabriele. *Rethinking Positive Thinking*. New York: Current, 2014.

Ohio State University. "'Losing Yourself' in a Fictional Character Can Affect Your Real Life." ScienceDaily, May 7, 2012. www.sciencedaily.com/releases/2012/05/120507131948.htm.

Orlick, Terry, and John Partington. "Mental Links to Excellence." *Sport Psychologist* 2, no. 2 (1988): 105–30. doi:10.1123/tsp.2.2.105.

Parker, Matt. *Things to Make and Do in the Fourth Dimension*. New York: Farrar, Straus and Giroux, 2014.

Peterson, Christopher. *Pursuing the Good Life*. New York: Oxford Univ. Press, 2012.

Pettit, Michael. "Raccoon Intelligence at the Borderlands of Science." *American Psychological Association* 41, no. 10 (2010): 26. www.apa.org/monitor/2010/11/raccoon.aspx.

Pfeffer, Jeffrey. *Managing with Power.* Boston: Harvard Business Review Press, 1993.

Polavieja, Javier G., and Lucinda Platt. "Nurse or Mechanic? The Role of Parental Socialization and Children's Personality in the Formation of Sex-Typed Occupational Aspirations." *Social Forces* 93, no. 1 (2014): 31–61. doi:10.1093/sf/sou051.

Polly, Matthew. *American Shaolin.* New York: Penguin, 2007.

Polly, Matthew. *Tapped Out.* New York: Avery, 2011.

Quiñones-Hinojosa, Alfredo, and Mim Eichler Rivas. *Becoming Dr. Q.* Berkeley: Univ. of California Press, 2011.

Rich, Frank. "In Conversation: Chris Rock." *Vulture,* November 30, 2014. www.vulture.com/2014/11/chris-rock-frank-rich-in-conversation.html.

Rock, David. *Your Brain at Work.* New York: HarperCollins, 2009.

Rooney, Andy. "Eliminating House Clutter." *Chicago Tribune,* October 21, 1984. http://archives.chicagotribune.com/1984/10/21/page/72/article/eliminating-house-clutter.

Root-Bernstein, Robert, Lindsay Allen, Leighanna Beach, Ragini Bhadula, Justin Fast, Chelsea Hosey, Benjamin Kremkow, et al. "Arts Foster Scientific Success: Avocations of Nobel, National Academy, Royal Society, and Sigma Xi Members." *Journal of Psychology of Science and Technology* 1, no. 2 (2008): 51–63. doi:10.1891/1939-7054.1.2.51.

"SEALs BUD/s Training, 2 of 4." YouTube video, 1:46. Posted by America's Navy, December 1, 2006. www.youtube.com/watch?v=0KZuA7o1NIY.

Seligman, Martin. *Authentic Happiness.* New York: Simon and Schuster, 2002.

Seligman, Martin. *Learned Optimism.* New York: Vintage, 2011.

Simpson, Joe. *Touching the Void.* Bournemouth, UK: Direct Authors, 2012.

Sims, Peter. *Little Bets.* New York: Simon and Schuster, 2013.

Skillman, Peter. "Peter Skillman at Gel 2007." Video, 18:42. Posted by Gel Conference, 2009. https://vimeo.com/3991068.

Society for Personality and Social Psychology. "How Thinking About Death Can Lead to a Good Life." ScienceDaily. April 19, 2012. www.sciencedaily.com/releases/2012/04/120419102516.htm.

Specht, Jule, Boris Egloff, and Stefan C. Schmukle. "The Benefits of Believing in Chance or Fate: External Locus of Control as a Protective Factor for Coping with the Death of a Spouse." *Social Psychological and Personality Science* 2, no. 2 (2011): 132–37. doi:10.1177/1948550610384635.

Staff. "The Benefits of Bonding with Batman." *PacificStandard,* August 21, 2012. www.psmag.com/business-economics/the-benefits-of-bonding-with-batman-44998.

Stanley, Thomas J. *The Millionaire Mind.* Kansas City, MO: Andrews McMeel, 2001.

Swartz, Tracy. "Dave Chappelle Show's No-Phone Policy Draws Mixed Emotions from Attendees." *Chicago Tribune,* December 2, 2015. http://www.

chicagotribune.com/entertainment/ct-dave-chappelle-cellphone-ban-ent-1203-20151202-story.html.

Thompson, Derek. "Quit Your Job." *The Atlantic,* November 5, 2014. www.theatlantic.com/business/archive/2014/11/quit-your-job/382402/.

Vagg, Richard. *The Brain.* Darlow Smithson Productions, 2010. Film.

Wilson, Timothy D. *Redirect.* Boston: Little, Brown, 2011.

Wiseman, Richard. *The Luck Factor.* Calgary, Canada: Cornerstone Digital, 2011.

Wrosch, Carsten, Michael F. Scheier, Gregory E. Miller, Richard Schulz, and Charles S. Carver. "Adaptive Self-Regulation of Unattainable Goals: Goal Disengagement, Goal Reengagement, and Subjective Well-Being." *Personality and Social Psychology Bulletin* 29, no. 12 (2003): 1494–508. doi:10.1177/0146167203256921.

Wrzesniewski, Amy, and Jane E. Dutton. "Crafting a Job: Revisioning Employees as Active Crafters of Their Work." *Academy of Management Review* 26, no. 2 (2001): 179–201. doi:10.5465/AMR.2001.4378011.

Zabelina, Darya L., and Michael D. Robinson. "Child's Play: Facilitating the Originality of Creative Output by a Priming Manipulation." *Psychology of Aesthetics, Creativity, and the Arts* 4, no. 1 (2010): 57–65. doi:10.1037/a0015644.

Zauberman, Gal, and John G. Lynch Jr. "Resource Slack and Propensity to Discount Delayed Investments of Time Versus Money." *Journal of Experimental Psychology* 134, no. 1 (2005): 23–37. doi:10.1037/0096-3445.134.1.23.

Zehr, E. Paul. *Becoming Batman.* Baltimore, MD: Johns Hopkins Univ. Press, 2008.

CHAPTER 4: IT'S NOT WHAT YOU KNOW, IT'S WHO YOU KNOW (UNLESS IT REALLY IS WHAT YOU KNOW)

"About: MIT Radiation Laboratory," Lincoln Laboratory, MIT website. www.ll.mit.edu/about/History/RadLab.html.

"The Acceptance Prophecy: How You Control Who Likes You." *Psyblog,* August 27, 2009. www.spring.org.uk/2009/08/the-acceptance-prophesy-how-you-control-who-likes-you.php.

Achor, Shawn. *The Happiness Advantage.* New York: Crown Business, 2010.

Algoe, Sara B., Shelly L. Gable, and Natalya C. Maisel. "It's the Little Things: Everyday Gratitude as a Booster Shot for Romantic Relationships." *Personal Relationships* 17 (2010): 217–33. doi:10.1111/j.1475–6811.2010.01273.x.

Apatow, Judd. *Sick in the Head.* New York: Random House, 2015.

"Anecdotes About Famous Scientists." *Science Humor Netring.* http://jcdverha.home.xs4all.nl/scijokes/10.html#Erdos_8.

Aron, Arthur, and Elaine Aron. *The Heart of Social Psychology.* Lanham, MD: Lexington Books, 1989.

Baker, Wayne E. *Achieving Success Through Social Capital.* San Francisco: Jossey-Bass, 2000.

Bandiera, Oriana, Iwan Barankay, and Imran Rasul. "Social Incentives in the Workplace." *Review of Economic Studies* 77, no. 2 (2010): 417–58. doi:10.1111/j.1467–937X.2009.00574.x.

Barker, Eric. "Do You Need to Be Friends with the People You Work With?" *Barking Up the Wrong Tree* (blog). August 11, 2011. www.bakadesuyo.com/2011/08/do-you-need-to-be-friends-with-the-people-you/.

Barrick, Murray R., Susan L. Dustin, Tamara L. Giluk, Greg L. Stewart, Jonathan A. Shaffer, and Brian W. Swider. "Candidate Characteristics Driving Initial Impressions During Rapport Building: Implications for Employment Interview Validity." *Journal of Occupational and Organizational Psychology* 85, no. 2 (2012): 330–52. doi:10.1111/j.2044-8325.2011.02036.x.

Bartlett, Monica Y., Paul Condon, Jourdan Cruz, Jolie Baumann Wormwood, and David Desteno. "Gratitude: Prompting Behaviours That Build Relationships." *Cognition and Emotion* 26, no. 1 (2011): 2–13. doi:10.1080/02699931.2011.561297.

Bendersky, Corinne, and Neha Parikh Shah. "The Downfall of Extraverts and the Rise of Neurotics: The Dynamic Process of Status Allocation in Task Groups." *Academy of Management Journal* 556, no. 2 (2013): 387–406. doi:10.5465/amj.2011.0316.

Bernstein, Elizabeth. "Not an Introvert, Not an Extrovert? You May Be an Ambivert." *Wall Street Journal,* July 27, 2015. www.wsj.com/articles/not-an-introvert-not-an-extrovert-you-may-be-an-ambivert-1438013534.

Bernstein, Elizabeth. "Why Introverts Make Great Entrepreneurs." *Wall Street Journal,* August 24, 2015. www.wsj.com/articles/why-introverts-make-great-entrepreneurs-1440381699.

Bolz, Captain Frank, and Edward Hershey. *Hostage Cop.* New York: Rawson Associates, 1980.

Booyens, S. W. *Dimensions of Nursing Management.* Cape Town, South Africa: Juta Academic, 1998.

Bosson, Jennifer K., Amber B. Johnson, Kate Niederhoffer, and William B. Swann Jr. "Interpersonal Chemistry Through Negativity: Bonding by Sharing Negative Attitudes About Others." *Personal Relationships* 13, no. 2 (2006): 135–50.

Bouchard, Martin, and Frédéric Ouellet. "Is Small Beautiful? The Link Between Risks and Size in Illegal Drug Markets." *Global Crime* 12, no. 1 (2011): 70–86. doi:10.1080/17440572.2011.548956.

Brafman, Ori, and Judah Pollack. *The Chaos Imperative.* New York: Crown Business, 2013.

Breen, Benjamin. "Newton's Needle: On Scientific Self-Experimentation." *PacificStandard,* July 24, 2014. https://psmag.com/newton-s-needle-on-scientific-self-experimentation-b8a2df4d0ff2#.4pb3vdh96.

Bruzzese, Anita. "On the Job: Introverts Win in the End." *USA Today,* April 28, 2013. www.usatoday.com/story/money/columnist/bruzzese/2013/04/28/on-the-job-introverts-vs-extroverts/2114539/.

Cain, Susan. *Quiet.* New York: Broadway Books, 2012.

Casciaro, Tiziana, Francesca Gino, and Maryam Kouchaki. "The Contaminating Effects of Building Instrumental Ties: How Networking Can Make Us Feel Dirty." NOM Unit Working Paper No. 14–108, Harvard Business School, Boston, MA, April 2014. www.hbs.edu/faculty/Publication%20Files/14-108_dacbf869-fbc1-4ff8-b927-d77ca54d93d8.pdf.

Casciaro, Tiziana, and Miguel Sousa Lobo. "Competent Jerks, Lovable Fools, and the Formation of Social Networks." *Harvard Business Review,* June 2005. https://hbr.org/2005/06/competent-jerks-lovable-fools-and-the-formation-of-social-networks.

Chabris, Christopher and Daniel Simons. *The Invisible Gorilla.* New York: Harmony, 2011.

Chan, Elaine, and Jaideep Sengupta. "Insincere Flattery Actually Works: A Dual Attitudes Perspective." *Journal of Marketing Research* 47, no. 1 (2010): 122–33. http://dx.doi.org/10.1509/jmkr.47.1.122.

Charness, Neil. "The Role of Deliberate Practice in Chess Expertise." *Applied Cognative Psychology* 19, no. 2 (March 2005): 151–65. doi:10.1002/acp.1106.

Chen, Frances S., Julia A. Minson, and Zakary L. Tormala. "Tell Me More: The Effects of Expressed Interest on Receptiveness During Dialog." *Journal of Experimental Social Psychology* 46, no. 5 (2010): 850–53. doi:10.1016/j.jesp.2010.04.012.

Christakis, Nicholas A., and James H. Fowler. *Connected.* Boston: Little, Brown, 2009.

Clark, Dorie. "How to Win Over Someone Who Doesn't Like You." *Forbes,* September 16, 2012. www.forbes.com/sites/dorieclark/2012/09/16/how-to-win-over-someone-who-doesnt-like-you/#742b8a8f4132.

Cohen, Daniel H. "For Argument's Sake." Filmed February 2013. TEDxColbyCollege video, 9:35. www.ted.com/talks/daniel_h_cohen_for_argument_s_sake?language=en.

Cohen, Don, and Laurence Prusak. *In Good Company.* Boston: Harvard Business Review Press, 2001.

Conti, Gabriella, Andrea Galeotti, Gerrit Müller, and Stephen Pudney. "Popularity." *Journal of Human Resources* 48, no. 4 (2013): 1072–94. https://ideas.repec.org/a/uwp/jhriss/v48y2013iv1p1072-1094.html.

Cottrell, Catherine A., Steven L. Neuberg, and Norman P. Li. "What Do People Desire in Others? A Sociofunctional Perspective on the Importance of Different Valued Characteristics." *Journal of Personality and Social Psychology* 92, no. 2 (2007): 208–31. http://dx.doi.org/10.1037/0022-3514.92.2.208.

Coyle, Daniel. *The Little Book of Talent.* New York: Bantam, 2012.

Cross, Robert L., Andrew Parker, and Rob Cross. *The Hidden Power of Social Networks.* Boston: Harvard Business Review Press, 2004.

Csikszentmihályi, Mihály. *Creativity.* New York: HarperCollins, 2009.

Dabbs Jr., James M., and Irving L. Janis. "Why Does Eating While Reading Facilitate Opinion Change?—An Experimental Inquiry." *Journal of Experimental Social Psychology* 1, no. 2 (1965): 133–44. http://dx.doi.org/10.1016/0022-1031(65)90041-7.

Diener, Ed, Ed Sandvik, William Pavot, and Frank Fujita. "Extraversion and Subjective Well-Being in a U.S. National Probability Sample." *Journal of Research in Personality* 26, no. 3 (1992): 205–15. doi:10.1016/0092-6566(92)90039-7.

Duhigg, Charles. *The Power of Habit.* New York: Random House, 2012.

Ein-Dor, Tsachi, Abira Reizer, Philip R. Shaver, and Eyal Dotan. "Standoffish Perhaps, but Successful as Well: Evidence That Avoidant Attachment Can Be Beneficial in Professional Tennis and Computer Science." *Journal of Personality* 80, no. 3 (2011): 749–68. doi:10.1111/j.1467-6494.2011.00747.x.

Enayati, Amanda. "Workplace Happiness: What's the Secret?" CNN.com. July 10, 2012. www.cnn.com/2012/07/09/living/secret-to-workplace-happiness/index.html.

Ensher, Ellen A., and Susan E. Murphy. *Power Mentoring.* San Francisco: Jossey-Bass, 2005.

Ericsson, K. Anders, Ralf T. Krampe, and Clemens Tesch-Römer. "The Role of Deliberate Practice in the Acquisition of Expert Performance." *Psychological Review* 100, no. 3 (1993): 363–406. http://dx.doi.org/10.1037/0033-295X.100.3.363.

Feiler, Daniel C., and Adam M. Kleinbaum. "Popularity, Similarity, and the Network Extraversion Bias." *Psychological Science* 26, no. 5 (2015): 593–603. doi:10.1177/0956797615569580.

Flora, Carlin. *Friendfluence.* New York: Anchor, 2013.

Flynn, Francis J., and Vanessa K. B. Lake. "If You Need Help, Just Ask: Underestimating Compliance with Direct Requests for Help." *Journal of Personality and Social Psychology* 95, no. 1 (2008): 128–43. doi:10.1037/0022-3514.95.1.128.

Friedman, Howard S., and Leslie R. Martin. *The Longevity Project.* New York: Plume, 2012.

"From Benford to Erdos." *Radiolab.* Season 6, episode 5. Radio broadcast, 22:59. Aired November 30, 2009. www.radiolab.org/story/91699-from-benford-to-erdos/.

Garner, Randy. "What's in a Name? Persuasion Perhaps." *Journal of Consumer Psychology* 15, no. 2 (2005): 108–16. doi:10.1207/s15327663jcp1502_3.

Gawande, Atul. "Personal Best." *New Yorker,* October 3, 2011. www.newyorker.com/magazine/2011/10/03/personal-best.

Gladwell, Malcolm. "Most Likely to Succeed," *New Yorker,* December 15, 2008. www.newyorker.com/magazine/2008/12/15/most-likely-to-succeed-2.

Gleick, James. *Isaac Newton.* New York: Vintage, 2007.

Gordon, Cameron L., Robyn A. M. Arnette, and Rachel E. Smith. "Have You Thanked Your Spouse Today?: Felt and Expressed Gratitude Among Married Couples." *Personality and Individual Differences* 50, no. 3 (2011): 339–43. doi:10.1016/j.paid.2010.10.012.

Gosling, Sam. *Snoop.* New York: Basic Books, 2009.

Gottman, John, and Nan Silver. *The Seven Principles for Making Marriage Work.* New York: Harmony, 1999.

Goulston, Mark. *Just Listen.* New York: AMACOM, 2015.

Grant, Adam. *Give and Take.* New York: Penguin, 2013.

Green, Sarah. "The Big Benefits of a Little Thanks." Interview with Francesca Gino and Adam Grant. *Harvard Business Review,* November 27, 2013. https://hbr.org/ideacast/2013/11/the-big-benefits-of-a-little-t.

Green, Walter. *This Is the Moment!* Carlsbad, CA: Hay House, 2010.

Groth, Aimee. "The Dutch Military Is Trying Out a New Secret Weapon: Introverts." *Quartz,* July 14, 2015. http://qz.com/452101/the-dutch-military-is-trying-out-a-new-secret-weapon-introverts/.

Harari, Yuval Noah. *Sapiens.* New York: Harper, 2015.

Harrell, Thomas W., and Bernard Alpert. "Attributes of Successful MBAs: A 20-Year Longitudinal Study." *Human Performance* 2, no. 4 (1989): 301–22. doi:10.1207/s15327043hup0204_4.

Hast, Tim. *Powerful Listening. Powerful Influence.* Seattle: Amazon Digital Services, 2013.

Hemery, David. *Sporting Excellence.* New York: HarperCollins Willow, 1991.

Heskett, James. "To What Degree Does the Job Make the Person?" Working Knowledge, Harvard Business School. March 10, 2011. http://hbswk.hbs.edu/item/to-what-degree-does-the-job-make-the-person.

Hodson, Gordon, and James M. Olson. "Testing the Generality of the Name Letter Effect: Name Initials and Everyday Attitudes." *Personality and Social Psychology Bulletin* 31, no. 8 (2005): 1099–111. doi:10.1177/0146167205274895.

Hoffman, Paul. *The Man Who Loved Only Numbers.* New York: Hachette, 1998.

Hoffman, Paul. "The Man Who Loved Only Numbers." *New York Times.* www.nytimes.com/books/first/h/hoffman-man.html.

Holiday, Ryan. "How to Find Mentors." *Thought Catalog.* August 5, 2013. www.thoughtcatalog.com/ryan-holiday/2013/08/how-to-find-mentors.

Hotz, Robert Lee. "Science Reveals Why We Brag So Much." *Wall Street Journal,* May 7, 2012. www.wsj.com/news/articles/SB10001424052702304451104577390392329291890.

Hove, Michael J., and Jane L. Risen. "It's All in the Timing: Interpersonal Synchrony Increases Affiliation." *Social Cognition* 27, no. 6 (2009): 949–61. http://dx.doi.org/10.1521/soco.2009.27.6.949.

Interview with Adam Grant by author. "Adam Grant Teaches You the Right Way to Give and Take." *Barking Up the Wrong Tree* (blog). April 9, 2013. www.bakadesuyo.com/2013/04/interview-wharton-business-school-professor-teaches-approach-give/.

Interview with Adam Rifkin by author. "Silicon Valley's Best Networker Teaches You His Secrets." *Barking Up the Wrong Tree* (blog). February 18, 2013. www.bakadesuyo.com/2013/02/interview-silicon-valleys-networker-teaches-secrets-making-connections/.

Interview with Albert Bernstein by author. "How to Make Difficult Conversations Easy." *Barking Up the Wrong Tree* (blog). December 28, 2014. www.bakadesuyo.com/2014/12/difficult-conversations/.

Interview with Alex Korb by author. "New Neuroscience Reveals 4 Rituals That Will Make You Happy." *Barking Up the Wrong Tree* (blog). September 20, 2015. www.bakadesuyo.com/2015/09/make-you-happy-2/.

Interview with Ben Casnocha by author. "Interview—NYT/WSJ Bestselling Author Ben Casnocha Teaches You the New Secrets to Networking and Career Success." *Barking Up the Wrong Tree* (blog). April 15, 2013. www.bakadesuyo.com/2013/04/interview-casnocha-networking/.

Interview with Chris Voss by author. "Hostage Negotiation: The Top FBI Hostage Negotiator Teaches You the Secrets to Getting What You Want." *Barking Up the Wrong Tree* (blog). January 7, 2013. www.bakadesuyo.com/2013/01/interview-negotiation-secrets-learn-top-fbi-hostage-negotiator/.

Interview with John Gottman by author. "The 4 Most Common Relationship Problems—And How to Fix Them." *Barking Up the Wrong Tree* (blog). December 7, 2014. www.bakadesuyo.com/2014/12/relationship-problems/.

Interview with Nicholas Christakis by author. "The Lazy Way to an Awesome Life: 3 Secrets Backed by Research." *Barking Up the Wrong Tree* (blog). July 26, 2015. www.bakadesuyo.com/2015/07/awesome-life/.

Interview with NYPD hostage negotiators by author. "NYPD Hostage Negotiators on How to Persuade People: 4 New Secrets." *Barking Up the Wrong Tree* (blog). November 22, 2015. www.bakadesuyo.com/2015/11/hostage-negotiators/.

Interview with Ramit Sethi by author. "NYT Bestselling Author Ramit Sethi Explains the Secrets to Managing Money, Negotiating, and Networking." *Barking Up the Wrong Tree* (blog). February 25, 2013. www.bakadesuyo.com/2013/02/nyt-bestselling-author-ramit-sethis-explains-manage-money-negotiate-improve/.

Interview with Richard Wiseman by author. "How to Attract Good Luck: 4 Secrets Backed by Research." *Barking Up the Wrong Tree* (blog). July 19, 2015. www.bakadesuyo.com/2015/07/how-to-attract-good-luck/.

Interview with Robin Dreeke by author. "How to Get People to Like You: 7 Ways from an FBI Behavior Expert." *Barking Up the Wrong Tree* (blog). October 26, 2014. www.bakadesuyo.com/2014/10/how-to-get-people-to-like-you/.

Jones, Janelle M., and Jolanda Jetten. "Recovering From Strain and Enduring Pain: Multiple Group Memberships Promote Resilience in the Face of Physical Challenges." *Social Psychological and Personality Science* 2, no. 3 (2011): 239–44. doi:10.1177/1948550610386806.

"Judd Apatow." *The Daily Show with Jon Stewart*. ComedyCentral.com. Online video of TV broadcast, 6:16. Aired June 15, 2015. http://thedailyshow.cc.com/videos/mkfc6y/judd-apatow.

"Judd Apatow: A Comedy-Obsessed Kid Becomes 'Champion of the Goofball.'" *Fresh Air*. Radio broadcast, 37:22. Aired June 17, 2015. www.npr.org/2015/06/17/415199346/judd-apatow-a-comedy-obsessed-kid-becomes-champion-of-the-goofball.

Judge, Timothy A., Chad A. Higgins, Carl J. Thoresen, and Murray R. Barrick. "The Big Five Personality Traits, General Mental Ability, and Career

Success Across the Life Span." *Personnel Psychology* 52, no. 3 (1999): 621–52. doi:10.1111/j.1744-6570.1999.tb00174.x.

Judge, Timothy A., Joyce E. Bono, Remus Ilies, and Megan W. Gerhardt. "Personality and Leadership: A Qualitative and Quantitative Review." *Journal of Applied Psychology* 87, no. 4 (2002): 765–80. doi:10.1037//0021-9010.87.4.765.

Kesebir, S., and S. Oishi. "A Spontaneous Self-Reference Effect in Memory: Why Some Birthdays Are Harder to Remember than Others." *Psychological Science* 21, no. 10 (2010): 1525–31. doi:10.1177/0956797610383436.

Kreider, Tim. *We Learn Nothing*. New York: Free Press, 2012.

Kuhnen, Camelia M., and Joan Y. Chiao. "Genetic Determinants of Financial Risk Taking." *PLoS ONE* 4, no. 2 (2009): e4362. http://dx.doi.org/10.1371/journal.pone.0004362.

Lajunen, Timo. "Personality and Accident Liability: Are Extraversion, Neuroticism, and Psychoticism Related to Traffic and Occupational Fatalities?" *Personality and Individual Differences* 31, no. 8 (2001): 1365–73. doi:10.1016/S0191-8869(00)00230-0.

"Lawbreakers." *Crowd Control*. Season 1, episode 1. National Geographic channel. Aired November 24, 2014. http://channel.nationalgeographic.com/crowd-control/episodes/lawbreakers/.

Levin, Daniel Z., Jorge Walter, and J. Keith Murnighan. "Dormant Ties: The Value of Reconnecting." *Organization Science* 22, no. 4 (2011) 923–39. doi:10.2307/20868904.

Levin, Daniel Z., Jorge Walter, and J. Keith Murnighan. "The Power of Reconnection—How Dormant Ties Can Surprise You." *MIT Sloan Management Review*, March 23, 2011. http://sloanreview.mit.edu/article/the-power-of-reconnection-how-dormant-ties-can-surprise-you/.

Liberman, Varda, Nicholas R. Anderson, and Lee Ross. "Achieving Difficult Agreements: Effects of Positive Expectations on Negotiation Processes and Outcomes." *Journal of Experimental Social Psychology* 46, no. 3 (2010): 494–504. http://dx.doi.org/10.1016/j.jesp.2009.12.010.

Lindstrom, Martin. *Brandwashed*. New York: Crown Business, 2011.

Lockwood, Penelope, and Ziva Kunda. "Superstars and Me: Predicting the Impact of Role Models on the Self." *Journal of Personality and Social Psychology* 73, no. 1 (1997): 91–103. http://citeseerx.ist.psu.edu/viewdoc/download?doi=10.1.1.578.7014&rep=rep1&type=pdf.

Lount Jr., Robert B., Chen-Bo Zhong, Niro Sivanathan, and J. Keith Murnighan. "Getting Off on the Wrong Foot: The Timing of a Breach and the Restoration of Trust." *Personality and Social Psychology Bulletin* 34, no. 12 (2008): 1601–12. doi:10.1177/0146167208324512.

Lyubomirsky, Sonya. *The Myths of Happiness*. New York: Penguin, 2013.

Macdonald, Kevin. *One Day in September*. Sony Pictures Classics, 2009. Film.

Malhotra, Deepak. "How to Negotiate Your Job Offer—Prof. Deepak Malhotra (Harvard Business School)." YouTube video, 1:04:23. Posted November 20, 2012. www.youtube.com/watch?v=km2Hd_xgo9Q.

Marche, Stephen. "Is Facebook Making Us Lonely?" *The Atlantic,* May 2012.
www.theatlantic.com/magazine/archive/2012/05/is-facebook-making-us-
lonely/308930/.

Marks, Gary, Norman Miller, and Geoffrey Maruyama. "Effect of Targets' Physical
Attractiveness on Assumptions of Similarity." *Journal of Personality and Social
Psychology* 41, no. 1 (1981): 198–206. doi:10.1037/0022-3514.41.1.198.

Marmer, Max, Bjoern Lasse Herrmann, Ertan Dogrultan, and Ron Berman. "Startup
Genome Report Extra on Premature Scaling: A Deep Dive into Why Most
Startups Fail." Startup Genome. August 29, 2011. https://s3.amazonaws.com/
startupcompass-public/StartupGenomeReport2_Why_Startups_Fail_v2.pdf.

Martin, Steve J. "Can Humor Make You a Better Negotiator?" Excerpt from original
article (unavailable). *Barking Up the Wrong Tree* (blog). November 28, 2011.
www.bakadesuyo.com/2011/11/can-humor-make-you-a-better-negotiator/.

Max-Planck-Gesellschaft. "Negative Image of People Produces Selfish Actions."
Public release. April 12, 2011. www.eurekalert.org/pub_releases/2011-04/m-
nio041211.php.

McMains, Michael J., and Wayman C. Mullins. *Crisis Negotiations.* 4th ed.
Abingdon-on-Thames, UK: Routledge, 2010.

McPherson, Miller, Lynn Smith-Lovin, and Matthew E. Brashears. "Social
Isolation in America: Changes in Core Discussion Networks over Two
Decades." *American Sociological Review* 71, no. 3 (2006): 353–75.
doi:10.1177/000312240607100301.

Mongrain, Myriam, and Tracy Anselmo-Matthews. "Do Positive Psychology
Exercises Work? A Replication of Seligman et al." *Journal of Clinical Psychology*
68, no. 4 (2012). doi:10.1002/jclp.21839.

Neal, Andrew, Gillian Yeo, Annette Koy, and Tania Xiao. "Predicting the Form
and Direction of Work Role Performance from the Big 5 Model of Personality
Traits." *Journal of Organizational Behavior* 33, no. 2 (2012): 175–92.
doi:10.1002/job.742.

Neffinger, John, and Matthew Kohut. *Compelling People.* New York: Plume, 2013.

Nettle, Daniel. "The Evolution of Personality Variation in Humans and Other
Animals." *American Psychologist* 61, no. 6 (2006): 622–31. http://dx.doi.
org/10.1037/0003-066X.61.6.622.

Niven, David. *100 Simple Secrets of the Best Half of Life.* New York: HarperCollins,
2009.

Nizza, Mike. "A Simple B.F.F. Strategy, Confirmed by Scientists." *The Lede*
(blog). *New York Times,* April 22, 2008. http://thelede.blogs.nytimes.
com/2008/04/22/a-simple-bff-strategy-confirmed-by-scientists/.

Ohio State University. "Young People Say Sex, Paychecks Come in Second to
Self-Esteem." Public release. January 6, 2011. www.eurekalert.org/pub_
releases/2011-01/osu-yps010611.php.

Paulhus, Delroy L., and Kathy L. Morgan. "Perceptions of Intelligence in Leaderless
Groups: The Dynamic Effects of Shyness and Acquaintance." *Journal of
Personality and Social Psychology* 72, no. 3 (1997): 581–91. http://neuron4.psych.

ubc.ca/~dpaulhus/research/SHYNESS/downloads/JPSP%2097%20with%20
Morgan.pdf.

Pavot, William, Ed Diener, and Frank Fujita. "Extraversion and Happiness."
Personality and Individual Differences 11, no. 12 (1990): 1299–306.
doi:10.1016/0191-8869(90)90157-M.

Peters, Bethany L., and Edward Stringham. "No Booze? You May Lose: Why
Drinkers Earn More Money than Nondrinkers." *Journal of Labor Research* 27,
no. 3 (2006): 411–21. http://dx.doi.org/10.1007/s12122-006-1031-y.

Pickover, Clifford A. *Strange Brains and Genius.* New York: William Morrow, 1999.

Pines, Ayala Malach. *Falling in Love.* Abingdon-on-Thames, UK: Routledge, 2005.

Pink, Daniel H. "Why Extroverts Fail, Introverts Flounder, and You Probably
Succeed." *Washington Post,* January 28, 2013. www.washingtonpost.com/
national/on-leadership/why-extroverts-fail-introverts-flounder-and-you-
probably-succeed/2013/01/28/bc4949b0-695d-11e2-95b3-272d604a10a3_
story.html.

PON Staff. "The Link Between Happiness and Negotiation Success." *Program
on Negotiation* (blog). Harvard Law School. September 20, 2011. www.pon.
harvard.edu/daily/negotiation-skills-daily/the-link-between-happiness-and-
negotiation-success/.

Reuben, Ernesto, Paola Sapienza, and Luigi Zingales. "Is Mistrust Self-Fulfilling?"
Economics Letters 104, no. 2 (2009): 89–91. doi:10.1016/j.econlet.2009.04.007.

Roche, Gerard R. "Much Ado About Mentors." *Harvard Business Review,* January
1979. https://hbr.org/1979/01/much-ado-about-mentors.

Rueb, Emily S. "A 1973 Hostage Situation, Revisited." *Cityroom* (blog). *New York
Times,* September 10, 2012. http://cityroom.blogs.nytimes.com/2012/09/10/a-
1973-hostage-situation-revisited/?_r=2.

Ryssdal, Kai, and Bridget Bodnar. "Judd Apatow on His Band of Comedians and
Radio Roots." *Marketplace,* June 24, 2015. www.marketplace.org/topics/life/
big-book/judd-apatow-his-band-comedians-and-radio-roots.

Schaefer, Peter S., Cristina C. Williams, Adam S. Goodie, and W. Keith Campbell.
"Overconfidence and the Big Five." *Journal of Research in Personality* 38, no. 5
(2004): 473–80. doi:10.1016/j.jrp.2003.09.010.

Schmitt, David P. "The Big Five Related to Risky Sexual Behaviour Across 10 World
Regions: Differential Personality Associations of Sexual Promiscuity and
Relationship Infidelity." *European Journal of Personality, Special Issue: Personality
and Social Relations* 18, no. 4 (2004): 301–19. doi:10.1002/per.520.

Seibert, Scott E., and Maria L. Kraimer. "The Five-Factor Model of Personality
and Career Success." *Journal of Vocational Behavior* 58, no. 1 (2001): 1–21.
doi:10.1006/jvbe.2000.1757.

Seibert, Scott E., and Maria L. Kraimer. "The Five-Factor Model of Personality and
Its Relationship with Career Success." *Academy of Management Proceedings,*
August 1, 1999 (Meeting Abstract Supplement): A1–A6. http://proceedings.
aom.org/content/1999/1/A1.2.full.pdf+html.

Seligman, Martin E. P. *Flourish.* New York: Atria, 2012.

Shambora, Jessica. "Fortune's Best Networker." *Fortune Magazine,* February 9, 2011. http://fortune.com/2011/02/09/fortunes-best-networker/.

Simonton, Dean Keith. *Greatness.* New York: Guilford Press, 1994.

Simonton, Dean Keith. *The Wiley Handbook of Genius.* Hoboken, NJ: Wiley-Blackwell, 2014.

Sims, Peter. *Little Bets.* New York: Free Press, 2011.

Sinaceur, Marwan, and Larissa Z. Tiedens. "Get Mad and Get More than Even: When and Why Anger Expression Is Effective in Negotiations." *Journal of Experimental Social Psychology* 42, no. 3 (2006): 314–22. http://dx.doi.org/10.1016/j.jesp.2005.05.002.

Singer, Monroe S. "Harvard Radio Research Lab Developed Countermeasures Against Enemy Defenses: Allied Scientists Won Radar War." *Harvard Crimson,* November 30, 1945. www.thecrimson.com/article/1945/11/30/harvard-radio-research-lab-developed-countermeasures/.

Snow, Shane. *Smartcuts.* New York: HarperBusiness, 2014.

Spurk, Daniel, and Andrea E. Abele. "Who Earns More and Why? A Multiple Mediation Model from Personality to Salary." *Journal of Business and Psychology* 26, no. 1 (2011): 87–103. doi:10.1007/s10869-010-9184-3.

Sundem, Garth. *Brain Trust.* New York: Three Rivers, 2012.

Sutin, Angelina R., Paul T. Costa Jr., Richard Miech, and William W. Eaton. "Personality and Career Success: Concurrent and Longitudinal Relations." *European Journal of Personality* 23, no. 2 (2009): 71–84. doi:10.1002/per.704.

Takru, Radhika. "Friends with Negatives," BrainBlogger.com. September 28, 2011. http://brainblogger.com/2011/09/28/friends-with-negatives/.

"Understanding the Science of Introversion and Extroversion with Dr. Luke Smilie." The Psychology Podcast with Dr. Scott Barry Kaufman, podcast, 1:10:47. July 26, 2015. http://thepsychologypodcast.com/understanding-the-science-of-introversion-and-extraversion-with-dr-luke-smillie/.

Uzzi, Brian, and Jarrett Spiro. "Collaboration and Creativity: The Small World Problem." *American Journal of Sociology* 111, no. 2 (2005): 447–504. doi:10.1086/432782.

Uzzi, Brian, and Shannon Dunlap. "How to Build Your Network." *Harvard Business Review,* December 2005. https://hbr.org/2005/12/how-to-build-your-network.

Valdesolo, Piercarlo. "Flattery Will Get You Far." *Scientific American,* January 12, 2010. www.scientificamerican.com/article/flattery-will-get-you-far/.

Walton, Gregory M., Geoffrey L. Cohen, David Cwir, and Steven J. Spencer. "Mere Belonging: The Power of Social Connections." *Journal of Personality and Social Psychology* 102, no. 3 (2012): 513–32. http://dx.doi.org/10.1037/a0025731.

Ware, Bronnie. *The Top Five Regrets of the Dying.* Carlsbad, CA: Hay House, 2012.

Weaver, Jonathan R., and Jennifer K. Bosson. "I Feel Like I Know You: Sharing Negative Attitudes of Others Promotes Feelings of Familiarity." *Personality and Social Psychology Bulletin* 37, no. 4 (2011): 481–91. doi:10.1177/0146167211398364.

Weiner, Eric. *The Geography of Bliss.* New York: Hachette, 2008.

Whisman, Mark A. "Loneliness and the Metabolic Syndrome in a Population-Based Sample of Middle-Aged and Older Adults." *Health Psychology* 29, no. 5 (2010): 550–54. http://dx.doi.org/10.1037/a0020760.

Wolff, Hans-Georg, and Klaus Moser. "Effects of Networking on Career Success: A Longitudinal Study." *Journal of Applied Psychology* 94, no. 1 (2009): 196–206. http://dx.doi.org/10.1037/a0013350.

Zagorsky, Jay. "The Wealth Effects of Smoking." *Tobacco Control* 13, no. 4 (2004): 370–74. doi:10.1136/tc.2004.008243.

Zelenski, John M., Maya S. Santoro, and Deanna C. Whelan. "Would Introverts Be Better Off If They Acted More Like Extraverts? Exploring Emotional and Cognitive Consequences of Counterdispositional Behavior." *Emotion* 12, no. 2 (2012): 290–303. http://dx.doi.org/10.1037/a0025169.

Zinoman, Jason. "Judd Apatow's New Book Is a Love Letter to Stand-Up Comedy." *New York Times,* June 14, 2015. www.nytimes.com/2015/06/15/books/judd-apatows-new-book-is-a-love-letter-to-stand-up-comedy.html?_r=0.

CHAPTER 5: BELIEVE IN YOURSELF . . . SOMETIMES

Adolphs, Ralph, Daniel Tranel, and Antonio R. Damasio. "The Human Amygdala in Social Judgment." *Nature* 393 (1998): 470–74. doi:10.1038/30982.

Aldhous, Peter. "Humans Prefer Cockiness to Expertise." *New Scientist,* June 3, 2009. www.newscientist.com/article/mg20227115.500-humans-prefer-cockiness-to-expertise.

Andrews, Evan. "The Strange Case of Emperor Norton I of the United States." History.com. September 17, 2014. www.history.com/news/the-strange-case-of-emperor-norton-i-of-the-united-states.

Baumeister, Roy F., Jennifer D. Campbell, Joachim I. Krueger, and Kathleen D. Vohs. "Does High Self-Esteem Cause Better Performance, Interpersonal Success, Happiness, or Healthier Lifestyles?" *Psychological Science in the Public Interest* 4, no. 1 (2003): 1–44. doi:10.1111/1529-1006.01431.

Beyer, Rick. *The Ghost Army.* Plate of Peas Productions, 2013. Film.

Beyer, Rick, and Elizabeth Sayles. *The Ghost Army of World War II.* New York: Princeton Architectural Press, 2015.

Bhattacharya, Utpal, and Cassandra D. Marshall. "Do They Do It for the Money?" *Journal of Corporate Finance* 18, no. 1 (2012): 92–104. http://dx.doi.org/10.2469/dig.v42.n2.51.

British Psychological Society. "Good Managers Fake It." *Science Daily.* January 10, 2013. www.sciencedaily.com/releases/2013/01/130109215238.htm.

Brunell, Amy B., William A. Gentry, W. Keith Campbell, Brian J. Hoffman, Karl W. Kuhnert, and Kenneth G. DeMarree. "Leader Emergence: The Case of the Narcissistic Leader." *Personality and Social Psychology Bulletin* 34, no. 12 (2008): 1663–76. doi:10.1177/0146167208324101.

Cabane, Olivia Fox. *The Charisma Myth*. New York: Portfolio, 2012.

Carney, Dana. "Powerful Lies." Columbia Business School, Ideas at Work. January 22, 2010. http://www8.gsb.columbia.edu/ideas-at-work/publication/703/powerful-lies [Site no longer accessible].

Chabris, Christopher, and Daniel Simons. *The Invisible Gorilla*. New York: Harmony, 2011.

Chamorro-Premuzic, Tomas. "The Dangers of Confidence." *Harvard Business Review,* July 2014. https://hbr.org/2014/07/the-dangers-of-confidence/.

Chamorro-Premuzic, Tomas. "Less-Confident People Are More Successful." *Harvard Business Review,* July 6, 2012. https://hbr.org/2012/07/less-confident-people-are-more-su.

Chance, Zoë, Michael I. Norton, Francesca Gino, and Dan Ariely. "Temporal View of the Costs and Benefits of Self-Deception." *PNAS* 108, supplement 3 (2011): 15655–59. doi:10.1073/pnas.1010658108.

Chen, Patricia, Christopher G. Myers, Shirli Kopelman, and Stephen M. Garcia. "The Hierarchical Face: Higher Rankings Lead to Less Cooperative Looks." *Journal of Applied Psychology* 97, no. 2 (2012): 479–86. http://dx.doi.org/10.1037/a0026308.

Colvin, Geoff. *Talent Is Overrated*. New York: Portfolio, 2010.

Constandi, Mo. "Researchers Scare 'Fearless' Patients." *Nature,* February 3, 2013. www.nature.com/news/researchers-scare-fearless-patients-1.12350.

Crocker, Jennifer, and Lora E. Park. "The Costly Pursuit of Self-Esteem." *Psychological Bulletin* 130, no. 3 (2004): 392–414. doi:10.1037/0033-2909.130.3.392.

Crockett, Zachary. "Joshua Norton, Emperor of the United States." Priceonomics.com. May 28, 2014. http://priceonomics.com/joshua-norton-emperor-of-the-united-states/.

Daily Telegraph Reporter. "Worriers Who Feel Guilty Before Doing Anything Wrong Make the Best Partners, Research Finds." *The Telegraph,* October 12, 2012. www.telegraph.co.uk/news/uknews/9602688/Worriers-who-feel-guilty-before-doing-anything-wrong-make-best-partners-research-finds.html.

Drago, Francesco. "Self-Esteem and Earnings." *Journal of Economic Psychology* 32 (2011): 480–88. doi:10.1016/j.joep.2011.03.015.

Dunning, David, Kerri Johnson, Joyce Ehrlinger, and Justin Kruger. "Why People Fail to Recognize Their Own Incompetence." *Current Directions in Psychological Science* 12, no. 3 (2003): 83–87. doi:10.1111/1467-8721.01235.

Feinstein, Justin S., Colin Buzza, Rene Hurlemann, Robin L. Follmer, Nader S. Dahdaleh, William H. Coryell, Michael J. Welsh, et al. "Fear and Panic in Humans with Bilateral Amygdala Damage." *Nature Neuroscience* 16 (2013): 270–72. doi:10.1038/nn.3323.

Feinstein, Justin S., Ralph Adolphs, Antonio Damasio, and Daniel Tranel. "The Human Amygdala and the Induction and Experience of Fear." *Current Biology* 21, no. 1 (2011): 34–38, http://dx.doi.org/10.1016/j.cub.2010.11.042.

Finkelstein, Stacey R., and Ayelet Fishbach. "Tell Me What I Did Wrong: Experts Seek and Respond to Negative Feedback." *Journal of Consumer Research* 39, no. 1 (2012): 22–38. doi:10.1086/661934.

Flynn, Francis J. "Defend Your Research: Guilt-Ridden People Make Great Leaders." *Harvard Business Review,* January–February 2011. https://hbr.org/2011/01/defend-your-research-guilt-ridden-people-make-great-leaders.

Furness, Hannah. "Key to Career Success Is Confidence, Not Talent." *The Telegraph,* August 14, 2012. www.telegraph.co.uk/news/uknews/9474973/Key-to-career-success-is-confidence-not-talent.html.

Gawande, Atul. "The Checklist." *New Yorker,* December 10, 2007. www.newyorker.com/magazine/2007/12/10/the-checklist.

Gino, Francesca. *Sidetracked.* Boston: Harvard Business Review Press, 2013.

Gladwell, Malcolm. "Malcolm Gladwell at HPU, North Carolina Colleges." YouTube video, 1:09:08. Posted by High Point University, January 16, 2012. www.youtube.com/watch?v=7rMDr4P9BOw.

Goldsmith, Marshall. "Helping Successful People Get Even Better." MarshallGoldsmith.com. April 10, 2003. www.marshallgoldsmith.com/articles/1401/.

Goldsmith, Marshall. "The Success Delusion." The Conference Board Review. MarshallGoldsmith.com. October 29, 2015. http://www.marshallgoldsmith.com/articles/the-success-delusion/.

Grant-Halvorson, Heidi. *Nine Things Successful People Do Differently.* Boston: Harvard Business Review Press, 2011.

Haidt, Jonathan. *The Happiness Hypothesis.* New York: Basic Books, 2006.

Hamermesh, Daniel S. *Beauty Pays.* Princeton, NJ: Princeton Univ. Press, 2011.

Hawthorne, Nathaniel. *Scarlet Letter.* Seattle: Amazon Digital Services, 2012.

Hmieleski, Keith M., and Robert A. Baron. "Entrepreneurs' Optimism and New Venture Performance: A Social Cognitive Perspective." *Academy of Management Journal* 52, no. 3 (2009): 473–88. doi:10.5465/AMJ.2009.41330755.

Horwitz, French, and Eleanor Grant. "Superhuman Powers." *Is It Real?* Season 1, episode 8. National Geographic channel. Aired August 20, 2005.

Human, Lauren J., Jeremy C. Biesanz, Kate L. Parisotto, and Elizabeth W. Dunn. "Your Best Self Helps Reveal Your True Self: Positive Self-Presentation Leads to More Accurate Personality Impressions." *Social Psychological and Personality Science* 3, no. 1 (2012): 23–30. doi:10.1177/1948550611407689.

Interview with Gautam Mukunda by author. "Gautam Mukunda of Harvard Explains the Secrets to Being a Better Leader." *Barking Up the Wrong Tree* (blog). March 18, 2013. www.bakadesuyo.com/2013/03/interview-harvard-business-school-professor-gautam-mukunda-teaches-secrets-leader/.

"Joshua A. Norton." Virtual Museum of the City of San Francisco website. www.sfmuseum.org/hist1/norton.html.

Kahneman, Daniel. "Don't Blink! The Hazards of Confidence." *New York Times Magazine,* October 19, 2011. www.nytimes.com/2011/10/23/magazine/dont-blink-the-hazards-of-confidence.html?_r=0.

Kaufman, Scott Barry. "Why Do Narcissists Lose Popularity Over Time?" ScottBarryKaufman.com. 2015. http://scottbarrykaufman.com/article/why-do-narcissists-lose-popularity-over-time/.

Keltner, Dacher, Deborah H. Gruenfeld, and Cameron Anderson. "Power, Approach, and Inhibition." *Psychological Review* 110, no. 2 (2003): 265–84. doi:10.1037/0033-295X.110.2.265.

Kendall, Todd D. "Celebrity Misbehavior in the NBA." *Journal of Sports Economics* 9, no. 3 (2008): 231–49. doi:10.1177/1527002507301526.

Kinari, Yusuke, Noriko Mizutani, Fumio Ohtake, and Hiroko Okudaira. "Overconfidence Increases Productivity." ISER Discussion Paper No. 814. Institute of Social and Economic Research, Osaka University, Japan. August 2, 2011. doi:10.2139/ssrn.1904692.

Kraus, Michael W., and Dacher Keltner. "Signs of Socioeconomic Status: A Thin-Slicing Approach." *Psychological Science* 20, no. 1 (2009): 99–106. doi:10.1111/j.1467-9280.2008.02251.x.

Lammers, Joris, and Diederik A. Stapel. "Power Increases Dehumanization." *Group Processes and Intergroup Relations,* September 3, 2010. doi:10.1177/1368430210370042.

Lammers, Joris, Diederik A. Stapel, and Adam D. Galinsky. "Power Increases Hypocrisy: Moralizing in Reasoning, Immorality in Behavior." *Psychological Science* 21, no. 5 (2010): 737–44. doi:10.1177/0956797610368810.

Lammers, Joris, Janka I. Stoker, Jennifer Jordan, Monique Pollmann, and Diederik A. Stapel. "Power Increases Infidelity Among Men and Women." *Psychological Science* 22, no. 9 (2011): 1191–97. doi:10.1177/0956797611416252.

Lazo, Alejandro, and Daniel Huang. "Who Is Emperor Norton? Fans in San Francisco Want to Remember." *Wall Street Journal,* August 12, 2015. www.wsj.com/articles/who-is-emperor-norton-fans-in-san-francisco-want-to-remember-1439426791.

Leary, Mark R., Eleanor B. Tate, Claire E. Adams, Ashley Batts Allen, Jessica Hancock. "Self-Compassion and Reactions to Unpleasant Self-Relevant Events: The Implications of Treating Oneself Kindly." *Journal of Personality and Social Psychology* 92, no. 5 (May 2007): 887–904. doi.org/10.1037/0022-3514.92.5.887.

Leder, Helmut, Michael Forster, and Gernot Gerger. "The Glasses Stereotype Revisited: Effects of Eyeglasses on Perception, Recognition, and Impression of Faces." *Swiss Journal of Psychology* 70, no. 4 (2011): 211–22. http://dx.doi.org/10.1024/1421-0185/a000059.

Linden, David J. "Addictive Personality? You Might Be a Leader." *New York Times,* July 23, 2011. www.nytimes.com/2011/07/24/opinion/sunday/24addicts.html?_r=0.

Machiavelli, Niccolò. *The Prince.* Inti Editions, 2015.

Marshall, Frank. "The Man vs. the Machine." FiveThirtyEight.com. October 22, 2014. ESPN video, 17:17. http://fivethirtyeight.com/features/the-man-vs-the-machine-fivethirtyeight-films-signals/.

Mingle, Kate. "Show of Force." 99% Invisible. Episode 161. April 21, 2015. http://99percentinvisible.org/episode/show-of-force/.

Misra, Ria. "That Time a Bankrupt Businessman Declared Himself Emperor of America." *io9* (blog). February 11, 2015. http://io9.gizmodo.com/that-time-a-bankrupt-businessman-declared-himself-emper-1685280529.

Moylan, Peter. "Emperor Norton." Encyclopedia of San Francisco online. www.sfhistoryencyclopedia.com/articles/n/nortonJoshua.html.

Neely, Michelle E., Diane L. Schallert, Sarojanni S. Mohammed, Rochelle M. Roberts, Yu-Jung Chen. "Self-Kindness When Facing Stress: The role of Self-Compassion, Goal Regulation, and Support in College Students' Well-Being." *Motivation and Emotion* 33, no. 1 (March 2009): 88–97. doi:10.1007/s11031-008-9119-8.

Neff, Kristin D., Ya-Ping Hsieh, and Kullaya Dejitterat. "Self-Compassion, Achievement Goals, and Coping with Academic Failure." *Self and Identity* 4 (2005): 263–87. doi:10.1080/13576500444000317.

Parke, Jonathan, Mark D. Griffiths, and Adrian Parke. "Positive Thinking Among Slot Machine Gamblers: A Case of Maladaptive Coping?" *International Journal of Mental Health and Addiction* 5, no. 1 (2007): 39–52. doi:10.1007/s11469-006-9049-1.

"Pathology of the Overconfident: Self-Deceived Individuals More Likely to Be Promoted over the More Accomplished." *Signs of the Times,* August 29, 2014. www.sott.net/article/284663-Pathology-of-the-overconfident-Self-deceived-individuals-more-likely-to-be-promoted-over-the-more-accomplished.

Pentland, Alex. *Honest Signals.* Cambridge, MA: MIT Press, 2010.

Pfeffer, Jeffrey. *Power.* New York: HarperBusiness, 2010.

Phillips, Donald T. *Lincoln on Leadership.* Marion, IL: DTP/Companion Books, 2013.

Pickover, Clifford A. *Strange Brains and Genius.* New York: William Morrow, 1999.

Richman, James. "Why Bosses Who Show Vulnerability Are the Most Liked." *Fast Company,* July 7, 2015. www.fastcompany.com/3048134/lessons-learned/why-bosses-who-show-vulnerability-are-the-most-liked.

Rock, David. *Your Brain at Work.* New York: HarperBusiness, 2009.

Rucker, Derek D., David Dubois, and Adam D. Galinsky. "Generous Paupers and Stingy Princes: Power Drives Consumer Spending on Self Versus Others." *Journal of Consumer Research* 37, no. 6 (2011). doi:10.1086/657162.

Shell, G. Richard. *Springboard.* New York: Portfolio, 2013.

Silver, Nate. "Nate Silver: The Numbers Don't Lie." YouTube video, 56:09. Posted by Chicago Humanities Festival, November 28, 2012. www.youtube.com/watch?v=GuAZtOJqFr0.

Silver, Nate. *The Signal and the Noise.* New York: Penguin, 2012.

Starek, Joanna E., and Caroline F. Keating. "Self-Deception and Its Relationship to Success in Competition." *Basic and Applied Social Psychology* 12, no. 2 (1991): 145–55. doi:10.1207/s15324834basp1202_2.

Stuster, Jack W. *Bold Endeavors.* Annapolis, MD: Naval Institute Press, 2011.

Tedlow, Richard S. *Denial*. New York: Portfolio, 2010.

Tost, Leigh Plunkett, Francesca Gino, and Richard P. Larrick. "When Power Makes Others Speechless: The Negative Impact of Leader Power on Team Performance." *Academy of Management Journal* 56, no. 5 (2013): 1465–86. doi:10.5465/amj.2011.0180.

University of Nebraska–Lincoln. "How Do I Love Me? Let Me Count the Ways, and Also Ace That Interview." ScienceDaily. April 2, 2012. www.sciencedaily.com/releases/2012/04/120402144738.htm.

Van Kleef, Gerben A., Christopher Oveis, Ilmo van der Löwe, Aleksandr LuoKogan, Jennifer Goetz, and Dacher Keltner. "Power, Distress, and Compassion Turning a Blind Eye to the Suffering of Others." *Psychological Science* 19, no. 12 (2008): 1315–22. doi:10.1111/j.1467-9280.2008.02241.x.

Verkuil, Paul R., Martin Seligman, and Terry Kang. "Countering Lawyer Unhappiness: Pessimism, Decision Latitude, and the Zero-Sum Dilemma." Public Law Research Working Paper 019, Benjamin N. Cardozo School of Law School, Yeshiva University, New York, NY, September 2000. doi:10.2139/ssrn.241942.

Vialle, Isabelle, Luís Santos-Pinto, and Jean-Louis Rulliere. "Self-Confidence and Teamwork: An Experimental Test." Gate Working Paper No. 1126, September 2011. http://dx.doi.org/10.2139/ssrn.1943453.

Wallace, Harry M., and Roy F. Baumeister. "The Performance of Narcissists Rises and Falls with Perceived Opportunity for Glory." *Journal of Personality and Social Psychology* 82, no. 5 (2002): 819–34. http://dx.doi.org/10.1037/0022-3514.82.5.819.

Wiseman, Richard. *The As If Principle*. New York: Free Press, 2013.

Wood, Graeme. "What Martial Arts Have to Do with Atheism." *The Atlantic,* April 24, 2013. www.theatlantic.com/national/archive/2013/04/what-martial-arts-have-to-do-with-atheism/275273/.

"World with No Fear." *Invisibilia*. Radio broadcast, 24:43. Aired January 15, 2015. www.npr.org/2015/01/16/377517810/world-with-no-fear.

Ybarra, Oscar, Piotr Winkielman, Irene Yeh, Eugene Burnstein, and Liam Kavanagh. "Friends (and Sometimes Enemies) with Cognitive Benefits: What Types of Social Interactions Boost Executive Functioning?" *Social Psychological and Personality Science,* October 13, 2010. doi:10.1177/1948550610386808.

Yong, Ed. "Meet the Woman Without Fear." *Not Rocket Science* (blog). *Discover Magazine,* December 16, 2010. http://blogs.discovermagazine.com/notrocketscience/2010/12/16/meet-the-woman-without-fear/#.VgsT_yBViko.

Zenger, Jack, and Joseph Folkman. "We Like Leaders Who Underrate Themselves." *Harvard Business Review,* November 10, 2015. https://hbr.org/2015/11/we-like-leaders-who-underrate-themselves.

Zhao, Bin. "Learning from Errors: The Role of Context, Emotion, and Personality." *Journal of Organizational Behavior* 32, no. 3 (2011): 435–63. doi:10.1002/job.696.

CHAPTER 6: WORK, WORK, WORK . . . OR WORK-LIFE BALANCE?

Abele, Andrea E., and Daniel Spurk. "How Do Objective and Subjective Career Success Interrelate over Time?" *Journal of Occupational and Organizational Psychology* 82, no. 4 (2009): 803–24. doi:10.1348/096317909X470924.

Achor, Shawn. *The Happiness Advantage.* New York: Crown Business, 2010.

Ackerman, Jennifer. *Sex Sleep Eat Drink Dream.* New York: Mariner, 2008.

Alfredsson, L., R. Karasek, and T. Theorell. "Myocardial Infarction Risk and Psychosocial Work Environment: An Analysis of the Male Swedish Working Force." *Social Science and Medicine* 16, no. 4 (1982): 463–67. doi:10.1016/0277-9536(82)90054-5.

Amabile, Teresa. "Does High Stress Trigger Creativity at Work?" *Marketplace,* May 3, 2012. www.marketplace.org/2012/05/03/life/commentary/does-high-stress-trigger-creativity-work.

American Psychological Association. *Stress in America.* October 7, 2008. www.apa.org/news/press/releases/2008/10/stress-in-america.pdf.

Arnsten, Amy F. T. "Stress Signalling Pathways That Impair Prefrontal Cortex Structure and Function." *Nature Reviews Neuroscience* 10, no. 6 (2009): 410–22. doi:10.1038/nrn2648.

Axelsson, John, Tina Sundelin, Michael Ingre, Eus J. W. van Someren, Andreas Olsson, and Mats Lekander. "Beauty Sleep: Experimental Study on the Perceived Health and Attractiveness of Sleep Deprived People." *BMJ* 341 (2010): c6614. http://dx.doi.org/10.1136/bmj.c6614.

Bandiera, Oriana, Andrea Prat, and Raffaella Sadun. "Managerial Firms in an Emerging Economy: Evidence from the Time Use of Indian CEOs." July 2013. www.people.hbs.edu/rsadun/CEO_India_TimeUse_April_2013.pdf.

Barker, Eric. "How Bad Is It to Miss a Few Hours of Sleep?" (Original article unavailable.) *Barking Up the Wrong Tree* (blog). November 5, 2009. www.bakadesuyo.com/2009/11/how-bad-is-it-to-miss-a-few-hours-of-sleep-jo/.

Barnes, Christopher M., John Schaubroeck, Megan Huth, and Sonia Ghumman. "Lack of Sleep and Unethical Conduct." *Organizational Behavior and Human Decision Processes* 115, no. 2 (2011): 169–80. doi:10.1016/j.obhdp.2011.01.009.

Beck, Melinda. "The Sleepless Elite." *Wall Street Journal,* April 5, 2011. www.wsj.com/articles/SB10001424052748703712504576242701752957910.

Behncke, Stefanie. "How Does Retirement Affect Health?" IZA Discussion Paper No. 4253, Institute for the Study of Labor, Bonn, Germany, June 2009. http://ftp.iza.org/dp4253.pdf.

Bianchi, R., C. Boffy, C. Hingray, D. Truchot, E. Laurent. "Comparative Symptomatology of Burnout and Depression." *Journal of Health Psychology* 18, no. 6 (2013): 782–87. doi:10.1177/1359105313481079.

Binnewies, Carmen, Sabine Sonnentag, and Eva J. Mojza. "Recovery During the Weekend and Fluctuations in Weekly Job Performance: A Week-

Level Study Examining Intra-Individual Relationships." *Journal of Occupational and Organizational Psychology* 83, no. 2 (2010): 419–41. doi:10.1348/096317909X418049.

Blaszczak-Boxe, Agata. "The Secrets of Short Sleepers: How Do They Thrive on Less Sleep?" CBSNews.com. June 27, 2014. www.cbsnews.com/news/the-secrets-of-short-sleepers-how-do-they-thrive-on-less-sleep/.

Boehm, Julia K., and Sonja Lyubomirsky. "Does Happiness Promote Career Success?" *Journal of Career Assessment* 16, no. 1 (2008): 101–16. doi:10.1177/1069072707308140.

Bradlee Jr., Ben. *The Kid.* Boston: Little, Brown, 2013.

Brown, Stuart. *Play.* New York: Avery, 2010.

Cain, Susan. *Quiet.* New York: Broadway Books, 2012.

Christensen, Clayton M., James Allworth, and Karen Dillon. *How Will You Measure Your Life?* New York: HarperBusiness, 2012. Kindle Edition.

Csikszentmihályi, Mihály. "Contexts of Optimal Growth in Childhood." *Daedalus* 122, no. 1 (Winter 1993): 31–56.

Csikszentmihályi, Mihály. *Finding Flow.* New York: Basic Books, 2007.

Currey, Mason, ed. *Daily Rituals.* New York: Knopf, 2013.

Doherty, William J. "Overscheduled Kids, Underconnected Families: The Research Evidence." http://kainangpamilyamahalaga.com/pdf/studies/Overscheduled_Kids_Underconnected_Families.pdf.

Drucker, Peter F. *The Practice of Management.* New York: HarperBusiness, 2010.

Duhigg, Charles. *Smarter Faster Better.* New York: Random House, 2016.

Eck, John E. "Sitting Ducks, Ravenous Wolves, and Helping Hands: New Approaches to Urban Policing." *Public Affairs Comment* 35, no. 2 (Winter 1989). Lyndon B. Johnson School of Government, University of Texas at Austin. https://www.researchgate.net/publication/292743996_Sitting_ducks_ravenous_wolves_and_helping_hands_New_approaches_to_urban_policing.

Ferrie, Jane E., Martin J. Shipley, Francesco P. Cappuccio, Eric Brunner, Michelle A. Miller, Meena Kumari, and Michael G. Marmot. "A Prospective Study of Change in Sleep Duration: Associations with Mortality in the Whitehall II Cohort." *Sleep* 30, no. 12 (2007): 1659–66. www.ncbi.nlm.nih.gov/pmc/articles/PMC2276139/.

Fincher, David. *Fight Club.* Twentieth Century Fox, 1999. Film.

Garbus, Liz. "Bobby Fischer Against the World." HBO Documentary, 2011. Film.

Gardner, Howard. *Creating Minds.* New York: Basic Books, 2011.

Gaski, John F., and Jeff Sagarin. "Detrimental Effects of Daylight-Saving Time on SAT Scores." *Journal of Neuroscience, Psychology, and Economics* 4, no. 1 (2011): 44–53. doi:10.1037/a0020118.

Gleick, James. *Faster.* Boston: Little, Brown, 2000.

Golden, Lonnie, and Barbara Wiens-Tuers. "To Your Happiness? Extra Hours of Labor Supply and Worker Well-Being." *Journal of Socio-Economics* 35, no. 2 (2006): 382–97. doi:10.1016/j.socec.2005.11.039.

Gould, Daniel, Suzanne Tuffey, Eileen Udry, and James E. Loehr. "Burnout in

Competitive Junior Tennis Players: III. Individual Differences in the Burnout Experience." *Sports Psychologist* 11, no. 3 (1997): 257–76.

Graham, Ruth. "The Unbearable Loneliness of Creative Work." *Boston Globe,* October 04, 2015. www.bostonglobe.com/ideas/2015/10/03/the-unbearable-loneliness-creative-work/5bY0LfwuWjZnMKLZTXOHJL/story.html.

Gujar, Ninad, Steven Andrew McDonald, Masaki Nishida, and Matthew P. Walker. "A Role for REM Sleep in Recalibrating the Sensitivity of the Human Brain to Specific Emotions." *Cerebral Cortex* 21, no. 1 (2011): 115–23. doi:10.1093/cercor/bhq064.

Halliwell, John F., and Shun Wang. "Weekends and Subjective Well-Being." *Social Indicators Research* 116, no. 2 (2014): 389–407. doi:10.3386/w17180.

"Hardcore History 43: Wrath of the Khans I." Dan Carlin website. www.dancarlin.com/product/hardcore-history-43-wrath-of-the-khans-i/.

Harden, Blaine. "Japan's Killer Work Ethic." *Washington Post,* July 13, 2008. www.washingtonpost.com/wp-dyn/content/article/2008/07/12/AR2008071201630.html.

Harter, Jim, and Saengeeta Agarwal. "Workers in Bad Jobs Have Worse Wellbeing than Jobless." Gallup.com. March 30, 2011. www.gallup.com/poll/146867/Workers-Bad-Jobs-Worse-Wellbeing-Jobless.aspx.

Henry, Paul. "An Examination of the Pathways Through Which Social Class Impacts Health Outcomes." *Academy of Marketing Science Review* 2001, no. 03 (2001). www.med.mcgill.ca/epidemiology/courses/655/SES%20and%20Health.pdf.

Hewlett, Sylvia Ann, and Carolyn Buck Luce. "Extreme Jobs: The Dangerous Allure of the 70-Hour Workweek." *Harvard Business Review,* December 2006. https://hbr.org/2006/12/extreme-jobs-the-dangerous-allure-of-the-70-hour-workweek.

Hitt, Michael A., R. Duane Ireland, and Robert E. Hoskisson. *Strategic Management Concepts.* 7th ed. Cincinnati: South-Western College Pub, 2006.

Hoang, Viet. "Karoshi: The Japanese Are Dying to Get to Work." Tofugu.com. January 26, 2012. www.tofugu.com/2012/01/26/the-japanese-are-dying-to-get-to-work-karoshi/.

"Inside the Teenage Brain: Interview with Ellen Galinsky." *Frontline.* (Documentary aired January 31, 2002.) www.pbs.org/wgbh/pages/frontline/shows/teenbrain/interviews/galinsky.html.

Interview with Barry Schwartz by author. "How to Find Happiness in Today's Hectic World." *Barking Up the Wrong Tree* (blog). February 22, 2015. www.bakadesuyo.com/2015/02/how-to-find-happiness/.

Interview with Benjamin Walker by Roman Mars. "Queue Theory and Design." 99% Invisible. Episode 49. March 9, 2012. http://99percentinvisible.org/episode/episode-49-queue-theory-and-design/transcript/.

Interview with Cal Newport by author. "How to Stop Being Lazy and Get More Done—5 Expert Tips." *Barking Up the Wrong Tree* (blog). August 10, 2014. www.bakadesuyo.com/2014/08/how-to-stop-being-lazy/.

Interview with Dan Ariely by author. "How to Be Efficient: Dan Ariely's 6 New

Secrets to Managing Your Time." *Barking Up the Wrong Tree* (blog). October 12, 2014. www.bakadesuyo.com/2014/10/how-to-be-efficient/.

Interview with Michael Norton by author. "Harvard Professor Michael Norton Explains How to Be Happier." *Barking Up the Wrong Tree* (blog). May 18, 2013. www.bakadesuyo.com/2013/05/harvard-michael-norton-happier/.

Interview with Scott Barry Kaufman by author. "How to Be Creative: 6 Secrets Backed by Research." *Barking Up the Wrong Tree* (blog). December 6, 2015. www.bakadesuyo.com/2015/12/how-to-be-creative/.

Interview with Shawn Achor by author. "Be More Successful: New Harvard Research Reveals a Fun Way to Do It." *Barking Up the Wrong Tree* (blog). September 28, 2014. www.bakadesuyo.com/2014/09/be-more-successful/.

Isaacson, Walter. *Einstein.* New York: Simon and Schuster, 2007.

Iyengar, Sheena S., Rachael E. Wells, and Barry Schwartz. "Doing Better but Feeling Worse: Looking for the 'Best' Job Undermines Satisfaction." *Psychological Science* 17, no. 2 (2006): 143–50. doi:10.1111/j.1467-9280.2006.01677.x.

"Jobs for Life." *The Economist,* December 19, 2007. www.economist.com/node/10329261.

Jones, Jeffrey M. "In U.S., 40% Get Less than Recommended Amount of Sleep." Gallup.com. December 19, 2013. www.gallup.com/poll/166553/less-recommended-amount-sleep.aspx.

Jones, Maggie. "How Little Sleep Can You Get Away With?" *New York Times Magazine,* April 15, 2011. www.nytimes.com/2011/04/17/magazine/mag-17Sleep-t.html?_r=0.

Judge, Timothy A., and John D. Kammeyer-Mueller. "On the Value of Aiming High: The Causes and Consequences of Ambition." *Journal of Applied Psychology* 97, no. 4 (2012): 758–75. http://dx.doi.org/10.1037/a0028084.

Kanazawa, Satoshi. "Why Productivity Fades with Age: The Crime–Genius Connection." *Journal of Research in Personality* 37 (2003): 257–72. doi:10.1016/S0092-6566(02)00538-X, http://personal.lse.ac.uk/kanazawa/pdfs/JRP2003.pdf.

"Kazushi Sakuraba: 'The Gracie Hunter.'" Sherdog.com. www.sherdog.com/fighter/Kazushi-Sakuraba-84.

Keller, Gary. *The ONE Thing.* Austin, TX: Bard Press, 2013.

Kendall, Joshua. *America's Obsessives: The Compulsive Energy That Built a Nation.* New York: Grand Central, 2013.

Kibler, Michael E. "Prevent Your Star Performers from Losing Passion for Their Work." *Harvard Business Review,* January 14, 2015. https://hbr.org/2015/01/prevent-your-star-performers-from-losing-passion-in-their-work.

Kuhn, Peter, and Fernando Lozano. "The Expanding Workweek? Understanding Trends in Long Work Hours Among U.S. Men, 1979–2006." *Journal of Labor Economics* 26, no. 2 (2008): 311–43, 04. doi:10.3386/w11895.

Kühnel, Jana, and Sabine Sonnentag. "How Long Do You Benefit from Vacation? A Closer Look at the Fade-Out of Vacation Effects." *Journal of Organizational Behavior* 32, no. 1 (2011): 125–43. doi:10.1002/job.699.

Laham, Simon. *Science of Sin*. New York: Harmony, 2012.

Levitin, Daniel J. *The Organized Mind*. New York: Plume, 2014.

Loehr, Jim, and Tony Schwartz. *The Power of Full Engagement*. New York: Free Press, 2003.

Maher, Brendan. "Poll Results: Look Who's Doping." *Nature* 452 (2008): 674–75. doi:10.1038/452674a.

"Man Claims New Sleepless Record." BBC.com, May 25, 2007. http://news.bbc.co.uk/2/hi/uk_news/england/cornwall/6689999.stm.

Martin, Douglas. "Robert Shields, Wordy Diarist, Dies at 89." *New York Times*, October 29, 2007. www.nytimes.com/2007/10/29/us/29shields.html.

Masicampo, E. J., and Roy F. Baumeister. "Consider It Done! Plan Making Can Eliminate the Cognitive Effects of Unfulfilled Goals." *Journal of Personality and Social Psychology* 101, no. 4 (2011): 667–83. http://dx.doi.org/10.1037/a0024192.

Maslach, Christina. "Burnout and Engagement in the Workplace: New Perspectives." *European Health Psychologist* 13, no. 3 (2011): 44–47. http://openhealthpsychology.net/ehp/issues/2011/v13iss3_September2011/13_3_Maslach.pdf.

Maslach, Christina, and Julie Goldberg. "Prevention of Burnout: New Perspectives." *Applied and Preventive Psychology* 7, no. 1 (1998): 63–74. http://dx.doi.org/10.1016/S0962-1849(98)80022-X.

Maslach, Christina, and Michael P. Leiter. *The Truth About Burnout*. San Francisco: Jossey-Bass, 2009.

Mazzonna, Fabrizio, and Franco Peracchi. "Aging, Cognitive Abilities, and Retirement." *European Economic Review* 56, no. 4 (2012): 691–710. http://www.eief.it/files/2012/05/peracchi_mazzonna_eer_2012.pdf.

McGill University. "Men Who Lose Their Jobs at Greater Risk of Dying Prematurely." Public release. April 4, 2011. www.eurekalert.org/pub_releases/2011-04/mu-mwl040411.php.

McLynn, Frank. *Genghis Khan*. Cambridge, MA: Da Capo Press, 2015.

Medina, John. *Brain Rules*. Edmonds, WA: Pear Press, 2008.

Meldrum, Helen. "Exemplary Physicians' Strategies for Avoiding Burnout." *Health Care Manager* 29, no. 4 (2010): 324–31. doi:10.1097/HCM.0b013e3181fa037a.

Monteiro, Mike. "The Chokehold of Calendars." *Medium*. July 18, 2013. https://medium.com/@monteiro/the-chokehold-of-calendars-f70bb9221b36#.fnje9u6jm.

Mullainathan, Sendhil, and Eldar Shafir. *Scarcity*. New York: Times Books, 2013.

MYOB Australia. "MYOB Australian Small Business Survey, Special Focus Report: Lifestyle of Small Business Owners." December 2007. https://www.myob.com/content/dam/myob-redesign/au/docs/business-monitor-pdf/2007/2-MYOB_SBS_Special_Focus_Report_Dec_2007.pdf.

Nash, Laura, and Howard Stevenson. *Just Enough*. Hoboken, NJ: Wiley, 2005.

Newport, Cal. *Deep Work*. New York: Grand Central, 2016.

Niven, David. *100 Simple Secrets of Great Relationships*. New York: HarperCollins, 2009.

Novotney, Amy. "The Real Secrets to a Longer Life." *Monitor on Psychology* 42, no. 11 (2011): 36. www.apa.org/monitor/2011/12/longer-life.aspx.

O'Connor, Anahad. "The Claim: Lack of Sleep Increases the Risk of Catching a Cold." *New York Times,* September 21, 2009. www.nytimes.com/2009/09/22/health/22real.html?_r=0.

Pais, Abraham. *Subtle Is the Lord.* Oxford: Oxford Univ. Press, 2005.

Peláez, Marina Watson. "Plan Your Way to Less Stress, More Happiness." *Time,* May 31, 2011. http://healthland.time.com/2011/05/31/study-25-of-happiness-depends-on-stress-management/.

Pencavel, John. "The Productivity of Working Hours," *Economic Journal* 125, no. 589 (2015): 2052–76. doi:10.1111/ecoj.12166.

Perlow, Leslie A. *Sleeping with Your Smartphone.* Boston: Harvard Business Review Press, 2012.

Pfeffer, Jeffrey. *Managing with Power.* Boston: Harvard Business Review Press, 1993.

Pfeffer, Jeffrey, and Robert I. Sutton. *Hard Facts, Dangerous Half-Truths, and Total Nonsense.* Boston: Harvard Business Review Press, 2006.

Pink, Daniel H. *Drive.* New York: Riverhead Books, 2011.

Proyer, René T. "Being Playful and Smart? The Relations of Adult Playfulness with Psychometric and Self-Estimated Intelligence and Academic Performance." *Learning and Individual Differences* 21, no. 4 (2011): 463–67. http://dx.doi.org/10.1016/j.lindif.2011.02.003.

Randall, David K. *Dreamland.* New York: W. W. Norton, 2012.

Redelmeier, Donald A., and Daniel Kahneman. "Patients' Memories of Painful Medical Treatments: Real-Time and Retrospective Evaluations of Two Minimally Invasive Procedures." *Pain* 66, no. 1 (1996): 3–8. doi:10.1016/0304-3959(96)02994-6.

Reynolds, John, Michael Stewart, Ryan Macdonald, and Lacey Sischo. "Have Adolescents Become Too Ambitious? High School Seniors' Educational and Occupational Plans, 1976 to 2000." *Social Problems* 53, no. 2 (2006): 186–206. http://dx.doi.org/10.1525/sp.2006.53.2.186.

Robinson, Evan. "Why Crunch Modes Doesn't Work: Six Lessons." International Game Developers Association. 2005. www.igda.org/?page=crunchsixlessons.

Rock, David. *Your Brain at Work.* New York: HarperCollins, 2009.

Rohwedder, Susann, and Robert J. Willis. "Mental Retirement." *Journal of Economic Perspectives* 24, no. 1 (2010): 119–38. doi:10.1257/jep.24.1.119.

Rosekind, Mark R., David F. Neri, Donna L. Miller, Kevin B. Gregory, Lissa L. Webbon, and Ray L. Oyung. "The NASA Ames Fatigue Countermeasures Program: The Next Generation." NASA Ames Research Center, Moffett Field, CA. January 1, 1997. http://ntrs.nasa.gov/archive/nasa/casi.ntrs.nasa.gov/20020042348.pdf.

Ross, John J., "Neurological Findings After Prolonged Sleep Deprivation."

Archives of Neurology 12, no. 4 (1965): 399–403. http://dx.doi.org/10.1001/archneur.1965.00460280069006.

Rothbard, Nancy P., and Steffanie L. Wilk. "Waking Up on the Right or Wrong Side of the Bed: Start-of-Workday Mood, Work Events, Employee Affect, and Performance." *Academy of Management Journal* 54, no. 5 (2011): 959–80. doi:10.5465/amj.2007.0056.

Rubens, Jim. *OverSuccess.* Austin, TX: Greenleaf Book Group, 2008.

Saad, Lydia. "The '40-Hour' Workweek Is Actually Longer—by Seven Hours." Gallup.com. August 29, 2014. www.gallup.com/poll/175286/hour-workweek-actually-longer-seven-hours.aspx.

San Diego State University. "Adults' Happiness on the Decline in U.S.: Researchers Found Adults over Age 30 Are Not as Happy as They Used to Be, but Teens and Young Adults Are Happier than Ever." ScienceDaily. November 5, 2015. www.sciencedaily.com/releases/2015/11/151105143547.htm.

Schaufeli, Wilmar B., Michael P. Leiter, and Christina Maslach. "Burnout: 35 Years of Research and Practice." *Career Development International* 14, no. 3 (2009): 204–20. doi:10.1108/13620430910966406.

Schwartz, Barry. *The Paradox of Choice.* New York: HarperCollins, 2009. Kindle Edition.

Schwartz, Barry, Andrew Ward, Sonja Lyubomirsky, John Monterosso, Katherine White, and Darrin R. Lehman. "Maximizing Versus Satisficing: Happiness Is a Matter of Choice." *Journal of Personality and Social Psychology* 83, no. 5 (2002): 1178–97. doi:10.1037//0022-3514.83.5.1178.

Sedaris, David. "Laugh, Kookaburra." *New Yorker,* August 24, 2009. www.newyorker.com/magazine/2009/08/24/laugh-kookaburra.

Sherman, Lawrence W., and David L. Weisburd. "General Deterrent Effects of Police Patrol in Crime 'Hot Spots': A Randomized, Controlled Trial." *Justice Quarterly* 12, no. 4 (1995): 625–48. doi:10.1080/07418829500096221.

Simonton, Dean Keith. *Greatness.* New York: Guilford Press, 1994.

Simonton, Dean Keith. *The Wiley Handbook of Genius.* Hoboken, NJ: Wiley-Blackwell, 2014.

Sims, Peter. *Little Bets.* New York: Free Press, 2011.

Smith, Dinitia. "Dark Side of Einstein Emerges in His Letters." *New York Times,* November 6, 1996. www.nytimes.com/1996/11/06/arts/dark-side-of-einstein-emerges-in-his-letters.html?pagewanted=all.

Streep, Peg, and Alan Bernstein. *Quitting.* Cambridge, MA: Da Capo Press, 2015.

Stuster, Jack W. *Bold Endeavors.* Annapolis, MD: Naval Institute Press, 2011.

Sullivan, Bob. "Memo to Work Martyrs: Long Hours Make You Less Productive." CNBC.com. January 26, 2015. www.cnbc.com/2015/01/26/working-more-than-50-hours-makes-you-less-productive.html.

Surtees, Paul G., Nicholas W. J. Wainwright, Robert Luben, Nicholas J. Wareham, Shiela A. Bingham, and Kay-Tee Khaw. "Mastery Is Associated with Cardiovascular Disease Mortality in Men and Women at Apparently Low Risk." *Health Psychology* 29, no. 4 (2010): 412–20. doi:10.1037/a0019432.

Tierney, John. "Prison Population Can Shrink When Police Crowd Streets." *New York Times,* January 25, 2013. www.nytimes.com/2013/01/26/nyregion/police-have-done-more-than-prisons-to-cut-crime-in-new-york.html?pagewanted=all&_r=1.

Todd, Benjamin. "How Good Are the Best?" *80,000 Hours* (blog). September 1, 2012. https://80000hours.org/2012/09/how-good-are-the-best/.

Twenge, Jean M., Ryne A. Sherman, and Sonja Lyubomirsky. "More Happiness for Young People and Less for Mature Adults: Time Period Differences in Subjective Well-Being in the United States, 1972–2014." *Social Psychological and Personality Science* 7, no. 2 (2016): 1–11. doi:10.1177/1948550615602933.

University of Massachusetts Amherst. "'Sleep on It' Is Sound, Science-Based Advice, Study Suggests." ScienceDaily. June 8, 2011. www.sciencedaily.com/releases/2011/06/110607094849.htm.

Visser, Mechteld R. M., Ellen M. A. Smets, Frans J. Oort, and Hanneke C. J. M. de Haes. "Stress, Satisfaction and Burnout Among Dutch Medical Specialists." *CMAJ* 168, no. 3 (2003): 271–75. PMCID:PMC140468.

Wagner, David T., Christopher M. Barnes, Vivien K. G. Lim, and D. Lance Ferris. "Lost Sleep and Cyberloafing: Evidence From the Laboratory and a Daylight Saving Time Quasi-Experiment." *Journal of Applied Psychology* 97, no. 5 (2012): 1068–76. doi:10.1037/a0027557.

Wang, Wei-Ching, Chin-Hsung Kao, Tsung-Cheng Huan, and Chung-Chi Wu. "Free Time Management Contributes to Better Quality of Life: A Study of Undergraduate Students in Taiwan." *Journal of Happiness Studies* 12, no. 4 (2011): 561–73. doi:10.1007/s10902-010-9217-7.

Ware, Bronnie. *The Top Five Regrets of the Dying.* Carlsbad, CA: Hay House, 2012.

Wargo, Eric. "Life's Ups and Downs May Stick." *Observer,* May 2007. Association for Psychological Science. www.psychologicalscience.org/index.php/publications/observer/2007/may-07/lifes-ups-and-downs-may-stick.html.

Weatherford, Jack. *Genghis Khan and the Making of the Modern World.* New York: Broadway Books, 2005.

Weiner, Eric. *The Geography of Genius.* New York: Simon and Schuster, 2016.

White, Gregory L., and Shirley Leung. "American Tastes Move Upscale, Forcing Manufacturers to Adjust." *Wall Street Journal,* March 29, 2002. www.wsj.com/articles/SB1017351317283641480.

Wohl, Michael, Timothy A. Pychyl, and Shannon H. Bennett. "I Forgive Myself, Now I Can Study: How Self-Forgiveness for Procrastinating Can Reduce Future Procrastination." *Personality and Individual Differences* 48, no. 7 (2010): 803–8. doi:10.1016/j.paid.2010.01.029.

Wood, Graeme. "What Martial Arts Have to Do with Atheism." *The Atlantic,* April 24, 2013. www.theatlantic.com/national/archive/2013/04/what-martial-arts-have-to-do-with-atheism/275273/.

Xu, Xin. "The Business Cycle and Health Behaviors." *Social Science and Medicine* 77 (2013): 126–36. doi:10.1016/j.socscimed.2012.11.016.

Yoo, Seung-Schik, Ninad Gujar, Peter Hu, Ferenc A. Jolesz, and Matthew P. Walker. "The Human Emotional Brain Without Sleep—A Prefrontal Amygdala

Disconnect." *Current Biology* 17, no. 20 (2007): pR877–78. doi:http://dx.doi. org/10.1016/j.cub.2007.08.007.

Zerjal, Tatiana, Yali Xue, Giorgio Bertorelle, R. Spencer Wells, Weidong Bao, Suling Zhu, Raheel Qamar, et al. "The Genetic Legacy of the Mongols." *American Journal of Hum Genetics* 72, no. 3 (2003): 717–21. doi:10.1086/367774.

CONCLUSION: WHAT MAKES A SUCCESSFUL LIFE?

Achor, Shawn. "Is Happiness the Secret of Success?" CNN.com. March 19, 2012. www.cnn.com/2012/03/19/opinion/happiness-success-achor.

Boehm, Julia K., and Sonja Lyubomirsky. "Does Happiness Promote Career Success?" *Journal of Career Assessment* 16, no. 1 (2008): 101–16. doi:10.1177/1069072707308140.

Chappell, Bill. "Winner of French Scrabble Title Does Not Speak French." NPR. Radio broadcast, 3:11. Aired July 21, 2015. www.npr.org/sections/thetwo-way/2015/07/21/424980378/winner-of-french-scrabble-title-does-not-speak-french.

Dweck, Carol. *Mindset.* New York: Random House, 2006.

"Entombed in My Own Body for Over 12 Years." BBC World Service online. 55 minutes. October 23, 2013. www.bbc.co.uk/programmes/p01jt6p6.

Heigl, Alex. "Man Memorizes French Dictionary to Win French Scrabble Tournament, Does Not Speak French." *People,* July 22, 2015. www.people.com/article/new-zealand-scrabble-champion-french-dictionary.

Petite, Steven. "Unscrambling Strings of Letters: The Beautiful Mind of Nigel Richards." *Huffington Post,* July 23, 2015. www.huffingtonpost.com/steven-petite/unscrambling-strings-of-l_b_7861738.html.

Pistorius, Martin. *Ghost Boy.* Nashville: Thomas Nelson, 2013.

Pistorius, Martin. "How My Mind Came Back to Life—and No One Knew," Filmed August 2015. TEDxKC video, 14:08. www.ted.com/talks/martin_pistorius_how_my_mind_came_back_to_life_and_no_one_knew.

Powdthavee, Nattavudh. "Putting a Price Tag on Friends, Relatives, and Neighbours: Using Surveys of Life Satisfaction to Value Social Relationships." *Journal of Socio-Economics* 37, no. 4 (2008): 1459–80. doi:10.1016/j.socec.2007.04.004.

Roeder, Oliver. "What Makes Nigel Richards the Best Scrabble Player on Earth." FiveThirtyEight.com. August 8, 2014. http://fivethirtyeight.com/features/what-makes-nigel-richards-the-best-scrabble-player-on-earth/.

"Secret History of Thoughts." *Invisibilia.* Radio broadcast, 59:07. Aired January 9, 2015. www.npr.org/programs/invisibilia/375927143/the-secret-history-of-thoughts.

Shenk, Joshua Wolf. "What Makes Us Happy?" *The Atlantic,* June 2009. www.theatlantic.com/magazine/archive/2009/06/what-makes-us-happy/307439/?single_page=true.

Simonton, Dean Keith. *The Wiley Handbook of Genius*. Hoboken, NJ: Wiley-Blackwell, 2014.

Stevenson, Howard, and Laura Nash. *Just Enough*. Hoboken, NJ: Wiley, 2005.

Vaillant, George E. *Triumphs of Experience*. Cambridge, MA: Harvard Univ. Press, 2012.

Valliant, George E. "Yes, I Stand by My Words, 'Happiness Equals Love—Full Stop.'" *Positive Psychology News*, July 16, 2009. http://positivepsychologynews.com/news/george-vaillant/200907163163.

About the Author

You don't meet what writes the books when you meet a writer. You meet where *it* lives.

—WILLIAM GIBSON

Eric Barker is the creator of the blog *Barking Up the Wrong Tree*. His work has been mentioned in the *New York Times, The Wall Street Journal, The Atlantic Monthly, Time Magazine, The Week, Business Insider,* and a bunch of other places he is far too lazy to Google right now. He is a former Hollywood screenwriter, having worked on projects for Walt Disney Pictures, Twentieth Century Fox, and Revolution Studios. Eric was part of the Wii team at Nintendo, worked on the BioShock franchise for Irrational Games, and helped Spider-Man creator Stan Lee turn the Backstreet Boys into superheroes (we all do things we're ashamed of when we're young). He is a graduate of the University of Pennsylvania and holds an MBA from Boston College and a Master of Fine Arts from UCLA. Eric has fenced in Russia with Olympians, grappled with MMA champions, and trained in Krav Maga with members of the Israeli Military. He has never killed anyone who did not have it coming. Eric thinks talking about himself in the third person is really awkward. His mother considers him a great success. Visit him online at www.bakadesuyo.com.